John Bunyan

By Ola Elizabeth Winslow (died 1977, age 92)

Jonathan Edwards, 1703–1758
Meetinghouse Hill, 1630–1783
Master Roger Williams
John Bunyan

John Bunyan

By OLA ELIZABETH WINSLOW

THE MACMILLAN COMPANY
New York

Second Printing 1968

The Macmillan Company, New York
Collier-Macmillan Canada Ltd., Toronto, Ontario

Printed in the United States of America

Library of Congress catalog card number: 61-6890

"Besides, sir, words easy to be understood do often hit the mark, when high and learned ones do only pierce the air."

John Bunyan, "To the Learned Reader"
The Holy City, 1665

Preface

After nearly three centuries, the available personal data concerning John Bunyan would seem to be on the record. Extant sources of many sorts have long been diligently and repeatedly explored, until at this late date, re-examination yields little with which to change or lengthen the familiar story. In terms of an established record of fact, this story is more scant than for most men who have been remembered so long. A baptismal record, a muster roll, a prison sentence, a release, a license to preach, various items in a Church Book, a portrait, a tombstone, and that is about all. In the Bedford Museum which bears his name, there are a few "relics": a table, a chair, a pulpit desk, a jug, a walking stick, a few manuscript pages, a homemade anvil, an iron fiddle, a prison door: pathetic memorials of a brave life. But a man's life does not consist in items on yellowed parchment, were the list many times as long, nor in "relics," even though they might require a house of many rooms to contain them.

This book promises no new discoveries of fact, no new unearthing of relics. It is written in the confidence that when available fact is on the record, one may still talk about a man whose work has had a vital continuity for nearly three hundred years.

Three recent books restrict somewhat the scope of a new inquiry, and make certain directions of emphasis unnecessary: Vera

Preface

Brittain's *In the Steps of John Bunyan*, London, 1950, New York, 1951; Henri Talon's *John Bunyan, The Man and His Works*, Paris, 1948, London, 1951; and Roger Sharrock's *John Bunyan*, in the Hutchinson University Library, London, 1954.

The materials for this study have been examined chiefly in the British Museum, and the book has been written in the Boston Athenaeum Library. It is a pleasure to acknowledge the helpfulness and unwearied service of the custodians of these resources and once more to record my gratitude to them. Specific acknowledgment for the permissions involved is made at the appropriate places in the text.

OLA ELIZABETH WINSLOW

Boston, March 21, 1960

Contents

Preface   vii

Prologue   1

I.   The Boy of Bunyan's End   4
     Harrowden, 1628–1644

II.   Soldier in Cromwell's New Model Army   24
     Newport Pagnell, 1644–1647

III.   Embattled Tinker   43
     Elstow, 1647–1653
     Bedford, 1653–1655

IV.   Field Preacher   65
     Bedford, 1655–1660

V.   Offender Before the Law   85
     Bedford, 1660

VI.   "The Lord's Free Prisoner"   102
     Bedford County Gaol, 1660–1672

VII.   "The Head of Goliath in My Hand"   118
     Grace Abounding to the Chief of Sinners, 1666

VIII.   Pastor of Bunyan Meeting   129
     Bedford, 1672–1688

ix

Contents

IX. *The Pilgrim's Progress*, 1678   140

X. Bishop Bunyan   159
      Bedford, 1676–1688

XI. "Our Author Bunyan"   169
      Bedford, 1680–1686
      The Life and Death of Mr. Badman, 1680
      The Holy War, 1682
      The Pilgrim's Progress, Part II, 1684
      Country Rhimes for Children, 1686

XII. "All the trumpets sounded for him on the other side"   198
      Bunhill Fields, 1688

      Postscript "It came from mine own heart"   205

      Notes   212

      Titles of Bunyan's Published Works   224

      Selected Bibliography   227

      Index   235

John Bunyan

Prologue

John Bunyan's life spanned one of the most tumultuous sixty years in English history. The Petition of Right in 1628 made one abutment, the Bloodless Revolution of 1688 the other. On the arch in between were the Civil Wars, the Protectorate, the Restoration, and all the endings of things old and the beginnings of things new which make up the chapter we call Puritanism. Although to some degree Bunyan was the product and also the victim of these convulsions, in his own thought he lived a life almost entirely apart from them. Political confusions, social upheavals, crumbling traditions, even the death of kings, were not to him events of greatest magnitude. He was also an alien to those new continents of thought which great original seventeenth century thinkers were opening up to the wonderment of men. His life spanned one of the most momentous and constructive periods in the history of human thought. Harvey, Kepler, Galileo, Pascal, Leibnitz, Spinoza, Locke, Newton, Descartes were his contemporaries, revolutionizing men's thought of themselves and of the world they lived in. But not for John Bunyan. He might almost as well have been living on a remote planet. Perhaps the moon is inhabited, men were saying. Perhaps some day we shall reach it from this earth. Perhaps we shall do commerce with its inhabitants. Perhaps the earth itself is not immobile. Bunyan had no share in the interest of these speculations.

His compass was set to no goal possible to human achievement and to no rewards of man's bestowal.

Nevertheless, in his own area of intense inner exploration he wrote history, English history. In a very true sense, he was history. By the singleness of his own individual conviction, he brought to expression the central core of the English medieval religious heritage in what was to be its final literary embodiment. He did so with a simplicity that requires little commentary. In so doing he also made articulate what thousands of ordinary men and women of his day believed, dreamed, hoped for, responded to, in things religious. He forged out a path of religious quest which became a main track for the following century. He helped to shape the cultural pattern of his own day and the day immediately after. In all this he was both an end and a beginning. The story of English Puritanism can hardly be understood without his contribution to the record. It is the common man's contribution.

Neither he nor the most farseeing prophets of his time could have supplied a hint as to why this should be so. As a troublesome Dissenter in the cataclysmic mid-seventeenth century, he was one obscure man among many hundreds. Nearly every detail of his sixty-year story can be paralleled in the dissenting ranks many times over and in every county of England: his humble origin, his lack of education, his agonized conversion, his obstinate nonconformity, his defiance of the law against lay preaching, his arrest, trial, and long imprisonment, his stoical endurance of poverty, abuse, humiliation, often revolting in their sordid reality. In all this he was the common thread in the web of English dissenting Puritanism. In the one great book the world has known for nearly three centuries, he was (to borrow a figure from Epictetus) the purple thread, which allows the garment to be worn only by the man of high degree. Such a paradox is by no means unique for Bunyan's day or for any other. Genius knows no laws save its own, observes no precedents, but wherever it occurs, it remains one of the perennial human mysteries. John Bunyan in his day personified that mystery.

In the present far-off sequel to his sixty-year record, his name and the title of his great book are inseparable. Hardly a country so remote or a language so obscure that one may not read in his own tongue the tale of the "man clothed with rags, standing in a certain place, a book in his hand and a great burden on his back." Time was, and that only a long lifetime ago, when this book was standard reading for not always reluctant boys and girls penned up indoors on Sunday afternoons. If Bunyan has an audience today, it is more likely to be of adults, not children, and if he has anything to offer to a time when other gods rule, other disasters impend, and other convictions determine the beliefs and actions of the rank and file, it is because the power of conviction in a single human life is one of the most compelling forces in human history. The story such a man's life has to tell is always relevant. Bunyan's own deeply troubled century, not unlike our own in many ways, cannot fully claim him or account for him.

His own life story is disarmingly simple, but for all that (perhaps because of it) there is a strong human pull to it. He was himself that lonely man, clad with rags, a book in his hand and a great burden on his back. This is the way I went, he wrote, and this is what I saw as I traveled. The landmarks are strangely familiar, the path is a recognizable road map, and the people he met are neighbors of us all. By making himself an anonymous wayfarer, John Bunyan became one of the most representative of men.

Chapter One

The Boy of Bunyan's End

John Bunyan's early story provides illustration for Ben Jonson's neat aphorism that the most worthy men have been rocked in mean cradles. In his words, "No great worke or worthy of praise or memory, but came out of poore cradles." [1] Not a verdict to be taken literally, of course, but let it invite a roll call of the cottage-born great ones of Bunyan's day, or of any other, and the company quickly becomes impressive. Be that as it may, however, the familiar fact is that John, first child of Thomas and Margaret Bunyan, was rocked in the "mean cradle" of their one-hearth cottage on the border between Harrowden and Elstow in Bedfordshire. The time was November of the turbulent year 1628, a year that in current thought, as in retrospect, was a funnel-shaped cloud on the English horizon. Before this infant son had passed his twelfth birthday, there would be no spot in all England so remote and untraveled as to escape the storm, but at quiet Bunyan's End in 1628, the thunder was still too distant for cottagers to be alarmed.

As the place name implies, the Bunyan family were no strangers to this corner of Bedfordshire. Had Thomas Bunyan been prideful in this sort, he might have traced his lineage back more than four centuries in this very spot, when in 1199, one William Bunion had owned land scarce a mile away from the thatched cottage where son John was born in 1628. During the intervening generations other

Thomas and William Bunyans, under various spellings of the name, had owned homesteads and farmlands in the Elstow-Bedford neighborhood. Presumably of Norman extraction, the earliest forebears had settled in Pulloxhill, some nine miles from Elstow, and later had moved to lands both north and south of this point.

In 1327, three hundred and one years before 1628, a William Boynon was living on the very site of John Bunyan's birthplace, and two hundred and twenty-one years later, in 1548, Thomas Bonyon, "labourer," was owing the yearly rent of three shillings, fourpence, for a "messuage" and certain lands of his father, William Bonyon. Always small, the landholdings of the earlier Bunyans had slipped away, until at the birth of John, the only fame-bearer of the name, the family fortunes were on a distinctly lower level.[2] The loss of acreage, however, was of far less importance than the four-century inheritance of a way of life and loyalties too deep for conscious knowledge. By virtue of this inheritance, John Bunyan was Midland English to the central axis of his being, and when, grown man, he spoke to his own countrymen, they understood something more than the words.

His father, Thomas Bunyan, was by the designation of his will, a "Braseyer," that is, a mender and purveyor of pots, pans, lanterns, and all manner of small household tools and utensils. Like others of his trade, he had a small forge beside his cottage, and was presumably a licensed itinerant, pushing his noisy cart along the Bedfordshire roads, beating his kettle at every man's door, as he served the farms and hamlets in the immediate vicinity of Elstow and Bedford. A humble occupation, truly enough, but to assume that it meant an unworthily low social rating and poverty in the squalid sense, is to wrong both the tinker and his trade. He supplied a service necessary to a rural population in his day, and no one pitied or despised him for it.

His father before him, also Thomas by name, had been a "Pettie Chapman," but neither did such a calling make him an Autolycus. When this Thomas Bonyon, grandfather of the famous John, died in 1641, he left a sixpence to his grandson, when he should reach the age of twenty-one. When John's father died in 1676, during his son's second imprisonment in Bedford County Gaol, he left him a shilling, to be paid one year after his death, and also one to each of his other three children, Thomas, Mary, and Elizabeth. Such small bequests may be found on almost any folio page of wills for any county in England during the seventeenth century. The fact that both Bunyan's grandfather and father made wills, as poor men seldom did, is far more significant, in terms of social dignity, than the size of their bequests. More important still, both men had lived their lives on ancestral acres, which it was their pride to pass on to their families. After his shilling bequest to each of his children, Thomas Bunyan left the residue of his estate, presumably including his Elstow cottage, to his wife Anne, "to doe with what she pleases and to be at her own disposing." Instead of signing his name, he made his mark.

John Bunyan's own apology for the low door through which he had been brought into the world,

"My father's house being of that rank that is meanest and most despised of all the families in the land," [3]

was purposely made more humble than it was currently accounted, in order that "thereby the goodness and bounty of God" toward him as a sinner might be "more advanced and magnified before the sons of men." Make your origins low and your sins grievous, that God may be the more glorified in your redemption; such was standard idiom in ministerial autobiographies. There is no reason whatever to think that as a boy in Elstow John Bunyan ever suffered local obloquy because of the brazier's cart and the forge beside the door.

Margaret Bunyan, mother of John, was Thomas Bunyan's second wife. She was born Margaret Bentley in Elstow in 1603, the same year as her husband. Like him, she belonged ancestrally to the Bedford neighborhood, at least for the generation of her parents, William and Mary Bentley (née Goodwin), and also of her grandmother, Mary Bentley, who died in 1613. The will of Mary Bentley, mother of Margaret, suggests that her station, like that of Thomas Bunyan, was humble, but by no means abject. She named her small possessions pridefully; to her daughter Elizabeth, the "lesser kettle" and the "biggest plater," a "flaxen sheet and a flaxen pillowbere, a trummel bed and a coffer in the chamber and the table sheet." To her daughter Anne she gave her "best hatte, best cuffe, my gowne, my best petticoate, the presse in the chamber, the best boulster and blankett, the coffe above, the skillet and a pewter platter, and the other trummle bed, a harder sheet and a pillowbere." They were all worthy gifts, and she bestowed them with dignity.[4]

When this Mary Bentley died in 1632, her daughter Margaret, whom she made executrix and to whom she gave all else, had been the wife of Thomas Bunyan for five years. Their marriage record reads,

"1627. Thomas Bonnion, Junr. and Margaret Bentley were married the three and twentieth of May."

Thomas Bunyan's first wife, Anne Pinney, whom he had married on January 10, 1623, had died shortly before this twentieth of May date. There had been no children.

John was the first child of this second marriage. His christening record, as entered in the Elstow Church Book, and now preserved in the Transcript Records of the Archdeaconry of Bedford reads:

"1628. John the sonne of Thomas Bonnionn, Junr. the 30th of Novemb."

This fateful and also dimly hopeful year was nearly over. On June 5th the Petition of Right had passed Commons, and on June 7th, with the king's reluctant assent, it had become a statute of the realm. On July 1st William Laud had been made Bishop of London. On August 23rd the Duke of Buckingham had been assassinated. In November, the month of John Bunyan's birth, Oliver Cromwell was returned to Parliament from Huntingdon, and three months later, on February 11, 1628/29, he would make his first speech in Commons. During this year the Massachusetts Bay Company leaders were in frequent session. Thomas Harvey published his treatise on the circulation of the blood. Shakespeare had been dead twelve years. George Fox was four years old. In this same year, 1628, an Englishman on the verge of middle age might have lived his entire life in peace, so far as enemy action against Britain was concerned, a condition which would not be true for his children or for any other generation even to the present day.

Very early in this year that was to be a turning point in English history, it was apparent, even on the surfaces of life, that the forces were gathering for vast overthrow, national tragedy, and the opening of new springs of life. On all levels of English society traditional loyalties were in flux, and in the midst of this widespread unrest, new types of leadership in both church and state were being unconsciously tutored. For one capable of leadership, or for a layman with courage enough to hold to unpopular ideas against danger to life itself, it may be a man's good fortune to be born into a world of tumult. It may also be his best key to remembrance. Except for the peculiar tumult of the mid-seventeenth century, the world might never have heard of John Bunyan.

Portents of ill became reality slowly, however, and in so far as is known, Bunyan's boyhood story was that of a fairly normal country boy for his time and neighborhood. In the cottage at Bunyan's End during the next five years after 1628, two more children were born to Thomas and Margaret Bunyan: a daughter, Margaret, christened March 7, 1630, and a son, William, December 1, 1633. Under the steep thatched roof at this far extremity of the parish, there would be childhood companionship for the eldest son. There would also be a few glimpses of a world beyond these border limits. Isolated, though not remote, the Bunyan cottage stood in a field at the foot of a gentle slope, from which the tower of Elstow church a mile away was plainly visible. In the nearer distance were other thatched cottages similar to that of Thomas Bunyan. By walking to the top of the slope he could see the spire of St. Paul's church in Bedford, scarcely farther than a mile away also. Except for marginal glimpses such as these, however, and the human associations they represented, life was little wider than the immediate cottage neighborhood. Bunyan's End was a dead-end street, and the village of Elstow, numbering no more than sixty families at this date, was as yet far removed from the whirlpool of public affairs which would change England.

A lifetime later, Celia Fiennes, a sidesaddle traveler in these parts, wrote that in the Bedfordshire section the miles were "longer than those about London and much in Lanes and woods." Seventy-five years earlier, when John Bunyan knew these miles as a boy, travelers would have found them still longer and the woods and lanes still more dense and untraveled. Even Bedford, the most considerable town in this part of the county, had no more than a thousand inhabitants at any time in John Bunyan's entire life, and in his boyhood it was much smaller.

> "Bedford town is an old Building, it's wash'd by the river Ouse, which Comes from Buckingham and is here Broader than in most places till it reaches Yorke,"

Celia Fiennes wrote.

> "There is nothing worth notice in the town, . . . severall streetes small and old, the middle streete which runns from ye Bridge is pretty broad, wherein stands ye market place and house which is on severall stone pillars and raill'd in."

She noted also the gate, the houses on the bridge, the "very good fish" with which the river was stored, the "trunkes," as she called them, along the brink, from which the fish were "taken out fresh for supper or dinner." Past the bridge, she noted the "severall notches of Ground" set with willows, the many "Little boats chained to the sides belonging to ye people of the town for their diversion," the well kept bowling-green, the seats, the summer houses. What she repeatedly called "large prospects," interested her particularly, and she must have climbed to the roof of the market house, in hope of another such view, for she remarked that from that point the prospect commanded the "whole town and Country round." [5]

One can still recognize Bedford in these details, for the modern town retains much of picturesqueness, thanks chiefly to the river with its clusters of swans under the bridge and along the banks, the many boats, large and small, the willows, the narrow streets, the gabled cottages, their thatched roofs gone in these later rebuildings, the lower stories often transformed into shops, and best reminder of these earlier days, the Moot Hall, half-timbered, half-stucco, still standing alone on the Elstow green, and the market cross now only a broken stump. In the open spaces around the Moot Hall the boys played their games: trapball in its various forms, Northern murr and spell, and most popular game of all, tipcat, closest to modern cricket. The popularity of this traditional game owed something to the fact that any number of boys could play and that everything needed could easily be homemade. Any boy could whittle the six-inch shuttle called the "cat" and also the bludgeon, or "catstaff," by which it was struck. The rules were simple enough for the youngest to follow. Stand in the center of the circle, hit your "cat" in turn, and then estimate how far it has gone beyond the circle bounds. Skill consisted as much in the estimate as in the stroke. A noisy, exciting game it was, exercising a fascination which long outlasted boyhood. Of all Sunday games in seventeenth century England, it was easily first choice, and thanks to Bunyan, it is still known by name down to present times.

Once a year, May 2nd to 5th, the Elstow green was a livelier place than on any playday, for this was the occasion of the annual fair dating back to the time when the Elstow church was part of the ancient abbey. During this festival time the whole area was laid out in streets, bordered with displays of merchandise, jugglers, puppet shows, perhaps a platform for stage plays, to entertain the great ones from afar and the hundreds of country folk for miles around. Days afterward the small boys on the green would imitate the strange feats of strength, the sleight of hand, the magician's tricks they would not see again until the next May 2nd to 5th.

At the time of Celia Fiennes' visit, John Bunyan had been asleep in Bunhill Fields, London, for a full decade, and at that time there was as yet no reason why a visitor from a higher level of English society should pause for a moment on the bridge, under the willows, in the market place, or scan the broad view from the market-house roof for his sake. Before another century had passed, however, certain details in that broad view would be familiar to many thousands who would never set foot in Bedford, but who had traveled with Christian every step of the way from the City of Destruction, through the Slough of Despond (just back of the Elstow birthplace), past the Interpreter's House on the near side of the bridge, and on to the Celestial City. But before John Bunyan was to see the transformed landscape of his dream, as the reading world knows it, he would have walked the Elstow-Bedford "wilderness of this world" a thousand times, known its landmarks and obscure corners, as only an adventurous, oversensitive, and perhaps lonely boy could know them.

For the first sixteen years of his life he looked out on this gentle landscape of wide spaces, broken here and there by clumps of willows, of meandering streams, of sloping meadows, blooming like gardens in the springtime and vocal with bird songs. A featureless landscape it is to some eyes, since it lacks high drama of nature's gift, but serene and good to live with. Looked at today, its serenity interrupted by the changes of modern life, it still seems a kindly background for the dreamer John Bunyan was sometimes to be. Surely only one who had been a country boy could have written *Pilgrim's Progress*. Had John Bunyan been born a Londoner in 1628 and lived his boy life in and out of crooked streets, crowded tenements, noisy city clamors, and in Defoe's word, "drawn his breath in sin," there would probably have been in his Dream no wicket gate yonder over the plain, no undiscovered path the other side of the stile, no sound of bells across the valley, no Enchanted Ground, no Delectable Mountains, no castle in the far distance. *Pilgrim's Progress* is a country book; in fact, a Midland country book, impossible to a mere sojourner in these same rolling spaces and soft sounds. Inevitably its geography was conceived by one who knew nature's ways without ever having consciously learned them, one whose earliest child pleasures had been the sights and sounds and fragrances of the changing seasons. The breath of the fields is in this book. There are wide spaces, secret dells, rocky slopes, fields stretching far away. There is dew on the grass, the music of brooks, a child's fear of dark places, the footprint of animals at dawn, a bundle of myrrh for the gathering, a robin with a spider in his mouth. The evidence of such association as belongs to one's early years is on many pages. It is evidence too deep for reminiscence, too deep for conscious learning. Clearly the imagination of this gifted boy had been nourished by country fact, early enough for the tutelage to be forgotten and too early for him to be aware of the treasure hoard he possessed.

His thought of what lay beyond this country world would have been teased now and then by what he saw on the High Road, which for a brief moment became the main street of Elstow village. Down this road en route to or from London, fifty miles away, a fleeting segment of the world passed by. Sometimes a company of forty men on horseback, sometimes only two or three travelers to the farther towns and villages from London way. Once in a long while a royal equipage, or the retinue of a visiting prince, scores in his train, nobles, ushers, courtiers, grooms of the packsaddle, stragglers and hangers-on. More often it would be a country judge riding his circuit, accompanied by barristers and servants, perhaps a royal messenger, bearing dispatches, a doctor in the saddle, soldiers riding behind a prisoner, who walked on foot, chains on his legs and a boy bearing part of the weight. It might be a funeral procession, the corpse tied to a board and carried on horseback, pack horses laden with market produce, a litter of pigs, a flock of geese, a group of rogues and vagabonds, contrary to law, a band of gipsies, a Tom o' Bedlam, ballad singers. Any day might bring the postboy who appears in one of Bunyan's *Country Rhimes for Children*,

> "With what haste and speed
> He travels the road,"

sounding his horn as he goes. Bunyan had seen and heard him many times.

Among these travelers who may have arrived just at nightfall, there were sometimes those who tarried for the night at the hostelry known as the Swan Inn by the river, where its successor still stands today. The different garb and far destinations of these passing strangers might have been matter of awe and wonder to the small boys on the green. What lay beyond the turn of the road whence they had come? Possibly there were adventurous longings in the morning when the bustle had ceased, and the strangers had ridden out of sight in the opposite direction, but if so, they were inarticulate, as the games around the Moot Hall began again.

There were other hints of a larger, or at least a very different, world from that of the forge and tinker's cart. Around the manor house of Sir Thomas Hillersdon, a little back from the High Road, southwest of the Elstow church, an unseen life went on in a dimension unknown to a brazier's son and his boy companions. In Bunyan's later memory certain details of this lordly mansion, its noble proportions, its arches and decorated panels, would grow in grace and magnificence, to unite with those of the still nobler Houghton House, several miles farther away, until presently the memory of both would contribute something to his dream of a stately palace, which had no earthly locale and was by name House Beautiful.

Bunyan's boyhood schooling was brief. "It pleased God," he wrote years later, to put it into his parents' hearts "to put me to school, to learn both to read and write." These were goals often missed by tinkers' sons, and the fact of such an ambition in Thomas and Margaret Bunyan's thought suggests perhaps something of plan or at least hope for their son beyond the forge and cart. The record of this early schooling is a blank, but its brevity is attested in Bunyan's own remark that he did "soon lose that little I learned." [6]

It was probably poor enough, for at that date village schoolmasters were often incompetent in their teaching and unscrupulous in their discipline, making it so severe as hardly to instill a desire to learn, much less a love of learning for its own sake. In Richard Baxter's boyhood village of Eaton Constantine in Shropshire, four clergymen in rapid succession, all of them, in Baxter's memory, of scant education and doubtful morality, "read Common Prayer on Sundays and Holy-days, and taught school and tipled on the Week-days, and whipt the Boys when they were drunk, so that we changed them very oft." [7]

At the Harpur School in Bedford, in 1629, the usher had been "violently removed" under charges of neglect and cruelty. On one occasion he had injured a boy so severely, having "mangled him in the throat and the mouth," that the doctor feared he would die. In Elstow, a little later, one William Varney had been dismissed for "grossly neglecting the school by frequent absence from it, by nightwalking, and mis-spending his time in taverns and ale-houses, and is very cruel when present to the boys." By these misdemeanors he had rendered the school "desolate" and caused parents to send their boys elsewhere. [8] Even so, country boys capable of it got an education. Baxter's father set him to reading the Bible, which Baxter reported,

John Bunyan

particularly in the historical part, "uniting with my Nature, greatly delighted me."

There was no grammar school in Elstow when Bunyan would have been ready for it, and as the Harpur School in Bedford was available for sons of Bedford property owners only, he would not have been eligible for instruction there. It is strongly probable that he attended school at Houghton Conquest, several miles from Elstow, although nothing survives that can be trusted as evidence of his attendance. We know only that Thomas Archer, rector of the Houghton Conquest church, had some knowledge of Bunyan's father, possibly some acquaintance with him, for it is in Archer's *Journal* that the oft-repeated tale of Thomas Bunyan's finding the three white rooks is recorded. They were in a nest in the Bery woods, "all white as milke and not a blacke feather on them."

Thomas Archer was dead before the boy Bunyan was of school age, but the Houghton Conquest school was in existence after 1632. A schoolmaster was provided by the will of Sir Francis Clarke, founder of the school, a lodging for the master, and also an alms-house. The fact that by the terms of the benefaction, he was to be appointed by Sidney Sussex College, to which Sir Francis had also given generously, suggests that the school was of grammar school rank. If so, attendance here would have meant dame school training previously, and as to that, Elstow records supply no hint. All that we know is Bunyan's statement of his parents' ambition for him and of the brevity of his training. Had his own religious awakening come prior to the ending of his school days, the urge to learn might have been stronger, but formal schooling was not his world, nor ever to be. Blessedly he had learned to read, and the key was in his hand. It would open many doors, most important of all for him, doors to knowledge of the Bible. There is no record of a parental spur in this direction, such as Richard Baxter reported, but somewhere very early in his own search for inner peace, Bunyan discovered the Bible for himself. It would be to him a school and college education; in fact, almost a total culture.

Looked back upon in the light of his whole life and achievement, the greatest event of not only his boyhood but of his whole mortal

Bunyan known to have used Geneva Bible also

span, had nothing whatever to do with Elstow or Bedford. It had taken place seventeen years before he was born and was none other than the publication of the King James version of the Bible in 1611. One can speak more largely and still speak truly. In the first quarter of the century perhaps only the sailing of the *Mayflower* and the founding of Plymouth colony are historical events commensurate in importance with putting this version of the Scriptures in the cottages of England. Henceforth it would become the household book of the land. It would be read by the rank and file as it had never been read before and has never been read since. It would fit every need of life. It would hold the answer to every question men could ask, personal as well as national. It would be the literal voice of God to individual men and women. Its meanings would be discussed and passionately debated not only by assemblies of divines, but by work-men at the bench and soldiers in the garrison. Men would go to prison and die for their own interpretations of its meaning. Their interpretations would be a sword in the church body and would split the ranks of believers into a multitude of sects. These interpreta-tions would bestow upon anyone who could read a power hitherto unmatched in print. William Tyndale had paid with his life for his ambition to put the Bible within popular reach. His alleged remark to the theologian came true:

> "If God spare my life, [he had said] ere many years, I will cause a boy that driveth the plough shall know more of the Scripture than thou dost." [9]

In a very true sense John Bunyan was one of Tyndale's plowboys.

The fifty-four men who gave England the King James version had built on the foundation of the work life had not allowed Tyndale to finish. They had also done more. They had achieved a common lan-guage for everyday communication, a language that became almost a native speech to Puritan England. It is the language of Cromwell's speeches in Parliament and of his private correspondence, as well as the language of the pulpit. In the words of the Preface to the King James version,

John Bunyan

"Translation it is that openeth the window, to let in the light; that breaketh the shell, that we may eat the kernel; that putteth aside the curtaine, that we may look into the most holy Place; that removeth the cover of the well, that wee may come by the water, even as *Jacob* rolled away the stone from the mouth of the well, by which meanes the flockes of *Laban* were watered. Indeede without translation into the vulgar tongue, the unlearned are like children at *Jacob's* well (which was deepe) without a bucket or something to draw with." [10]

After 1611 no English cottager need be without the bucket.

Had any schoolmaster urged John Bunyan in his schooldays to read "Great Books" in the English language and literature, the shelf was already long. Spenser, Shakespeare, Montaigne, Bacon were waiting; also Sidney's *Arcadia*, More's *Utopia*, Cervantes' *Don Quixote*, Holinshed's *Chronicles*, Hobbes' *Leviathan*, Burton's *Anatomy of Melancholy*, Hooker's *Ecclesiastical Polity*, but there is no likelihood that he had ever so much as handled any one of them. His life reading was on a single track, and in his criteria of choice literary merit did not exist. Religion was reality above all else. Belief could take you to prison or to the scaffold any day during those decades. Religion had no rival in print. Best sellers were religious tracts, and sermons were almost the whole intellectual life of the rank and file. For Bunyan, as for thousands more on his social level, the Bible alone was sufficient, as it was for thousands on higher levels as well.

Fortunately, however, in his boyhood years another printed resource came early enough to give his imagination a characteristic bent. His mental world was enriched and stimulated by the fables and tales of medieval adventure that other English boys were reading. Sir Bevis of Hampton, Guy of Warwick, Sir Eglamoure of Artoys bewitched them all; "Corrupted my affections and lost my time," Richard Baxter was to say, after he had freed himself from their spell, but he like Bunyan had spent hours of delirious pleasure in company with these gallant ones. It is remembered of Cardinal Newman that as a boy he used to wish *The Arabian Nights* were true. If one reads them early enough, they are true, and medieval romances were probably so for John Bunyan in the years to which they belonged. In the light of the guilt he was later to feel for such indulgence, it may seem unkind to say that his early exposure to a world that never was, is one of the most fortunate chapters in his experience. One hopes also that it provided something of a balance for the anguish he suffered during these early years for his alleged sins. Surely the picture of the Elstow boy lost in a medieval world of tournaments and battles with giants and dragons, throws a broad shaft of light on much that he was later to write, particularly on *Pilgrim's Progress.*

To reread some of these lordly tales with *Pilgrim's Progress* in mind is to meet on page after page prototypes of Giant Despair, Apollyon, Giant Grim, Bloody Man, and to recognize analogues of tyrannies, dangers, victories along Christian's or Christiana's journey. These tales unlock a world of wonder: Sir Bevis, saddling his horse for high adventure, tracking the wild boar, the terror of Ermyn's court, to his foul den along the road "wholly covered by the litter of human bones"; Sir Bevis, blowing his horn to prolong the boar's slumber and then thrusting his spear down the foul creature's throat. No more could he refuse acorns and demand human flesh. Sir Bevis, attacking a giant thirty feet long, bristling like a sow and with a foot of space between his brows; Sir Bevis, confined in a deep dungeon, guarded by two dragons accustomed to devouring their prisoners, and then after seven years escaping by climbing the chain that fastened him to the rock; why must such a story ever end? [11]

So it would be with Guy of Warwick unhorsing his opponents at the tournament, winning the prize, battling the man-eating monster that could not be wounded from the nave upward, fighting the giant so big no horse could carry him, and finally being borne to heaven by a thousand and seven angels. All these encounters, triumphs by violence or skill with a magic sword, contributed something of detail and more of atmosphere, not of actual English earth, to the perils that would someday beset Christian: the lions in his path, the foul dungeon of Giant Despair, the fiery tortures of Faithful, the fierce barking of the great mastiff at the wicket gate, the deep pits, the mists and darkness of caverns emitting foul odors. The deep imprint these fantastic stories had made in Bunyan's boy mind, and the childhood terrors they had invited, enabled him somehow to carry into adulthood the memory of the feelings they had excited: the immediacy of doom and the hopelessness of escape. He had the rare kind of emotional memory which preserved for him the sense of how it would be to see the jaws open at close range and to feel the dragon's heat on his face. The folklore of the Elstow neighborhood would supply a locale for similar dangers. Once he had read the stories of these long-ago terrors, he would go well out of his way to avoid such danger spots as the mound in the neighboring parish of Eastcotts known as the Devil's Jumps.

To an adult reader the pattern of these romances is so heavily moral as to endanger the adventure for the sake of the preachment. Christian champions won because they were on God's side; those whom they beheaded or pierced to the heart were always the devil's underlings, whether king, giant, or beast. But to a seventeenth century boy to whom sermons had been a part of life since he first knew the meaning of words, this ethical pattern would have been so completely taken for granted that he would hardly have been conscious of it. Like any other boy in any other age, he read for the adventure alone. Did the champion win? How was the dragon slain? To be God's champion was to be the victor; to be against God was to be destroyed. The boy interest was in the *how* of each success, the stroke by which the beast was left roaring in his wounds, the agility of the victor with sword or truncheon, the speed of the horse as invincible as his rider, the secret discovery by which the hero extricated himself from the dungeon, or untied the knots which fastened him to the rock. Also for a champion to put on palmer's weeds and henceforth lead the holy life in a hermit's cell was wholly expected. The religious framework was basic and inevitable; only the details changed, and in these lay the boy's interest.

In these romances time waits; logic is defied. Raging lions prove "gentle beasts"; horses recognize their masters in disguise and neigh loudly at the critical moment when a horse is needed. Robert the Devil, promised to the devils by his mother at his conception, is converted and becomes a bright example of Christian virtue. As an infant he had been fed with a horn because he bit his mother's breasts; as a boy he cast stones, scratched out eyes, killed his school-master; as a young knight he killed so many at his first tournament that his father stopped the tilting. Presently wondering why he was so wicked, he strode into his mother's presence and demanded to know. When told that he had been given to the devil body and soul, he first fainted, then vowed henceforth to do nothing but good, did penance as directed by the hermit, humbled himself, acted the fool, and then did great deeds on the battlefield. It was the "deeds" which stretched the boy imagination and lured him on to the next romance.

By his own words of recall for his tender years, this world of monsters, dragons, devils, wicked spirits, took shape for Bunyan in personal terms by nightmarish visions of hell fiends, lying in wait to drag him off to the bonds of eternal darkness. Night by night, he wrote in his *Grace Abounding*, God did thus "scare and affright" him with "fearful dreams" and "dreadful visions," so that he was often so "overcome with despair of life and heaven" that he wished either there had been no hell or that he himself had been a devil so that he might rather be a tormentor than himself the tormented.[12] Santayana's phrase "the agonized conscience of Calvinism" needs no clearer illustration than the monstrous sense of guilt which matched these nighttime horrors in a small boy's thought and suggested to him so childish a way of escape.

There was nothing unique about them. Bunyan's anguished dreams can be paralleled many times in contemporary reminiscence. The pulpit was usually responsible. Another ten-year-old, only one year older than John Bunyan, John Rogers, a schoolboy of Maldon, Essex, tells of having been thrown into paroxyms of terror by the preaching of William Fenner, a man "full of zeal." Gazing straight at this startled boy, the preacher had thundered, beat the pulpit and shouted,

"Oh, you knotty! rugged! proud piece of flesh! you stony, rocky flinty, hard heart, what wilt thou do when thou art roaring amongst the damned?" [13]

The sequel to this horrifying directness of warning was that John Rogers was first startled, then troubled, then so "scared and frighted" that he "fell to duties," heard more sermons, read the Bible, not knowing what he read, prayed prayers, hardly knowing what he prayed, and went to sleep every night with his hands clasped in the attitude of prayer in case the devils came. Prayers were the only charm he knew against the devil's clutch, and for good measure he said them twice. Once, a little later, when Stephen Marshall, another preacher, caught him napping during service, he thought he had lost his chance of salvation forever. He made a covenant with himself never to sleep in meeting again, kept himself awake by writing all he could catch of the sermon, memorized it, and repeated it entire every night as a part of his bedtime devotions. His story is more extravagant than John Bunyan's, but the parallel is precise, and for both boys this early mental suffering retained its sharp cruelty into their mature years.

As he looked back on his early despair in maturity, John Rogers wrote,

"All this while I was labouring for life . . . and I did much covet to know the things of God." [14]

So did John Bunyan. Even as a child he was fleeing from what he sought, and unfortunately his Hound of Heaven was born of doctrines which repelled by their harshness. The fright and resentment they caused impelled a sensitive, confused boy to a spirit of bravado which did not represent him, and as he fled ever faster, his recklessness outran his fears.

Terrifying sermons such as John Rogers reported would not have been preached by John Kellie, who ministered in the Elstow parish during John Bunyan's early years, but as in all other country parishes, visiting clergymen passed by and were often invited to preach. Bedfordshire had a strong taint of Dissent, and an evangelical accent would not have been unwelcome to many in the congregation. Moreover, there was nothing unorthodox in the sermons which had so affrighted John Rogers. The two ministers were of good standing. Stephen Marshall was a Presbyterian, a frequent preacher before the Long Parliament, and often consulted by men of affairs in religious matters. The fright their words had caused was a matter of noisy zeal rather than of the doctrines they announced. Moreover, the soil was ready. The consciences of children had been subjected to a schooling as to what constituted sin and righteousness, and the assumption that they were by nature on the corrupt side was unquestioned. Counting up one's sins by the day and pleading forgiveness before one closed his eyes was standard practice, and not with ten-year-old boys alone.

Richard Baxter did likewise, but his boy list of iniquities is more suited to his age. His toll numbered eight: lying, when he feared detection, "excessive gluttonous eating of Apples and Pears," stealing them in neighboring orchards when there were plenty at home, excessive addiction to play, the reading of romances, fables, and old tales, indulgence in "idle, foolish chat & scurrilous foolish Words and Actions," pride in his schoolmaster's commendation and "unreverence" toward his parents.[15] Unlike John Bunyan, he "durst not swear." Take away swearing, and Bunyan as a nine-year-old would probably have been as pure as George Fox, who could say, and mean it, that

> "When I came to eleven years of age I knew pureness and righteousness; for while a child I was taught how to walk to be kept pure." [16]

Not so John Bunyan. Profanity was his major talent, to believe him literally in his self-condemnation. As he put it,

> "Considering my years, which were yet tender, I had few equals, . . . both for cursing, swearing, lying, and blaspheming the holy name of God." [17]

Had he dared to spell out a sample of his surpassing profanity on the written page, the guilt might have seemed paler to modern eyes. John Rogers did so, and the passage is illuminating.

Once while running at play with other children, he "threw out vain words to himself," crying aloud, "O, Lord!" His heart was so suddenly smitten with the enormity of the oath he had uttered, that he ran so fast he could not stop. At this pace, so goes the tale, he suddenly saw before him a gateway in which was set a naked sword, glittering with a fearful edge, set from one post to the other. He screamed, but having no power to stop, he ran through the gate and believed himself cut in two, until when he turned around, gate, sword, children and all had vanished. Amazed to find himself all in one piece, he was so "deeply and woefully wounded within" at this deliverance, that "never since, as I know of, have I had such extravagant, preposterous expressions pass from me." He had said "O, Lord!" His subsequent anguish for his sins, his fastings, prayers, sermon reading, psalm singing, fears of hell and night visions of devils are a match for John Bunyan's.[18] In the mature story of both men, the extravagance of these early experiences of terror was recognized for what it was, but the sufferings were real while childhood lasted. Such fears had root in part in the tensions of the Laudian era, as well as in a sensitivity which should have been shielded from such exploitation.

As John Bunyan looked back on his personal boyhood story in the perspective of his thirty-eighth year, he saw that, unknown to himself during these careless years, he had been marked as a dedicated spirit and protected for that reason. In his memory, as in that of his brother preachers who wrote their memoirs, divine protection was often given trivial application. Once he had fallen out of a boat in Bedford River, once he had struck an adder with his stick, and while she was stunned, had "plucked her sting out with my fingers," and gone unharmed. Richard Baxter's list of near disasters, also recalled in maturity, is even longer. Once his horse had slipped on a snowy road and thrown him almost (but not quite) under the wheels of a wagon he was meeting; once his bookshelves fell on him; at another time he swallowed a gold bullet, but after three weeks and the fastings and prayers of good neighbors, he was "delivered of it." [19] The record of divine watchfulness over these "set apart" men, as they recalled their wayward boyhoods, grows from one autobiography to the next. One and all they swallowed peach stones, fell into open wells, were attacked by beasts, lost their way in woods and swamps, but always God was there. They recorded these deliverances in all seriousness, not in boyhood diaries, but as mature men of reputation and influence whom God had saved for

The Boy of Bunyan's End

His own purpose. Bunyan's list is less spectacular than many others, but he showed the same sense of special preservation that he in turn might save others, eternally.

In the perspective of three more centuries, John Bunyan's boyhood would seem to have forecast the central secret of his life, but not clarified the pattern by which he would discover, much less unravel, it. In his introspective moments he knew himself to be a creature of sin and he was oppressed by the helplessness of his doom. At such times there was not a ray of light on his path, but seeking no guidance, he suffered alone. There is no reason to doubt his self-accusations as to coarseness of speech and manners or indulgence in vices common to his age and the village mores. As a brazier's son he would have been neighbor to coarseness and also to such refinements as Elstow offered, very probably in his own home and the persons of his father and mother.

Boyhood ended for him, and ended abruptly, in the summer of 1644, when he was fifteen years old. On June 20th his mother, Margaret Bunyan, died in her forty-first year. One month later, on July 24th, his sister Margaret, the close companion of his childhood, was also carried across the fields to Elstow churchyard. Less than one month later, his father, Thomas Bunyan, brought a new wife to the cottage at Bunyan's End. In sequel to his own grief and loneliness and sense of a world awry, the fifteen-year-old son probably watched the increasing number of soldiers under slow march down the High Road, now that the reality of war came closer to Bedford's very doors. In darkness greater than he had ever yet known, he waited for November 30th. The army door opened. The door of the Elstow cottage closed behind him. Boyhood was over.

Chapter Two

Soldier in Cromwell's
New Model Army

On his sixteenth birthday he became a soldier. The muster roll of Lieutenant Colonel Richard Cockayne's regiment records that on November 30, 1644, "John Bunion" was enrolled among the privates or "centinels" of the Parliamentary army.[1] At this date enlistment would not have been a matter of free choice, for in June, 1644, Sir Samuel Luke, Commissioner for Bedfordshire, had issued warrants requiring all men between the ages of sixteen and sixty to report immediately for military duty. Bunyan may have responded to the order previous to his November 30th birthday, when his enrollment might legally be recorded, but in no case could induction into military life have come as a surprise.

The most critical year of the war had been 1643, and Cromwell's presence in Bedford from time to time had repeatedly dramatized the urgency of Parliament's need for men. In January his regiment of horse had been quartered in Bedford. Two months later he was at the Swan Inn waiting for a thousand foot soldiers to come from Cambridge, Norfolk, and Suffolk, and he was also seeking additional help from Bedford to cope with the king's men under Viscount Camden.

These appeals continued throughout the summer and autumn of

24

1643, as defeat, sickness, and desertion reduced Manchester's army to about a third of its former strength. In June royal forces marched across Bedfordshire in search of supplies. This meant the taking of fat sheep and oxen, the raiding of barns and gardens, the setting of posts and stretching of chains across private gateways. In October, Bedford town was briefly in royal hands, and though Essex quickly restored it to Parliament, the previous assurance that the county was safe Parliamentary territory had been seriously shaken. Meanwhile royal victories had gained ground for the king, until by the end of the year his forces were in control of all the north except Lancaster and Hull, and all of the west except Gloucester, Plymouth, and a few towns in Dorset. Parliament's need for men was all but desperate, and if they were to be found in time it was the Eastern Association to which Bedfordshire belonged that must supply them.

This was the urgency to which Bunyan's enlistment belonged. Day by day throughout the immediately preceding months, along with the other Elstow residents, he had responded to the ringing of the church bells, summoning all to hear further appeals or news reports. Day by day and no doubt impatiently he had watched recruits passing in groups along the High Road. Now it was his turn to go. In this dark summer of his personal life, he probably welcomed the call.

It was not sudden, however. Well before November word of the Parliamentary warrant for compulsory service had penetrated to nearly every village of the realm, and as the drummers went through the streets war took on a new and ominous reality. Colonel Cockayne, to whose regiment Bunyan would belong, recruited his men personally, according to custom, and then formed them into a company, henceforth to be considered his own special property and responsibility. His arrival in Harrowden, Houghton Conquest, Elstow, and other neighboring villages would have caused tenseness and may have aroused hostility, as in some other towns. Some sixteen-year-olds went into hiding. Others escaped after being enrolled. Still others came forward to enlist voluntarily, as impressment knocked at every door, and the number of men enlisted reached a male majority in nearly every village.

Those who were left took sides and then changed back and forth as loyalties wavered. Although the sympathy of Bedfordshire had been with Parliament quite solidly, sharp divisions and reversals came about continually, as in any civil war. Neighbors were against neighbors, fathers against sons, brothers against brothers. Each side called the other traitor, "without giving a syllable of reason for it," Richard Baxter recalled. In his own village of Kiddermaster, what he called "the fury of the rabble" had led to such violence as on one occasion sent him into hiding for fear of his life. "And, I think," he added, "there were few parishes where at one time or other blood had not been shed." [2]

Whether violence had come to Elstow is not recorded, but one may be sure that the confusions of the years 1643–1644 had not spared even this remote village. In 1642 Bedfordshire residents had addressed a petition to the king, saying,

"Many are the miseries your Subjects suffer, and our fears are beyond our miseries." [3]

By November, 1644, these miseries were sadly increased, as resentment and suspicion followed each successive encampment of either royal or Parliamentary forces within county borders.

Bunyan's enlistment on November 30th corresponded closely with the authorization of the New Model Army to replace the depleted forces of Manchester, Essex, and Waller. Originally made up of trained bands, these forces had lacked the dependability of a standing army. They were local units only, with something of legal right on their side when the men refused to fight beyond their own neighborhood. When ordered to march afield, many among them merely laid down their arms and went home. Ill fed, ill clad, ill quartered, and often unpaid for long periods, they gave little more than halfhearted service. Even before midsummer, 1644, it had become increasingly apparent that unless something were done immediately, Parliament would soon have no army. Forced impressment with promise of regular pay was the beginning toward a solution. Looked back upon, this decision virtually determined the outcome of the war as a Parliamentary victory.

The decision having been made, action upon it had followed

immediately. In June, 1644, both Houses called for a new force of three thousand horse and ten thousand foot soldiers to be ready by July 20th, on a permanent basis with pay assured. On July 2nd, eighteen days before the deadline, came the dramatic victory of Marston Moor, when in Cromwell's word,

"God made them as stubble to our swords."

In immediate sequel to this victory, a compromise settlement with the king looked more possible than at any time in the preceding two years of war, but Cromwell saw otherwise. A negotiated peace? No. Nothing but a complete military victory would justify the cost of the two preceding years of war and make a new beginning possible. Furthermore, nothing but complete concentration on military success could achieve such a victory. The divisive issues of Presbyterianism and Independency must be put aside in the urgent need for wholehearted unity of purpose or all would be lost. Cromwell's scathing speech in Parliament after the second battle of Newbury, on October 27th, expressed what he believed to have been the cause of Manchester's ineffectiveness as a leader; namely, lack of unity among his men. Such lack must end, and at once.

This disastrous second battle of Newbury was the last engagement of the old army. The king had escaped. The forces of Manchester were sadly disorganized. Manchester himself was immediately accused of ineffectiveness and faced with impeachment. What might have been a long period of inaction while this charge against him was being considered and a verdict pending, was ended by Cromwell's speech on December 9th, when he revived both hope and lagging energy by demanding that instead of all this inquiry into whose fault it is that we have not prospered in war,

"Let us apply ourselves to the remedy. Let us put the army into a new method."

Commons had already had warning that such a proposal was coming, for on November 23rd the Committee of both Houses, of which Cromwell was a member had been asked,

27

"to consider of a frame or model for the whole Militia, and present it to the House."

The answer to Cromwell's December 9th speech was action on this proposal. The Committee went to work, and after due consideration of their findings, the New Model Army became a fact. On January 11th, 1644/45, England's first standing army, twenty-one thousand in number, was authorized. It was to be built on the model of Cromwell's Ironsides. On January 21st Sir Thomas Fairfax was made commander. Thereafter plans went forward with great speed, and as one proclamation followed another, the result was electric. By April the organization was complete, and by May the army was ready to go into action.[4]

As a new recruit of Colonel Cockayne's company, John Bunyan was assigned to the garrison of Newport Pagnell, twelve miles from Elstow, between Bedford and Stony Stratford, and as soon as the recruits from Bedford and the small villages around were assembled, the long, slow march began. It took a complete day. Bunyan had often pushed the tinker's cart along the first miles of this long road, but on the day he marched away from home with scores of strangers, sixteen to sixty, the familiar landmarks might suddenly have seemed strange. If so, this was only the beginning of strangeness. He would soon be one among many hundreds of strangers, looking out not only on a different scene within the garrison, but through newly opened windows of experience, of danger, of evil, of human brutishness, of courage, and most important of all, new windows into himself.

In the fortress of Newport Pagnell, now strengthened by Parliament at Cromwell's insistence, he would spend his two and a half years as a soldier in the People's Army. It would hardly prove "a warm nest for the soldier in winter," as *Mercurius Britannicus* had remarked the preceding October 23rd. Nor would it be the powerful base of operations against royalist activity from the west, as had been hoped, when it suddenly came into Parliament hands late in 1642. Strategically situated beyond low meadows, and encircled by the Ouse and Lovat rivers, it occupied a midway position between the counties of the Eastern Association and the London stronghold of the king, and might well have been of great military importance. Instead, it became little more than a center from which small forays were sent out against minor strongholds, chiefly in the near neighborhood. By these nibbling engagements more territory was slowly brought under Parliamentary claim, but the results hardly justified the elaborate and expensive fortifications completed during the summer of 1644, under the direction of Sir Samuel Luke of Cople Wood End, newly appointed governor of the fortress.[5]

John Bunyan arrived too late to take part in these preparations. Sir Samuel's notebook gives hint of their magnitude in the listing of his need for three hundred shovels and spades, two hundred pickaxes, five hundred wheelbarrows, four hundred spars, and one thousand "deal boards," along with the forced labor of workmen from neighboring towns. He also missed a chance to take part in the July 2nd victory of Marston Moor, which practically determined the outcome of the first half of the civil war. Although it might not have seemed so to a new recruit, his two and a half years of service would be lacking in tension as compared with the two preceding years.

He probably saw no large-scale fighting, but took part in various small forays against royal strongholds in the neighborhood. Such attacks, spoken of as sieges, usually involved no more than several score of men (possibly less) both horsemen and foot soldiers, carrying pikes or staves, and wearing cuirasses. The encounter usually lasted no longer than several hours. Soldiers took their turn in these engagements, usually as volunteers. Bunyan himself referred to a soldier who on one such occasion had volunteered to go in his stead and had been killed in the action.[6] This deliverance was later to be interpreted as meaning that God had saved him for a special service to Himself, but at the time Bunyan may merely have thought that he was lucky and his substitute unlucky. The oft-repeated assumption that Bunyan was present at the siege of Leicester is unfounded, since his name on a muster roll shows him to have been serving under Major Boulton at Newport Pagnell from May 22nd to 27th, 1645.[7] The siege of Leicester began on the following day.

His associates in the ranks would have been for the most part men of his own class. The New Model Army, as its popular name, the People's Army, suggests, was made up of a cross section of different religious affiliations as of different trades and callings. On the extreme right were the Presbyterians and ex-royalists; in the middle, the conservative Dissenters or Congregationalists, and on the extreme left, the Levellers, Baptists, and Fifth Monarchists. Sir Samuel Luke, governor of the fortress, was an uncompromising Presbyterian, even intolerantly so, but in high favor with Cromwell, to whom he was distantly related through Cromwell's aunt, Elizabeth Hampden. Cromwell had discovered that the army he needed in the 1644 emergency could not meet his earlier thought, when he had announced that he desired to have none in his army but such as are of independent judgment. At least it could not be Independent written with a capital letter. Nor could he quite hope for the

"plain russet-coated captain that knows what he fights for and loves what he knows,"

rather than one who is called a gentleman and is nothing else. Essential homogeneity in religious loyalty, as in other matters, was impossible, and unity, in so far as it existed, was not of creed and church polity, but of some share in Cromwell's own unshakable faith that beyond all question he and his men were on God's side.[8] The statue of Cromwell in the shadow of the Houses of Parliament, with his Bible and his sword in hand, is Cromwell as his soldiers knew him. Carlyle understood his man when he wrote,

"No one can ever be so sure again as Cromwell was that God was on his side."

That is the kind of certainty that is infectious, and it was infectious in the New Model Army. Cromwell knew the strength of religious zeal in his men, and encouraged it. As he saw it, a thousand swords were feeble against the iron conviction of those who wielded less than half the number.

"Sir, they are trusty,"

he wrote to Speaker Lenthal after the battle of Naseby.

"I beseech you, in the name of God, not to discourage them." [9]

His thought went beyond sectarian bounds. It was religion that was real, and the particular sect did not matter.

In such an army, John Bunyan, along with every other new recruit, would have been quickly aware that this was a religious war and that he fought as a Christian soldier against the enemies of God. *The Souldier's Pocket Bible*, issued in August of the preceding year,[10] would have been part of his equipment, and as the prefatory statement reads, this tiny volume would supply "the want of the whole Bible, which a Souldier cannot conveniently carry about him." Intended as a manual, this little book consisted of selected verses from the Old Testament, arranged under headings, to show the proper scriptural qualifications of a man who is "a fit Souldier to fight the Lord's Battels, both before the fight, in the fight, and after the fight, and may bee usefull for any Christian to meditate upon, now in this miserable time of Warre."

Wisely the verses under each heading were few enough in number and sufficiently stressed in camp sermons to be known almost by heart. The headings announced the soldierly virtues beyond misunderstanding. Among them:

A Souldier must not doe wickedly.

He must put his confidence in God's wisdome and strength.

He must be valiant for God's cause.

He must denie his owne wisdome, his owne strength, & all provision for war.

He must pray before he goe to fight.

He must consider and believe God's gracious promises.

He must not feare his enemies.

He must love them as they are his, and hate them as they are God's enemies.

He must crie unto God in the very instant of the battell.

He must consider that sometimes God's people have the worst in battell as well as God's enemies.

If victory comes, he must give all glory to God . . . and say, The Lord is a man of warre, his name is Jehovah.

The last verses in *The Souldier's Pocket Bible* are a personal promise
and a vow:

> Psa. 116, 9, "I will walke before the Lord in the Land of the
> living."
> Psa. 119, 109, "I have vowed, and I will performe it, that I will
> keepe thy righteous judgements."

The importance of this small volume, still extant in several copies,
is less in its detailed preachments than in its testimony to the
religious emphasis which was seldom allowed to be absent from a
soldier's consciousness. Religion and life were still inseparable, and
no matter on which side a man fought, or whether he professed
godliness or not, few in the ranks or out of them doubted that God
ruled the world and that His will would prevail.

Bunyan would also have been provided with *The Souldier's
Catechism*,[11] a companion volume to the *Pocket Bible*, and an excellent piece of propaganda for the Parliament cause, skillfully adapted
to its time and occasion. The title page announces that it was
written for the "Incouragement and Instruction of all who have
taken up Armes in this Cause of God and his People; especially the
common Souldier." From the first word the common soldier could
understand it. The question-and-answer form is direct and eco-
nomical of words; the order of the questions such as to lead him
along one step at a time and never a long step. The answers invite
assent, not argument. It begins:

> What Profession are you of?
> I am a Christian and a souldier.
> Is it lawfull for Christians to be Souldiers?
> Yes, doubtlesse. We have Arguments enough to warrant it. [Abra-
> ham, David and the martyrs are called to witness.]
> What side are you of, and for whom do you fight?
> I am for the King and Parliament, or in plainer terms, I fight to
> recover the King out of the hands of a Popish Malignant Company.
> I fight in the defence and maintenance of the Protestant Religion.

The first-person answers were an excellent device, for as the soldier turned these pages, he heard himself acknowledging convictions for which, unaided, he would have lacked the words:

> What is it that moves you to take up Arms, and to ingage yourself in this Civill Warre?
> The love I beare to my Country.
> But is it not against the King that you fight in this Cause?
> No surely; our onely aime is to rescue the King out of the hands of his and the Kingdome's enemies.

In the long days of camp boredom Bunyan probably read and reread these oversimplified questions and answers and heard himself embracing the cause of the People's Army, whether with or without enthusiasm or patriotic fervor, there is no knowing. He had heard many of these stereotyped phrases all his life as a Bedfordshire boy, and the hours of argument they now invited from the more zealous of his soldier companions may not have enlisted his sympathies or incited him to fervor against such evils as "antichristian prelacy," or moved his endeavor toward the "reformation of a corrupt clergy and the preservation of the gospel to our posterity," but there was no escaping familiarity with these objectives in the daily emphasis of camp life.

More insistent demands on his attention would have been made by the sermons, prayers, psalm singing, which were as regular a part of garrison routine as training in the field. The religious emphasis was strong on both sides, but in the Parliamentary army the familiar pattern of worship was discarded and emotional fervor often substituted for dignity. Because there were not enough chaplains, sermons were often preached by fellow soldiers, who exhorted freely according to their own model of Independency. Justification of lay preaching made much of it as a necessity; otherwise "we could scarce have had so much as any solemne forme of godliness found amongst us." Sermons could be heard on weekdays as well as on Sundays, and in every regiment. Such lay preaching was forbidden and arrests were numerous, but ineffective. Prayers were "without the Book," such prayers as "for their faith and familiarity with God" made William Dell "stand wondering at the grace." He wrote:

"I have seen more of the presence of God in that army, than amongst any people that ever I conversed with in my life." [12]

Richard Baxter, also a chaplain, in reporting his own experience, wrote that a few "proud, self-conceited, hot-headed Sectaries had got into the highest places, and were Cromwell's chief Favourites, and by their very heat and activity, bore down the rest, or carried them along with them." Although few in number, they were, in Baxter's thought, "the Soul of the Army." His acquaintance was with the horse rather than the foot, but his report of the incessant arguing about religion was true in both ranks.

"My Life among them was a daily contending against Souldiers," he said, "and gently arguing with the more Tractable." He found "the greatest part of the Common Soldiers, especially of the Foot, were ignorant men, of little Religion." The "smallest part of them" were "active Sectaries," but because of their ignorance, they were "ready Instruments for the Seducers." [13] His temperate report commends itself as believable, and makes a place for John Bunyan among the two or three thousand men who were his associates for the next two and a half years. According to Bunyan's own report of his earlier Elstow life, religion was not yet his goal, and he may have been indifferent to the exhorting, preaching, and arguing about religion which went on around him, but he could not have escaped incessant exposure to all this, and in the periods of inactive garrison life he probably sat on the fringe of such gatherings for uncounted hours.

After the first awesome beginnings, the unaccustomed discipline of army life may have frequently put Bunyan in trouble, for unfamiliar as he was with even the mild rigidities of a grammar school day, induction into military life may have meant for him the beginning of formal discipline and control by outside authority. Had he been enrolled only a matter of months earlier, he would have found discipline exceedingly lax and unevenly administered. Absenteeism, desertion, plundering, and ruthless destruction of property had gone almost past prohibition. In some regiments there had been abundance of religious zeal, but it had hardly been zeal according to orderliness. The soldiers of Essex, we are told, kept fasts, listened to "Heavenly sermons," advanced to the siege singing psalms, and if victorious, sang again among the bodies of the slain. But the battle being over, if there were a parish church near by, religious zeal took a destructive turn. First they burned the rails, destroyed the images, seized the vestments, as nonconforming loyalty permitted them to do, and then proceeded to pillage neighborhood homes, selling the contents for private gain.

Nehemiah Wharton, a subaltern officer in Denzil Holles' regiment, in a quite routine report of 1642, wrote that at Acton men of his regiment pillaged a priest, "defaced the antient and sacred glased pictures and burned the holy railes." At Hollington, "the railes beinge gone, we got the surplesse, to make us handkerchers, and one of our soldiers ware it to Uxbridge." At Southam "we pillaged the minister and tooke from him a drum and severall armes"; in Bailey, "our soldiers pillaged the parson of the town, and brought him away prisoner with his surplice and other relics." At Coventry horsemen brought in "an old base priest, the parson of Lowe, . . . and led him ridiculously about the city." "Sabbath day wee peaceably injoyed with Mr. Obadiah Sedgwick, who gave us two heavenly Sermons." The night before the siege of Worcester, when they had small comfort because of the rain, "we continued singing of psalms until the morning." Religious zeal was the inspiration of the pillaging as well as of the psalm singing. Several days after an order against plundering had been issued, Wharton wrote, "by commission from his Excellency, our soldiers marched seven miles to Sir William Russell's house, and pillaged it unto the bare walls." Regretfully, he added that on this occasion he got none of the loot, "the ruder sort of soldiers" being the fortunate ones.[14] Bunyan would have heard tales of all this, and accustomed as he had been all his life to regarding ritualistic worship with awe, as he himself says, such reports of sacrilege would seem to have made his own early village mischiefs tame by comparison.

In the New Model Army he had joined, such conditions were no more. Punishment of religious offenses was severe to harshness. The first three Lawes and Ordinances of Warre on both sides involved a soldier's duty to God, with penalties to suit. In the Parliamentary army "to blaspheme the holy and blessed Trinity" or "the knowne Articles of our Christian Faith," meant either to suffer the tongue to be bored through with a hot iron, or "to ride the wooden horse" (a sharp ridge formed by two boards nailed together with four posts for legs). The offender would also have a musket tied to his heels "to keep his legs wide" and on his back a placard announcing his offense. A less harsh penalty was to suffer a cleft stick on the tongue or to stand on a joint stool, wearing the placard. In addition, to be profane, even in a single oath, cost threepence and might cost as many as twelve, or fourpence more than a private soldier's complete daily pay. To neglect "divine worship" meant severe censure.[15]

Such penalties proceeded from the assumption that each unit of the New Model Army was a congregation as well as a military unit, and therefore that its members were subject to such disciplinary action as might have obtained within a communion of saints. Other offenses were likewise severely punished. Drunkenness cost a full week's pay. Contempt of authority meant public whipping and might bring a man to the gibbet. Drunkenness on watch meant death, as also "to fly away" in battle, fling away arms or powder, go a mile out of camp or to pillage without license. Vigor in enforcing these regulations was uneven, and even with the tightening of authority under Cromwell's leadership, many offenders escaped the penalty, but almost any soldier would have witnessed the hanging of one of his companions for one offense or another. With all this strictness, however, Sir Samuel Luke could speak of his men as "an ungodly crew," and say of them,

"I think these New Modelles knead all their doe with ale, for I never saw soe many druncke in life in so short a tyme." [16]

In time improvement came, to some degree, along with better equipment, better maintenance, and more regular pay. Bunyan would have had at least a partial uniform, as had not been possible for the foot soldiers in the army of Essex. His men had usually worn the garments in which they enlisted, supplementing them by plunder as best they could. In consequence it was not "always discernable who is a soldier and who is not." After Cromwell's appointment as lieutenant general, on January 21, 1644, an effort was made to clothe soldiers sufficiently for quick identification and to allot each man seventeen shillings "for additional comforts in clothing." Bunyan would have drawn eightpence a day and would have been regularly paid. This was sixpence more than the average earning of a farm laborer in his day.

So far as social status went, he would have been thoroughly comfortable among his fellow foot soldiers of Colonel Cockayne's company. Denzil Holles' disparaging remark as to an army officered by "brewers, tailors, goldsmiths, shoemakers and such like," was essentially correct, as indicating its rank-and-file character, but not its officers. Predominantly the men were drawn from the lower classes of English society. This was Bunyan's world. Elstow had already introduced him to numerous examples of a "such like" company. Now he saw them drawn together by hundreds. Sensitively observant as he later proved himself to be, as to the springs of men's thought and action, he could hardly have spent these years among such a varied cross section of English workingmen without being unconsciously confirmed in a bias toward this stratum of society, as opposed to rank and privilege. Not that he was incited to personal resentment against the inequality of possession and privilege, as others of his class were. His later writings show little of the militant restlessness which was becoming increasingly vocal in this same level of English society. The more privileged classes to which most of the officers and drillmasters belonged, had nothing that he wanted. Titles did not exist in his vocabulary or in his searching interest as to what went on underneath a man's words and actions.

In the monotony of life within the fortress, local happenings bordering on the sensational took on extravagant proportions, especially when they offered a chance for partisan sympathy. Such an incident was the arrest ordered by Sir Samuel of Lieutenant Paul Hobson and Captain Beaumont for holding an unauthorized preaching service on Sunday, June 15, 1645. During its hour the noise stirred up by this incident could be heard almost anywhere in England, as rumor brought the word and as soldiers and civilians

promptly took sides. The fact that these two men were officers serving under one commander, ordered arrested by another, denied
witnesses to their offense (as Paul Hobson declared), and as he also
said, treated abusively, made their case what amounted to a front-
page sensation. For later times some light is cast on the current religious situation, as a man in the ranks might view it, by this minor
tempest.

The two offenders were members of Captain Fleetwood's company, en route to London, and while tarrying briefly at Newport
Pagnell, they had absented themselves from a service of thanksgiving,
ordered by Sir Samuel after the victory at Naseby. Instead, they
had held a service of their own at the neighboring village of Lath-
bury, where Paul Hobson, a Baptist, had preached the sermon. Apparently their service was better attended than the official thanksgiving at the garrison, for in a letter to his cousin Ford, Sir Samuel
wrote,

> "They were preaching all ye weeke long & I left them alone, &
> now when I had ordered a publiqe thankesgiving for Gods un-
> speakable mercy onto us, for ym to draw my Parishoners away &
> soe leave ye church empty I could noe longer endure." [17]

He had cause surely, but at a sensitive time his severity proved to be
unwise. The two men were deprived of their commands, their arms
taken from them, and they were imprisoned. Their arrest was clearly
less for the nature of the sermon preached than for disobedience
to the governor of the garrison in which they were guest officers.
A council of war was called to hear the case, and if Sir Samuel's
command of the garrison had not expired while the furor was at its
height, more trouble might have come of it. Instead, Colonel
Cockayne, temporarily in charge of the garrison while Sir Samuel
went back to Commons, became conciliatory to General Fairfax, to
whom the case had been taken, and the affair was concluded with
apologies on both sides. It was in such passing tempests as this that
the Sectaries won their way with large numbers of men who were
beginning to taste freedom in matters of worship. It would have been
impossible to be a soldier in Newport Pagnell garrison and not have
taken sides on this occasion.

From one of Paul Hobson's sermons of the same year, 1645, it is easy to see why he had a following for more reasons than the doctrine he preached. His sermon, entitled "A Garden Inclosed," is the very opposite of contentious. He appeals to the heroic in his hearers and challenges them to be strong, stand your ground, enjoy what is intended for the saints. This enjoyment is worth more than all besides. In another sermon, entitled "Practicall Divinity," he said:

"Be not disturbed at charges against you.
All the men in the world cannot hurt a Saint; nor all the Divells in Hell.
A man will never feare his Enemie, especially when he knows he is kild before he comes neare him.
Love the cross. Love the frowns of the world.
If thou losest farthings, and gainest pounds, if thou losest strawes, and gainest pearles, what losse hast thou?
Let men go on to revile and abuse the Saints, . . . and if they should proceed to persecution, as they may, and imprisonment, no matter. There comes a new supply from Christ answering to their sufferings."

Whatever such words meant both to the preacher and those who flocked to hear, there was power in them for a nervous time.

In other matters than religion Newport Pagnell was remembered as a seat of unrest, at times close to mutiny. During the month of the Hobson ferment, there was considerable opposition to Sir Samuel Luke as commander, both from the soldiers and also from the residents of the town, fomented, no doubt, by friends of Colonel Cockayne, who hoped to succeed him. Cockayne lost, however, and after Luke's resignation, Charles O'Doyly was made governor. During the interval between commanders, there had been less than six hundred men in the fortress; discipline had been so lax that on reports of violence, Parliament had granted a plea for martial law until quiet could be restored. At that time Bunyan still had a year to serve.

In all of his later writings there is little evidence that he would have satisfied Cromwell's hope for the ideal soldier, who knew what he fought for and loved the cause. Bunyan probably had only a dim idea why he was in uniform. Nowhere in his writings is there any expression of ardent partisan sympathy with the civil war struggle. He had nothing to say as to the great issues, civil and religious, which divided England during these years, nor is there any strong likelihood that as a village boy he had a rational understanding of them. Later he was capable of passionate difference of opinion and ardent controversial zeal, but such were reserved for doctrinal issues. As a boy of sixteen to eighteen, he was probably one of thousands of men in the rank and file of any army, then as now, who accept the necessity to enlist, to drill, to obey orders, take part in the engagements to which they are assigned, and then in due course leave the ranks without their thought having been stirred or perhaps even touched below the merest surface.

In terms of preparation for the work of his maturity, in addition to having religious issues thrust on him day by day, perhaps the most valuable deposit of these soldier years came from the day-to-day jostling, the give-and-take exchanges with Mr. Pliable, Mr. Live-loose, Ignorance, Mr. Much-afraid, Pickthank, and always Talkative. In the daily routine of camp life, he met them all. They are individuals of no particular social stratum. They belong to no century and have no nationality. They are members of the human race to be found everywhere. Bunyan's early close association with so richly varied an assortment of humankind was the best possible spur he might have had to the kind of observation and sympathy which would later distinguish both his preaching and writing. Fortunately it came early enough to establish a lifelong habit. One likes to think that somewhere in the Newport Pagnell fortress there was an officer who unknowingly sat for the portrait of Captain Boanerges, or better still, Mr. Greatheart. Some of Bunyan's most individual and sharply drawn characters are soldiers. One hopes also that somewhere in the ranks of his associates he found such a friend as Faithful. But of his personal alliances and experiences there is scarcely a hint, except in such a phrase as "When I was a soldier"; "I heard once a story from a soldier"; or the oft-quoted mention of the "siege," for which another who volunteered in his stead was killed.

This silence, as though these two and a half years were a blank, is not surprising. At the sixteen- to eighteen-year-old stage he was still a boy of limited horizons, uprooted for the first time and suddenly thrust into the company of more human beings than he had ever seen before in one place at one time. Hitherto, as would have been true of almost any other ungrown boy of his time and station, his world had offered few surprises. Every sound of the forge beside the cottage door had been as familiar as the motion of hand that had produced it. On the village green and in the long Elstow street he had known everyone he met except at the time of the annual fair. On Sunday each worshiper in the village church had taken the seat he had always taken. By contrast the life at Newport Pagnell had been life on another planet.

A few associations in his later life appear to date from acquaintance during these war years, that with Mathias Cowley, Bookseller, whose name stands on the title page as seller of Bunyan's first book, *Some Gospel Truths Opened*, in 1656, and also of the second, *A Vindication of Some Gospel Truths*, in 1657. The third book, *The Doctrine of the Law and Grace Unfolded*, in 1659, was "printed for Mathias Cowley." He may well have been a fellow soldier. John Gibbs, only a year older than John Bunyan, vicar of the church in Newport Pagnell, was another possible acquaintance. He wrote a commendatory letter to Bunyan's *A Few Sighs from Hell* in 1658. Gibbs was the son of a cooper residing in St. Mary's parish in Bedford, and Bunyan may have known him previous to his enlistment, although this is unlikely. It is possible that the nonconformity of Gibbs may have given some early impulse to Bunyan's own thought. Certainly the later helpfulness of both Cowley and Gibbs would seem to have been built on some association dating from this earlier war time.

What the army experience meant for Bunyan in the light of the central purpose and direction of his life, and what his imagination and his pen would make of this experience in later years, would not be limited to the mere mention of the externals of garrison life, or the literal sights and sounds of seventeenth century forms of combat. Years later, in his introductory verses to *The Holy War*, to be sure, he wrote:

"I saw the colours waving in the wind,

. . . .

I saw the mounts cast up against the town,
And how the slings were placed to beat it down.
I heard the stones fly whizzing by mine ears,

. . . .

I saw them fall, and saw what work they made."

He mentions the battering rams, the shouts of the captains, the cries, the captives in chains, the armed men coming

"By troops, by thousands to besiege the town."

Certainly. Such details belong to seventeenth century warfare, as also to earlier times, but mention of them is neither surprising nor deeply significant. Also, that one of his allegories should find its pattern in the story of a besieged town, and that this picture should owe something to his own memories of soldier life as well as to traditional resources, was natural enough; inevitable perhaps, but incidental to his purpose.

The end of military service for him came suddenly when the two companies ordered to Ireland were disbanded by Parliament. Nearly a year previously, on August 6, 1646, Parliament had also voted to demolish the Newport Pagnell fortress and disband the men who wished to serve no longer. Further service for the relief of Ireland was put on a volunteer basis, as this Irish campaign was exceedingly unpopular. John Bunyan was one of those willing to go. His name appears in the muster roll of Captain O'Hara's regiment, June 17, 1647, as one of the seventy-nine privates who had volunteered.[18] The men were given a month's advance pay and marched to Chester, to be ready to embark for Ireland. Then, apparently without warning, they were ordered back to Newport Pagnell and disbanded on July 21, 1647. Bunyan's two and a half years as a soldier were over. They had been another chapter in his education, which was never to be from books.

Chapter Three

Embattled Tinker

Wars are dividing lines in the lives of men as in the history of nations, and so it would seem to have been in the life journey of John Bunyan. The five years immediately following his discharge from the Parliamentary army were the determining years of his life, turning it into directions hitherto unguessed. Outwardly, during these years he would change his local reputation from that of a ringleader in all manner of mischief, and as he would have it, also of evil, into that of a regular churchgoer, Bible student, and young man of exemplary behavior. Before the five years had passed, he would also have begun to exchange his trade at the forge and behind the tinker's cart for the itinerant preacher's calling, and in this new rôle he would already have a small following in several villages along the same route he had traveled as a mender of pots and pans. He would also have begun to discover the secret of moving men to action by a natural gift of oratory that as an eighteen-year-old veteran he did not know he possessed.

Inwardly, during these years he would live an embattled life. He would explore the abyss of self and grope for meanings that would still elude him. He would alternately experience tortures that were all but insupportable and ecstasies that could not be told. Somehow out of it all he would put himself in line with the purpose of human life as he saw it, and pledge unswerving loyalty to that end alone.

A more detailed record than we have of these determining years, in their outward sequence, might clarify many things as to the man he would be, although they might explain nothing as to his eventual fame or the likelihood of it. Except for a few hints, however, and these largely conjectural, we know for the outer life only of his return to the tinker's trade, and his marriage possibly two years later. Otherwise the day-to-day reality of his story is almost a complete blank. The inner story he himself told in great detail nineteen years later, when he was twice the age of the returning veteran of 1647.[1] Recalled thus in early maturity, this private record supplies the clue to his lifelong quest and the assurance that by the time he had reached his twenty-fourth or twenty-fifth year, he was headed straight toward the unseen perfection he sought. The changed direction of his life appears to have had no direct relation to his soldier years, but was rather the outcome of the disordered time that followed his homecoming. However, the roots of change in a young life are deeply hidden, and John Bunyan himself might have been the last to know when or whence the implanting from which they first took hold.

As he walked the twelve miles from Newport Pagnell to Elstow, he may very naturally have been conjuring up pictures of the life he had left behind two and a half years before, and assuming that he would return to what he had left, aged sixteen. If so, he would be quickly disillusioned, for like all other returning soldiers from all other wars, he would discover that he had come back to a very different world, and in nothing would these differences be more compelling than in that which had once been most familiar.

On first sight the very look of the town would be strange. During this month of July, Bedford was headquarters for the army of Fairfax, and the town was full of soldiers. Twenty thousand were billeted here and in the immediate environs, turning the familiar scene into an army camp. Cromwell and Ireton were present pending negotiations with the king, who had been brought to Woburn. It was a time of great sickness, particularly with spotted fever, which was taking heavy toll in many places. "Agues abounding more than in all my remembrance," Ralph Josselin wrote in his *Diary* for this month. He also mentioned the heavy rains, fruit rotting on the trees, cattle dying, and in consequence, all provision "excessive deare & scarce to be gotten for our money." The kingdom was in "strange unsettled frame," the people tense and discouraged.[2]

Within the small cottage at Bunyan's End, there was the stepmother John Bunyan hardly knew. His brother William, now aged thirteen, would also be almost a stranger. A half-brother, Charles, had died in infancy. On the village green, which to Bunyan's eye would now have shrunk to smaller dimensions, other fourteen- to sixteen-year-olds romped, shouted, played tipcat, and rang the church bells out of turn. Many of his former boy companions were gone, some never to return. In the Sunday congregation there were some strange faces and some vacant seats. History had caught up with Elstow village, which now showed a vaguely different face. Homecoming meant adjustment to all these outward differences, and in time it would come. The greater changes within himself would take longer. He was not now the boy who had marched down the High Road in November, 1644. His time for living his own independent life had come, and very soon he would know it.

The discovery of a homemade anvil, or brazier's spike, on which are cut the words

J. Bunyan, Helstowe, 1647

would seem to suggest, by the date, that the first chapter of this independence came immediately after his discharge from the army.[3] This necessary tool, crudely fashioned and weighing some sixty pounds, was presumably his own work and marked the resumption of the tinker's trade. Whether he began in his own right immediately or remained for a time at his father's forge beside the cottage at Bunyan's End is not known, but since he was returning to civilian life with presumably only the one month's advance pay (one pound) which his enlistment in the Irish campaign had brought him, necessity would seem to have sent him back to his father's roof and table, at least for a time. His seven-year apprenticeship, as required by the Statute of Apprentices, would have lacked only a few months after

45

the time of his return, and he would have been free to set up for himself as an independent tinker after his twentieth birthday, November 30, 1648.

His marriage probably came about this same time. His own word for it is,

"Presently after this, I changed my condition into a married state, and my mercy it was to light upon a wife whose father was counted godly." [4]

The precise date, as well as the name of the woman he chose, has not yet come to light, despite the persistent search of Bunyan scholars for several generations. The tradition that she was not of Elstow persists, perhaps with good reason, although the fact that the marriage does not appear on the Elstow parish records is not in itself conclusive proof. There are enough gaps in these records to account for the omission on other grounds, as is also true for the civil register. Better reason for the assumption that she was not of the Elstow neighborhood comes in Bunyan's own statement that after their marriage, she often used to tell him of her godly father and the righteous life he had lived. Had he belonged to Elstow, Bunyan would have known this without being told.

This remark supplies the only hint we have as to her individual quality, carrying with it the suggestion that her religious upbringing and her own active piety may have been among the causes of Bunyan's own torture because of his own unregenerate state, and also a spur toward his own search for peace. In recalling the time of their marriage, he remarks that her father had died, leaving her very poor, and adding that they had begun their life together with not so much "household stuff as a dish or a spoon betwixt us both." [5] More important, however, for Bunyan's future, they had a library, consisting of two pious books, as her complete dowry from her godly father. There was probably also a Bible to make three, quite enough for John Bunyan. The fact that at this unregenerate stage he chose a wife to whom religion mattered tells something very significant about him. Twenty-year-old ringleaders in evil ways usually make other choices.

How the two young people weathered the "without a dish or spoon" period is a blank. Presently, however, they were occupying the first of the two cottages that were to be their home for these married years. It stood just at the curve of the road, on the site now occupied by the later replica, and from the extant print, appears to have been as simple and humble as one might expect this young tinker's first home to be. In marrying one as poor as himself, he had stayed within his own social class, and a small cottage such as this would have been a natural zenith of his hope for a home of his own. Since his own story of these years omits all that belonged to the cottage side of his life, it is only fair to stress strongly the fact of this small home, a trade for a living, neighbors who had known him since childhood, and presently the birth of a child to supply at least a measure of personal happiness during his prolonged anguish of spirit in these years. At the birth of this first daughter, Bunyan was twenty-two years old. She was christened Mary, possibly for her mother, as the Bunyan family through previous generations had kept family names. She was born blind, reason enough that of all his six children, it would be Mary who would claim the utmost of her father's tenderness and affection.

As John Bunyan looked back on these early years of independence, he kept to the single track of his tortured progress toward religious peace. His own indications of time are loose, but by sorting them out one gathers that this was a five- or six-year struggle. In fact, it had begun much earlier in the nightmarish dreams of his childhood. He had been marked for a religious quest from his first conscious memory, but it was the years between nineteen and twenty-five when the struggle possessed him. It is a painful story, one of the most painful among records of similar struggles of other great souls. Not that the fact of anguish is in itself surprising or unusual. The history of any individual capable of a deep religious experience is a solitary journey, but it need not be so painful as Bunyan's. It was not painful to an excessive degree to his great contemporary religionist Richard Baxter. Baxter's worry had consisted chiefly in his inability to name the precise time and place of his conversion, but luckily, in the midst of his distress, aged fifteen, he had found in a pedlar's pack a copy of Edmund Bunny's edition of

Robert Parsons' *Resolution,*[6] and by it was convinced that "God breaketh not all hearts alike." Unfortunately, John Bunyan was to travel a much longer path before even so much as a helpful book came to his hand.

He tells the story of this long journey in great detail, but since religion was to be the realm in which he realized himself most fully, the emphasis is not disproportionate. Carlyle may not have been right for all men when he wrote that "a man's religion is the chief fact in regard to him," but he was certainly right for John Bunyan. His conversion story is the great story of his life, and it was life-long. Like Christian in his own *Pilgrim's Progress,* he often stumbled, lost the path, despaired, then somehow regained his bearings and his faith and went on. "Great works take time," Newman wrote, and for John Bunyan, the "great work" of conversion took all the time he had.

The opening scene of the drama is familiar to anyone who knows anything at all of Bunyan's life. The time was Sunday afternoon; the place, the village green of Elstow; the spectators, village residents of all ages. There were music, shouting, jollity, relaxation. Some were dancing, some playing games, some, the older ones, sitting along the Moot Hall, watching. By ecclesiastic fiat a generation earlier (1617) Sunday afternoon merriment of this sort had been made entirely legitimate. Go to church in the morning and then take the liberty of such simple refreshment with a clear conscience. *The Book of Sports* was the warrant.[7]

But to Puritan England of the midcentury the case was quite otherwise. *The Book of Sports* was odious. In 1643 Parliament had ordered it burned by the common hangman, and in the following year had passed an act for the better observance of Sunday. But the people, particularly country people, were loath to comply after nearly a generation of indulgence in their Sunday freedom, with the result that both the act itself and the failure to observe it had made Sunday sports a controversial issue which broke out period-ically in nearly every parish. Christopher Hall,[8] pastor of Elstow church during Bunyan's young manhood, was of the stricter Puritan way on this subject, and on this particular Sunday morning he had aroused feeling freshly on both sides by preaching on the sacredness of the holy day and the great evil of profaning it by "labor, sport, or otherwise."

As Bunyan listened to the sermon, he "fell in his conscience" under the theme. He had heard these same arguments many times, with Scripture to support them, but this morning because of something in the emphasis or in his own mood, they reached him, and he went home from the service with "a great load" on his mind. However, after dinner his trouble being somewhat relieved, he shook the sermon out of his mind and went to the green as usual. His companions were there, and he joined them in the favorite game of tipcat.

When it was his turn to play, as he remembered, he had just struck the "cat" one blow from the hole with his "catstaff," and was about to strike it a second time, when a voice did suddenly "dart from heaven" into his soul, saying,

"Wilt thou leave thy sins and go to heaven, or have thy sins and go to hell?"

Put to an "exceeding maze" by the voice, he left his "cat" upon the ground, and stood silent in the midst of his play. The other players stared, but he told them nothing. They had not heard the voice. Standing motionless and looking up to heaven whence the voice had come, "as if I had with the eyes of my understanding, seen the Lord Jesus looking down upon me," he faced the alternatives set before him. Heaven? He "fell to musing." No, his sins were too many and too grievous for any hope of forgiveness. It was too late. He mused again. No, forgiveness was not for him. Very well, he would go on in sin, and sin better. "I had as good be damned for many sins as to be damned for few." Accordingly, despair in his heart, he returned to his play, struck the "cat" a second time, and the game went on.[9] His momentary inaction was quickly forgotten by his companions, but the voice from heaven, as he believed it to be, was never forgotten by John Bunyan. He had experienced one of the memorable moments of his lifetime. As for the literal reality of what had happened, he had not a figment of doubt, neither at the moment or ever afterward. In his own record, this was one of the first times that

49

conviction had "seized on my soul" to the destruction of his peace for years of days. Thereafter at times "the very clouds were charged with the wrath of God."

The assumption that his experience was unique has added to the difficulty of understanding John Bunyan, except as an abnormal, half-crazed young man. The fact is that in this experience he was quite within the texture of his own time, so far as religious conversion was currently recognized. He was also firmly within the company of a few great souls in all ages and lands, for religious conversion is a fact in human experience. History knows these great souls in their sudden change of direction and also in the individual differences between one man's call to the good life and another's: Saul on the Damascus road, "breathing out threatenings and slaughter against the disciples of the Lord," but changed in a moment, as he remembered, by a great light that shined from heaven and a voice that called him by name. "Lord, what wilt thou have me to do?" he answered, and then spent the rest of his life doing it. St. Augustine, through the writings of this same Saul, achieved first the intellectual satisfaction which his nature demanded, and then after a prolonged struggle yielded submission to the God in whom he believed. For a long time he had been, as he said, "a great riddle" to himself, but when the long-delayed submission was at last accomplished,

"It was like coming into port after a rough sea."

This was also Cardinal Newman's figure. His search was for the end of a thousand doubts and uncertainties, and conversion for him meant acceptance of an authority which guaranteed the truth of something incomprehensible to man. For St. Francis, Martin Luther, George Fox, Richard Baxter, Pascal, Charles Wesley, Brother Lawrence, and an easy score of others, who have laid bare their souls at this crisis of their personal history, conversion was shaped by differing temperaments, a different set of circumstances, and the overhanging ideas of different times and places. Essentially, however, the differences are less impressive than the central similarity of agonizing struggle, surrender, and peace after storm. The intensity of the

struggle and its length are different; the stages are constant. For
John Bunyan, in the beginning, conversion meant salvation, and
salvation meant escape from damnation and the winning of what he
called eternal life. He was trying to escape a literal hell and achieve
a literal heaven. If this seems an unworthily selfish goal, or a pitifully
lesser one, the fault is ours in failing to understand the shape of seventeenth century thought as to wherein religion's goal consisted.

Perhaps adequate understanding is impossible. One remembers
Albert Schweitzer's wise word:

"We must abandon forever the hope of really understanding the
past."

Certainly in an age when religion takes a place well below the first,
complete understanding is not likely to be ours. Security, as everyone knows, is a word of our modern age in a very specific sense.
Security is the hope of every age really; only the content of that
assurance changes. For Bunyan's century security meant salvation,
certain and everlasting, and all men, even the ungodly, desired it
above all else.

In Schweitzer's religious consecration there is nothing comparable
to John Bunyan's agony of spirit. Why should there be? He is a
man of a different temperament, training, and time, and in this present day he is the least typical of men. As he tells his own story, he
had been committed to a selfless goal since early childhood. The
only question was where to find it. One evening, aged thirty, when
he was going through his mail, his eye caught the title of an article
about the need for workers in the Gaboon, northern province of the
Congo Colony. The writer expressed the hope that his appeal would
lead workers to offer themselves for this urgent need. His conclusion ran, "Men and women who can reply simply, 'Lord, I am coming,' these are the people whom the Church needs." Schweitzer's
answer had come. He wrote,

"Having finished the article, I quietly began my work. My search
was over." [10]

A new beginning can be as quiet as that, and often has been. So far as Schweitzer has told of his own inner experience, *quietly* is the keynote, as it has been of the service he renders.

Bunyan's experience stands at the opposite pole. His struggle was anguish, intermittent and in differing degrees over a period of five or six stormy years. Theologically, it was orthodox every step of the way, as his time spelled orthodoxy. To a later day, the literalness of seventeenth century orthodox belief of the sort Bunyan espoused as to things unseen is repellent. All was conceived in tangible form and understandable to finite minds. The Bible was an oracle. God had spoken, and the words of Scripture meant exactly what they meant in current speech. The devil was a black shape in the darkness; heaven was white robes, golden streets, and legions of angels; hell was literal fire which would burn forever. Bunyan was the inheritor of these concepts. At the time of the tipcat incident, he was a bewildered young man. All his life he had listened to sermons, and he knew what the preacher's words meant in current interpretation. Conviction, repentance, forgiveness were literal steps toward heaven, and as yet he had not taken them. Out of the tumble of half-understood pulpit words, something in him was crying out for peace and security, as he had heard it preached. His conscience was awake, but according to orthodox preachment, he was "lost."

We know nothing of the religious accent of his earlier home life, but the absence of recorded penalties against his parents for non-performance of parish duties would suggest (but does not prove) that they had attended church services regularly, observed fast days and festival seasons in orthodox manner. Bunyan himself testified to being uplifted by the externals of a ritualistic worship: "the high place, priest, vestment, service, and what else belonging to the church, counting all things holy that were therein contained." [11] All this was part of his inheritance, and in his boyhood he took it for granted. To these familiar assumptions, the army experience had most certainly offered challenge. He had heard men without education speak of this inheritance as idolatry and the delusion of Antichrist. In its place they had put their own strange visions. They had confuted Scripture with Scripture and told of revelations made to them by God Himself. If Bunyan had been arrested by these strange views, he could hardly have escaped the question, Who is right?

In the army he had also been exposed to coarseness, to irreverence, to excess, and in his own word had given rein to his lusts and "delighted in all transgression against the law of God." It had been his "delight to be taken captive by the devil at his will," so much so, that had not "a miracle of precious grace prevented," he might have been brought to "disgrace and open shame before the face of the world." Whatever this means in specific misconduct, the sense of condemnation rested heavily on him, until in his own eyes his iniquity seemed monstrous, and his severity with himself was proportionate. In his own word he was "tossed between the devil and my own ignorance, and so perplexed, especially at some times, that I could not tell what to do." [12]

It is a great pity that he had no wise counselor at this stage but was shut up entirely to his own resources, having "in this matter broken my mind to no man." He took to reading his Bible with great eagerness, and also the two pious books his wife's dowry had brought into their home: Arthur Dent's *The Plaine Man's Pathway to Heaven*, "wherein every man may clearely see whether hee shall be saved or damned," and Lewis Bayley's *Practice of Piety*, "Directing a Christian how to walk that he may please God." [13] At the distance of three centuries, the light which shines from these once best-selling religious guides seems pale indeed, but that they spoke not only to "plaine men" in their day is apparent from the record of their amazing popularity. They also afford more clues to the overhanging ideas and attitudes of Bunyan's day than any score of sermons.

The Plaine Man's Pathway is in dialogue form. Four men, Theologus, a divine; Philogathus, an honest man; Asunctus, an ignorant man; and Antilegon, a caviler, sit down in an arbor and talk from one o'clock until sundown. From the first question to the last answer, there is not an inspired touch anywhere in these pages, yet thousands of men and women of high and low degree, and all degrees in between, wore out this book, as edition after edition continued to supply the demand. Bunyan probably had the nineteenth edition, published in 1625, a volume of 392 pages. Leaving all controversial matters aside, the dialogue marches on through man's natural corruption, his deserved damnation, the signs of it, the grievous sins that lead to it, the nine bars to heaven, the nine gates to hell, the groundwork of salvation by which he may avoid his doom, and a warning that very few shall escape. The simplicity of what passed as "the plan of salvation" as set forth in this summary is such that a child of ten could understand it without straining his powers too much; that is, a seventeenth century child, who thanks to exposure to sermons through almost as many Sundays as his life was long knew by heart the doctrine spread over these pages before he had read the first question and answer.

The suggested picture of young John Bunyan, puzzled as he was to the brink of despair, reading the pages of this small bulky book by candlelight, after his day's work was over, is deeply moving. He had the desire, he had the capacity, he had the desperate sense of the urgency of that for which he yearned, but as he pored over these stereotyped phrases of a schematized salvation, he was not helped by what he read. The modern reader, however, is helped very much toward an understanding of the "plaine man's" intellectual climate by persevering through these dull pages.

Bunyan probably went back many times to that portion of the dialogue concerning swearing,[14] his own special accomplishment in sin, as he would have us believe. Theologus estimates that there are 100,000 oaths sworn in England every day, and declares that he knows men who swear as many as a hundred a day, a figure that would probably touch Bunyan where he lived. "You will even hear little boyes and children rappe out oaths in a most fearefull manner," he continues. "It would make a mans heart quake to heare them." He then lists some of the more common oaths.

"You cannot lightly talke with a man, but he will flush out some of them in his ordinarie speech."

The list is enlightening: "By my faith, By my troth, By our Lady, By Saint Mary, By God, As God shall judge me."

The Ignorant Man cannot believe it is sinful to swear by one's faith or troth, only to be told that these are the most precious jewels we have and that the sin is proportionate to their worth. He tries again. "I know somebody," he says, "who swears by Cock or Py, or Mouse-foot. I hope this is not so bad. He is an honest man." "On the contrary," Theologus answers, "I do not thinke he is so honest as you make him, for it is no small sin to swear by creatures." "What then can we swear by?" asks Asunctus, who is apparently addicted. "Swear not at all," is of course the answer, as the dialogue moves on to Lying.

The pace of this book is accommodated to the mental processes of one hard to convince. Doubt is met patiently, never hurriedly, so that what might seem a long book for one accustomed to print, is not a page too long for an untaught cottager. Doctrine is clarified through everyday experience. Direct questions demand direct answers; in fact, confession. Do you pray much? Do you have by-thoughts during prayer? Have you ever been angry? Did you ever lie? "Yes, assuredly," Asunctus answers, and most of his readers answer yes with him.

Since this is a guidebook to heaven, of course there is only one way to end it, and as the sun draws low and the dialogue must end, according to agreement of the speakers, the Ignorant Man appropriately says: "I do feel the burden of my sins. I am greatly grieved for them. I am weary of them. I am sorry that I ever sinned against God, or that I should be such a wretch, as to incur his displeasure. . . . I pray you, . . . minister to me out of God's word." [15] In sequel, of course he is converted and on his way to heaven.

For his own day, Arthur Dent was a wise counselor. He knew how to make the cause of salvation all-important, how to hold the biblical mirror up to the sinner so that he saw himself headed the wrong way, and then step by step to turn him in the opposite direction willingly. As the "Epistle to the Reader" announces,

"This Booke meddleth not at all with any controversies in the Church, or anything in the state Ecclesiastical, but onely entereth into a Controversie with Satan and Sinne."

It was quite enough. Sunday sermons would be immensely clearer after this conversational approach to doctrine. It spoke a familiar language and found people where they lived, as Thomas à Kempis would not have done at this time, or *The Saint's Everlasting Rest,* which was not yet written.

The second pious book in Bunyan's library is exactly what its title announces it to be, *The Practice of Piety,* a "how-to" book of pious behavior.[16] It makes no appeal to reason, does not argue the case, but as a manual for a daily Christian life, offers a rule for as many situations in life as its 1,031 pages in the 1613 edition can hold. To a modern ear, its flatness and utter literalness are unsavory in the extreme, and the marvel of its continuing popularity down even to the nineteenth century is small credit to either the shepherd or the sheep. Its effectiveness, however, is not open to question. Every Puritan owned it, and became more deserving of the name because of it. It won the distinction of being placed in the *Index Purgatorius,* and out of scores of editions, a surviving copy is hard to find. A manual so well suited to all classes is rare indeed in any age.

Its genius for the purpose intended is its definiteness and the connecting of preachment with the details of actual life. Readers are told how to begin the day, how to read the Bible through with profit and ease in one year's time, what to meditate on when going to bed, getting up in the morning, on going to church, by the way, after entering the door, while the preacher is expounding the word, when prayers begin, when the sermon is ended, on the way home, when dinner is over. For those who took these instructions as their plan of life, as hundreds did, there was almost no space in the whole day unfilled. For those who knew its counsels and disregarded them, condemnation followed their every step. There would be no peace anywhere, no chance to think an unscheduled thought, or pray an individual prayer. All are here in readiness. Use them.

For a long time John Bunyan tried to match his behaviors to the counsels of these two books. The sequel was that "some desires to religion" were begotten in him. His awareness of his own sins was greatly increased, with despairs to fit. It is ironical that such stereotyped counsels could help him find the way and that after he had found it, the burden of his own counsel to others would make a life by such rules not religious at all. Religion to him was something far more private than any page in either of these books dared to suggest. He had been helped by reading them, but it was human agents who spurred him to active improvement in his own behavior, and to the search for an experience of his own. The rebuke of a shopkeeper, whom he described as "a loose, ungodly wretch," silenced him and put him to secret shame. While he stood in her ungodly presence, hanging down his head, he wished with all his heart that he might be a little child again and be taught to speak without swearing. Neither *The Plaine Man's Pathway* nor *The Practice of Piety* could have done this for him.

About this time some conversation with a poor man who professed religion and spoke pleasantly of the Bible kindled his interest and he began to read the historical books, keep the Commandments, and reform his conduct. He was well pleased with his own reformation, and as he wrote, "I thought I pleased God as well as any man in England." To his neighbors he was a changed man, and under their commendation he persevered in this new righteousness for more than a year. He gave up the bell-ringing, although his mind still "hankered" after it. He used to go to the church and look on, "though I durst not ring." After a long struggle, he also gave up dancing, and had some peace with his conscience for so doing. Then came the day when his tinker's cart took him to a Bedford street, where four women sat at a door in the sun. They may have been knitters of bone lace, an industry of the town, the workers mentioned by travelers as sitting along the street and on the bridge in the sun. Bunyan listened to these four women as they talked together, and discovered that they had an experience from which he was shut out. They discounted their own righteousness, and instead, talked of a "new birth" which supported them against temptation. They spoke, he wrote, "as if joy did make them speak," [17] and as if they had found a world in which they dwelt apart. Their talk strangely affected him, and he went back again and again, until he began to see his own righteousness in a new light.

What might have been his undoing at this stage of his search, before he came out in the clear light, was his acquaintance with several Ranters, one of them a close friend in Elstow. Bunyan was repelled by his excesses and "shook him off." In his tinkering down

57

country lanes he met a group of other Ranters who tried to persuade him to join them, and briefly he almost yielded. "Their temptations were suitable to my flesh," he wrote, but something of essential decency in him was repelled by their frenzied emotionalism, their looseness of conduct, and abandonment of moral restraint. He turned away "to look into the Bible with new eyes."

From this time forward—and a long time it was—a new kind of struggle began for him. His tortures increased manyfold, but they became chiefly mental. The sins which cast him to the depths and seemed to shut all doors toward heaven were no longer the profanity, the indulgence of lust, anything that had tangible shape. Instead he was beset by doubt, pride, lack of faith, or even belief that faith was possible—intangibles all, to be met not by resolution and the will to turn away from them, but, as he thought, by scriptural assurance alone. He was seeking for light, for certainty, for an authoritative decree of acceptance of John Bunyan by God Himself, and seeking so determinedly that he read the whole Bible through again to find one verse he had heard of but could not find. All the while he "was in a flame to find the way to heaven and glory," and nothing could "beat me off" from the search.

The verse as he had remembered it read, "Look at the generations of old and see; did any ever trust in the Lord, and was confounded?" Page by page and day by day he read on until a whole year had passed and still he had not found it, until one day, picking up the Apocrypha, he found it in Ecclesiasticus, 2,10. At first he was troubled because it was not in the canonical Scriptures, but presently, as it "shone before my face," he took assurance from it.

As he went about his trade, or walked alone in the fields, other single verses "darted" into his mind, either for comfort or torture. Was he indeed "called," as the disciples had been? Would there be room for him in heaven? Had he indeed sold his birthright? Had he sinned the unpardonable sin beyond hope? It was a mental suffering. Often he obeyed a "great bending" in his mind and went back to the poor women of Bedford, told them his condition, but could hardly be comforted by their assurance. He must have it for himself. They might as well "have bade me reach the sun with my finger" (Blake's figure), he wrote, as to have bidden him receive or rely on these promises.

One alleviating interval during this dark period came with the counsels of John Gifford, pastor of a small group meeting at St. John's Church, Bedford. He invited Bunyan to his house, walked with him in the garden, and comforted him in his distress. He was a good choice in counsel. Formerly a major in the royalist army, taken prisoner after the battle at Maidstone in 1648, he had suddenly escaped and found his way to Bedford. For a time he had practiced medicine, was converted, preached, and in 1650 became pastor of twelve Bedford Christians whom he united into a church. The four poor women were members of his congregation. His helpfulness to John Bunyan probably had foundation in his own earlier way-wardness and desperate thoughts of his own doom. At any rate his kindness was healing, and he was gratefully remembered as being the prototype of Evangelist in *Pilgrim's Progress*.

Nevertheless the mental suffering for Bunyan went on, alleviated at times but never for long. To read this story of alternate despair and hope at this stage is to see him advancing steadily toward the assurance he sought, but not knowing that he progressed. There were times, he wrote, when he would have given ten thousand pounds for one tear, if only he could shed one, but the tear would not come; times when the devil still plucked him by the coat, or when he felt bound in the wings of the temptation, sin as it were "bubbling" out of his heart. He often lived with the wish that he had been born anybody but himself. On one occasion, as he sat down on a settle in a neighboring town, and "fell into a very deep pause" about his fearful state, it seemed the very tiles on the rooftops bent themselves against him. He thought himself unfit to live in a world of sunlight.

At such points in his story it is well to be reminded that his suffering has abundant parallel in the personal records of other young men of his day. For example, George Fox, "stiff as a tree and pure as a bell," as his Scarborough jailer characterized him, spent three years of comparable distress, although more for the sins of others and the moral failures of Christianity than for a sense of sin in himself. Taking only his Bible, he sat in hollow trees and lonesome places, and in the night walked mournfully by himself.

"When it was day I wished for night, and when it was night I wished for day," [18]

was his refrain. When the light finally came, it was insupportable. Hence the abnormal manifestations, the trances, the visions, which have no counterpart in John Bunyan's experience.

The agency of a book has proved a helpful detail in the distress of many young men caught in a similar web, particularly the web of doubt. With St. Augustine one such book was Cicero's *Hortensius*. With Martin Luther it was the *Theologia Germanica*, to which he said he owed more than to any other book except the Bible and St. Augustine. With John Bunyan it was to be Luther's *Commentary on the Galatians*, which came to his hand in an old copy "ready to fall piece from piece if I did but turn it over." Bunyan had been longing to see "some ancient godly man's experience, who had writ some hundreds of years before I was born," with his story unshaped by what others had written. The very look of this sadly tattered volume pleased him and he read eagerly, to his great comfort and profit.

Luther had become a monk in order to save his soul, but like John Bunyan he had begun in the wrong way by striving to obtain favor with God for keeping the Commandments. His struggle likewise had been long and inconclusive, until he abandoned his legalistic position, and instead of trying to make himself righteous, had merely accepted God's righteousness and forgotten his own. Under Luther's example, Bunyan took exactly the same step, gave up trying to reform his outward life in order to deserve salvation, and merely accepted it as a free gift. Both men stopped thinking of God as a magistrate and accepted Him as a Father. As He became to them a new kind of God, the struggle ceased. This discovery to which both men arrived by different paths suggests one reason why Luther's *Commentary* became to John Bunyan a book which seemed to have been written out of his own heart.

"I do prefer this book . . . excepting the Holy Bible, before all the books that ever I have seen as most fit for a wounded conscience." [19]

Luther's *Commentary* is a long book and by no means an easy book to read. One's impression of John Bunyan, the unschooled tinker, is subject to some alteration, as we see him turning these pages of closely written exposition, and being carried out of himself by Luther's attempt to clarify the mystery of faith. Without formal education and, as he said of himself, knowing not Plato or any other philosopher, he had been exposed since boyhood to doctrinal instruction from Puritan pulpits. For some five years he had spent as much time reading his Bible and religious books as many university students spent on logic, philosophy, metaphysics. He was not without what with some justice can be called the beginnings of culture. He had acquired some ability to think abstractly. In addition, he had the perceptiveness, and by this time the knowledge of himself, to see his own stubborn resistance to what Luther called a passive attitude of faith in opposition to all active strivings. Submit, accept, take hold of "free grace," Luther wrote, and the troubled conscience will at last be quiet. Bunyan read, believed, and found Luther's counsel to be true for him also.

Peace comes in its own way and to no two alike. We only know that it comes. St. Augustine sat in the garden with Alypius, reading the story of Anthony, who was changed inwardly and his mind "stripped of the world." Augustine's own preparation was complete. He had only to make the decision no longer to turn and toss but to go. He knew what he had to do and also that he would do it, but he had not yet taken the last step. "I said unto myself, 'Be it done now,' and as I spoke, I all but enacted it . . . but did not. And I essayed again . . . and all but touched and laid hold of it, and yet came not at it. This controversy in my heart was self against self only." He cast himself under a fig tree, weeping. Then he heard the voice of the child, saying "Tolle, lege" (Take up and read). He opened the book and read, "But put you on the Lord Jesus Christ."

"No further would I read, nor needed I, for instantly at the end of this sentence, by a light as it were of serenity infused into my heart, all the darkness of doubt vanished away." [20]

All of Augustine's subsequent life was determined by that moment.

Bunyan's subsequent experience would be different. Time after time doubts flooded back, black fears that he would yet be shut out at the very gate of heaven. He was honest enough to admit doubt. What he never quite realized was that the perfection he sought is unattainable on earth, but he was in the path at last, and to the end of his days his purpose and resolution were as clear as sapphire.

William James's definition of conversion fits Bunyan's experience in that for him it was a process rather than an event. "A process, gradual or sudden," James wrote, "by which a self hitherto divided, and consciously wrong, inferior and unhappy, becomes unified and consciously right, superior and happy, in consequence of its firmer hold on religious realities." [21] With John Bunyan the process from darkness to light came with no dramatic suddenness. He could never say, as John Wesley once did, "about a quarter before nine," the mystery came to pass. For John Bunyan the process would be lifelong.

At some time late in this long struggle, he suffered what would seem to have been a severe illness. His own word for it is that he was "somewhat inclining to a consumption," and so "violently seized with weakness" that he thought he could not live. His references to this condition suggest that it continued for some time. He was unable to work, and deeply depressed in spirit. A hint that the sustained mental anguish was back of his indisposition comes in the statement that suddenly temptation vanished, words of Scripture darted into his mind and did "sweetly revive my spirit."

"At this I became both well in body and mind at once, for my sickness did presently vanish, and I walked comfortably in my work for God again." [22]

In 1653 he became a member of Pastor John Gifford's congregation who were worshiping in St. John's Church, Bedford, by permission of the Bedford Corporation and the practice of Cromwell's Establishment, which held to no single form of church organization. Bunyan's name appears halfway down in the first column of the page headed Members of the Congregation. As one of this newly formed fellowship, he would continue to enjoy the friendly counsels of John Gifford, who had two more years to live. His preaching, Bunyan wrote, was "much for my stability." These were two of the most important years of Bunyan's young manhood. Learning years they were, when his purpose not only had found a new direction, but when he was making a beginning toward the knowledge and training which would make the new purpose effective. Stability was precisely what he needed most, along with a grounding in the doctrine he himself would henceforth proclaim. John Gifford's friendship had comforted him during the darkest hours of his struggle with himself, and his continuing counsels during these important two years were fortunate indeed.

Pastor Gifford's congregation belonged to the Open and Particular Baptists, who did not insist on immersion as requisite for communion with them. Water baptism was an outward rite only. This was the view Bunyan accepted and later expressed in his treatise *Differences in Judgment about Water Baptism no Bar to Communion*. But this was in 1673, twenty years later, when he was himself the pastor, and in 1653, when he joined the congregation, he may have subscribed to the usual pattern for a new member and been baptized again. Neither the Church Book nor Bunyan himself makes mention of a second baptism, which, if it occurred, would have taken place in a small inlet of the river Ouse, shaded by a great elm tree, near what is now the corner of Duck Mill Lane. One may still walk the path to this half-hidden spot, where under cover of night darkness the rite would have been solemnized. Lack of record makes it uncertain. The statement of the "unknown friend" who adds this baptism detail to his story in the seventh edition of *Grace Abounding* is without authorization. The second part of his statement that Bunyan "speedily became a very zealous professor" is borne out by many details in Bunyan's own account and is in line with all that we know of him both then and thereafter. He could never have been lukewarm in the service of either God or the devil. He had been a "ringleader" in mischief; now he was out front in the opposite direction.

Probably because he had found a church home and was enjoying the guidance and sympathy he so much needed at the beginning of this new chapter at the turning of the ways, he moved from the Elstow cottage to one in St. Cuthbert's Street, Bedford, probably early in 1655. Henceforth this would be his home for all the years he would be a free man. It stood near what is now the center of the town, on the site now occupied by Numbers 17 and 19. In his day there was an open view at the rear and a small garden. There was also a shop for the forge and the cart while he still carried on the tinker's trade. In 1654, shortly before the move, another daughter, Elizabeth, had been born. Her birth was entered in the Elstow register as of April 14, 1654. At this time blind Mary was nearly four years old. In 1656 there would be a son, John, and in 1658 a second son, Thomas.

The experience of conversion which had cost him the long struggle would determine nearly everything yet to come in his life. It would make a preacher of him, and before life was over, his would be a pulpit name known to many hundreds. It would send him to prison and rob him of twelve active years. It would put his name on the title pages of more than sixty books, and on a far distant day, which he would never see, one of these would enroll him among English Men of Letters. Another would be studied by distant generations, as an example of the conversion experience as reported step by step according to his memory of it. But he was not yet ready to write this book. While his painful progress was so recently behind him was not the time to try to understand what had happened. He must begin to live it first.

Chapter Four

Field Preacher

One of the great experiences of this new chapter in John Bunyan's life went unrecorded, as is true for most lives. He may not have marked the occasion himself, or even remembered it, but in the light of his whole career it held a determining promise. That was the day on which for the first time he discovered that he could stand before a company of men and women met in a private house, a barn, a clump of trees in the woods, and by his own words, the words of John Bunyan, the tinker, move them to decision and to action. As his hearers sat immovable before him, the words came, he hardly knew whence; he felt strangely at ease and also exhilarated. The discovery of this power, hitherto unrecognized by him, and the effect of it on others, was the beginning of his story as his own day was to know him, for until the last decade of his life, to the thousands who flocked to hear him, he was a man of the pulpit, not the printing office.

Even after it became gradually known that he had written a book, it was not the reputation of an author, but of a man whose eloquence was power, that impelled men to arrive at dawn in order to hear him at noon. Perhaps the tradition of his power in the pulpit has outrun truth at some points, but it is too widespread and too persistent to be seriously doubted. Here was a man with a gift, a compulsive power in his preaching, a speaker of personal magnetism, who gripped his hearers, and not those of humble classes only. Men of training and books who came to hear him went away amazed.

Hardly more than once in a generation does religion claim such a man, and sometimes waits much longer. A century later it would be George Whitefield, who when church doors in England were closed against him, preached on the steps, on gravestones, in the fields, wherever he happened to be, and with only a herald's announcement sent on ahead, he would find hundreds waiting. When he came to New England in the 1740's, his success quickly became a legend. Wherever he went, shops were closed, village life was all but disrupted during his stay, and when he rode on to the next town, he was followed by part of the throng he had just addressed, and met halfway by welcomers of the next settlement. Whitefield's success had something to do with the golden voice with which nature had endowed him, something with his gift for drama. He made his pulpit a stage and gave New England a taste of entertainment that had no previous parallel in their lives. But most of all, his power lay in the freshness of what he had to say and the intensity of conviction with which he said it.

So it would be with John Bunyan. No one recorded the quality of his voice and there is no reason to think it was extraordinary. Nothing in the text of his printed treatises would suggest that it was quiet, like Newman's, and surely nothing in the hints of his physical robustness. His own word that "I bowed myself with all my might, to condemn sin and transgression wherever I found it," [1] suggests a vigor and energy which may be near the mark. On his printed pages the many sequences of questions, addressed directly to the hearers as individuals, may contain another hint of his effectiveness. Apparently, like Jonathan Edwards, he knew how to isolate each member of his congregation, as though no one else were listening, and then press the inquiry home to a climax of tension. No revival preaching is more irresistible than that which seems to be one man preaching to one man listening. Many of John Bunyan's printed pages suggest that he was aware of this secret of power.

Unfortunately, no single sermon survives as it was originally preached, unless perhaps his last one, and of that only a summary.

Some sermons were later expanded into treatises, greatly changing the pace and immediacy of the original discourse. The matter as printed in these treatises is solid, heavily doctrinal, interlarded with Scripture, and spare of anecdote. There is not the slightest hint of the sensational. Bunyan used no tricks. To read these hundreds of pages developed from what in skeleton were once sermons heard behind guarded doors, or in the woods at midnight by men and women who had walked miles to listen after a hard day's work, is to wonder exceedingly about this man and his power. In so far as it is an open secret, the answer would seem to lie first in the utter certainty with which he spoke, confident that the authority of God's own word was behind what he said. The answer also lies in that curious alchemy by which something about an individual man, something about the idea he is expressing, and something about the moment in which he speaks, conjoin in such proportion as to make his words more powerful than logic can explain. In this case the man was a mechanic preacher, the idea, what was called "eternal salvation," and the moment, a time when old systems of religious thought and practice were deeply suspect. Not singly, but in combination, these three gave John Bunyan, George Fox, and many others whom fame passed by, their chance in the 1650's, and they took it.

It was not only the unlearned field preachers who attracted the populace in this restless decade. Both learned and humble gathered in vast crowds to hear Richard Baxter, a man of erudition and dignity. There were great congregations at St. Paul's and the Abbey, as well as at Paul's Cross. Samuel Pepys speaks of crowded churches throughout London. People were not going to church by compulsion at this date, and the crowds who followed the field preachers would not have continued to go for novelty alone. The public asks more than mere hypnotic exhibitions, particularly in such a crisis as midcentury England was experiencing in this decade. With all their extravagances and regrettable excesses, the field preachers fed the hungry crowds who followed them.

The time was one of overwrought nerves both politically and religiously. "The black Providence of the King's death" lay heavy on every Englishman's conscience. Corruption in church and state could be seen by anyone with his eyes half open. Who could be trusted? In such a time new voices have their chance, and if there is life in what they proclaim, their message will outlive its crudities. From such voices the one thing most desirable is authority, and at the moment it resided in neither authorized civil nor ecclesiastical representatives. The Bible in the hand of the lay preacher, chapter and verse at his command, helped to supply it. Edward Hyde, Earl of Clarendon, is reputed to have said, "The Bible in English under every weaver's and chambermaid's arms hath done us much hurt." The facts of English history attest the truth of his observation.

In the middle fifties, when John Bunyan's preaching career began, the uproar about lay preachers, merely because they were laymen, had fairly well subsided. Tradesmen in the pulpit, tub thumpers in the market place had come to stay, and they were not to be silenced by church decrees, arguments, ridicule, or even, on occasion, mob violence. Ten years earlier, when they were making headlines in the penny broadsides, it had been their right to preach, and the Scripture warrant they produced to justify it, that had had the emphasis. "A Swarme of Sectaries and Schismatiques," John Taylor, the "Water Poet," had called them in 1641.[2] "Cobblers, Tinkers, Pedlers, Weavers, Sow-gelders, and Chymney-Sweepers, who preach

> "Extemp'ry without any meditation,
>   But only by the Spirit's revelation.
>   Tis madnesse, that a crew of brainless blocks,
>   Dares teach the learned what is Orthodoxe.
>   These kind of Vermin swarm like Caterpillars
>   And hold Conventicles in Barnes and Sellars.
>   Some preach (or prate) in woods, in fields, in stables,
>   In hollow trees, in tubs, on tops of tables,
>   To the expence of many a Tallow Tapor,
>   They tosse the holy Scripture into Vapor."

Samuel How, a cobbler, who "took upon him beyond his last," had been a particularly vulnerable target. His shoemaker's trade invited puns, and for a time it was enough merely to ridicule him:

"His text he clouted, and his Sermon welted,
  His audience (with devotion) almost melted,
  His speech was neither studied, chew'd or champ'd
  Or ruminated, but most neatly vamp'd."

Later, however, when he broke into print with his justification of lay preaching, his pamphlet, *The Sufficiencie of the Spirits Teaching without Humane-Learning*,[3] demanded serious consideration. Denied publication in England, it was printed in Holland, and quickly ran through eight editions. Within weeks a spate of English pamphlets had replied. Such immediate and widespread opposition to his plea for the uneducated preacher owed something to the current uneasiness because of the common man's protest against class privilege, which was beginning to be vocal in unexpected quarters, but such protest had been no part of Samuel How's purpose. Instead he was proclaiming a new kind of individual faith, and in this direction he was squarely in the center of a current of religious thinking which would presently sweep away more barriers than his opponents could set up to block him. But they saw the danger and were ready with abuse and serious argument:

"How durst then this lump of ignorance assume so much boldnesse, with reasons drawne *ab absurdo* . . . or with his blacke Thumbe wax so impudent to touch, much less to handle humane Science and Learning." [4]

Nevertheless he dared, and thereby broke a strong lock to a hitherto forbidden door, letting in not only himself but the whole reviled "Swarme," and in the thought of many of his hearers, making lack of education almost a qualification for preaching. As he saw it, learning was a handicap to the soul. To him knowledge meant knowledge of God, and the learned ones were those who truly understood the Scriptures. Human teaching could not give such understanding. "The Christ within the saint, like Christ in the temple, knows better than all the doctors of the universities," he said, and there he left it.

At first confuting him and his lay-preacher colleagues, in their

seeming justification of ignorance, had seemed easy, and the established clergy piled up scriptural evidence in support of their position.
But Scripture was How's weapon too, and by the word-for-word
literalness of his interpretation, and never mind the context, he
could make the Bible prove anything. God had chosen the foolish
things of the world to confound the wise, and that was final.
He slipped out of every critical net made of Scripture, as soon
as it was drawn around him. Moreover, though learned ones could
refute him by logic, they could not gainsay his essential meaning that the power of preaching is inner, not outer. He proved his
case by his own example and the size of the crowds that followed
him. His martyrdom also helped the cause he stood for as much
as his preaching; possibly more. Meanwhile both ridicule and serious criticism of lay preaching blunted themselves by their vehe-
mence, as pamphlets continued to pour forth from printing houses.
The unspoken protest of the field preachers against class privilege
would win in due time, and also the new kind of individualistic faith
they were proclaiming.

Critics tried another theme, and listed the heresies these self-
appointed laymen were announcing to the danger of orthodoxy.
Abundant material awaited them, for the more sensational of the
lay preachers saw their chance to be as famous as Samuel How,
and proclaimed extravagant denials of approved doctrine. Penny
broadsides, "adorned with cuts," listed heresies clergymen had dealt
with seriously, and amused their readers thereby, probably without
much help to the cause.

A broadside of 1647 pictured the church as a woman in a boat,
seated on a throne, the Bible in her right hand, a palm in her left.
In the sea around her were representatives of the various sects, also
Pope Nero, Jesuits, Turks, infidels, each bearing his own emblem
in his hand. Beneath was a list of thirty-one heresies, some concerning doctrine, some practice. Another broadside of the same year
shows cuts of a confectioner, a smith, a shoemaker, a tailor, a saddler,
a porter, a box-maker, a soap-boiler, a glover, a meal-man, a chicken-
man, a button-maker, and announces, "These Tradesmen are Preachers in and about the City of London." A list of forty-nine heresies
follows the cuts. Some of those most common to all such lists were:

God does not foreknow all things.
Is not almighty.
Is not eternal.
Is not perfectly holy.
The Scriptures are not his Word.
Ordinances are of no use.
Children have no original sin.
A man has power of his own free will to repent.
There will be no judgment after death.
The Sabbath is not to be observed.
The souls of men are mortal and none is immortal but God.
Man had life before God breathed it into him.
There is no resurrection of men's bodies after this life.
Universities are of the devil and human learning is of the flesh.
It is unlawful to sing psalms.
All the heathen shall be saved, because they are not guilty of unbelief.
No man has to do with his conscience.
No man will be cast into hell for sin, but only because God will have it so.
Many shall be saved who are not elected.

Inevitably such lists begot other lists. The heresies listed can be sorted out as belonging to Ranters, Seekers, and other extremists, most of them not deserving of serious concern, some merely burlesque, some shockingly irreverent, others merely vulgar. The more sensational the heresy, the bigger the audience, the more sale for the broadside.

John Bunyan's preaching at no point denied orthodox belief or partook of such chaotic nonsense as broadside writers exploited, but in popular thought he belonged to the same "unlearned crew," and the fact that he spoke extemporaneously also brought him under the charge of "enthusiasm," for which no one had a good word. The learned wrote treatises on it. "Nothing else but a misconceit of being inspired," Henry More announced. Richard Baxter likewise deprecated it. Many score of pamphlet pages marshal the arguments against it, as it would seem endlessly, and yet the eloquence of a man who had the look of a simple countryman, not a university graduate, moved his hearers and worried the civil authorities.

Thomas Ellwood's remark, as he compared Edward Burrough, a young man of exceeding ready tongue, as he preached at Isaac Pennington's house on one occasion, with James Nayler, one of the most sensational of the itinerant preachers, is a typical, rather than an individual verdict:

"But what dropped from James Nayler had the greater force upon me, because he looked but like a plain, simple countryman, having the appearance of a husbandman or a shepherd." [5]

To his lay-preaching audience, the tinker's cart, like George Fox's leather breeches, helped John Bunyan to win his first audiences as much as anything he said. Browning wrote with imaginative understanding when he made Ned Bratts say,

"His language was not ours. 'Tis my belief, God spake:
No tinker had such powers."

Initially the marvel was more powerful than the preachment.

As a preacher without a settled living, or even a pulpit, John Bunyan had joined a company whose wayfaring mission stretched far back into English history. Ever since the coming of the Dominican and Franciscan friars, early in the thirteenth century, there had been a place in English life for the itinerant preacher. These preaching friars had brought something into life that the cathedrals and great churches did not supply. Their preaching had met a need, albeit a need that they had helped to create. The sermons they preached had brought religion closer to life as it was being lived; their human-interest stories had dramatized their teaching and made it easier to understand as well as easier to remember. It had changed both the appetite for sermons and the technique of the sermon itself. Later generations in their turn continued to meet the need and also still further to change the pattern set for them. The schematized sermon structure of the great seventeenth century preachers, Lancelot Andrewes, Thomas Preston, William Perkins, Thomas Adams,

Thomas Goodwin, owed something to the sermon techniques of the early friars, although the indebtedness had been long forgotten.

Wycliffe's "evangelical men" had still further strengthened the tradition of wayside preaching. Barefooted, carrying staves, these russet-clad evangelists in their day became familiar figures all over England. Like the preaching friars, they aimed their teachings at the common people, preaching wherever they could find them, in the churchyard, at the market place, in the street, or in the fields. They were gladly heard, and when presently sharp criticism, born of suspicion of militancy against the Crown, broke these large congregations into small conventicles, their followers still met in barns, stables, and other solitary places. Danger brought new life and a spirit of brotherhood into these secret meetings, and also an increased recklessness on the part of both preacher and congregation.

It is impossible to assess what remained of this Lollard experience in seventeenth century religious tradition after two centuries,[6] but the secret conventicle as the answer to prohibited preaching, and the enjoyment of an intimate fellowship of danger behind locked doors, were firmly a part of the English religious heritage in London as well as in the remote countryside. Once more John Bunyan, George Fox, and itinerants under many other loyalties found an existing tradition to which they gave new vitality. Traditions persist, underground as it were. One does not consciously learn them, or even know that he is heir to them. They also grow and branch, and the new expression may bear scant resemblance to the earlier form, but there is a recognizable continuity. In his insistence on the authority of the Bible against every teaching of man, Bunyan was in the Wycliffe tradition, as well as in the "cry aloud, spare not" bravery of the preaching friar. In his own seventeenth century day he too had fallen on "preaching times," and since he possessed in generous measure the peculiar gifts of eloquence and personal magnetism that mark the evangelist in any age, he would be singled out and watched, as a man to be put behind bars at the first provocation.

His preaching career began modestly. The Bedford Church Book does not show the date, but from various references in his own account it would seem that his gift in speaking was recognized by the brethren of the congregation before he himself knew that he possessed it. He speaks of himself as excessively shy in the beginning and it is easy to believe that he was. The brethren had their first chance to observe and judge the likelihood of his effectiveness in speaking when, according to custom, he was obliged to give evidence of his conversion before being accepted into the membership. This testimony would have been made to a small group and in the presence of Pastor Gifford. He would also have been obliged to repeat his story publicly for the membership, which at that date was a small company.

Presumably after this public recital, several of the brethren suggested that occasionally he speak a word of exhortation at their meetings. He did so, first at two private assemblies, and he was encouraged when his hearers were both "affected and comforted." Somewhat later, when members of the group went into the country to teach, he sometimes spoke "a word of admonition," at which those who heard, testified that their "souls were edified." The brethren were encouraged, and appointed him to a "more ordinary and public hearing of the word." The beginning of his preaching career was as simple and practical as that. There was no spectacular call, such as is in print for many of his fellow itinerants. He merely acknowledged a "secret pricking forward thereto," and after he had made an approved beginning, his path was clear before him.[7]

From an entry in the Church Book in September, 1657, stating that he could not act in a service for which he had been nominated, because he was "otherwise employed, taken off by the preaching of the Gospel," and another for March, 1658, concerning "what to doe with respect to the indictment against bro. Bunyan at ye Assizes for preaching at Eaton," it would seem that at least by 1657, and probably before, his preaching career, as sponsored by the Bedford congregation, was well launched. If John Gifford's interest and guidance were back of his appointment, as would seem likely, this employment would have come before 1655, the year Gifford died. This date is corroborated in Bunyan's own account of his arrest and trial of 1660, stating that he had been preaching about five years.[8]

Most of these early preaching occasions would have been secret, with the congregation assembled in a private house, a barn, or some secluded spot in the woods. Several of these places are identified by local tradition: Colman Green in the parish of Sandridge, Wainwood Dell near Hitchin, a cottage in Preston, a shed with an escape door in the rear at Bendish, Mobbs Hole, near by, and also a tree at Tinker's Hill. A few pulpits were also open at times. Itinerants would have been welcome in a dozen small villages of Bedfordshire, Cambridgeshire, and Buckinghamshire, among them that of John Gibbs of Newport Pagnell, Bunyan's probable acquaintance from soldier days; William Dell of Yielden, who later invited him to preach on Christmas day; John Donne of Pertenhall and William Wheeler of Cranfield. Seven or eight men, sponsored by a single church, might through these occasional invitations, and in the many more secret meetings, not only leaven the orthodoxy of a scattered area considerably in the space of a year, but also change somewhat what people asked of religious leaders, as was quickly realized by religious and civil authorities. Well might they be concerned, if they remembered England's religious history.

Very probably Bunyan's earliest sermons were exhortings based on his own conversion experience. He had a good story to tell, of its kind, and from the vigor with which later he turned it into drama on the printed page, one may suppose that with youth, voice, gesture added, he made it a moving recital. He mentions that when he told it in Elstow, "almost the whole town would go out to hear, also some of them perceiving that God had mercy upon me, came crying to Him for mercy too." [9] Bunyan had the gift of being able to put emotional compulsion behind his words, and he also knew how to bring the here and now of the urgency home to his hearers. For one who, as he said for himself, wished "to carry an awakening word," he was thus far qualified for effective evangelism, but aside from what one might call native gifts, and a compelling urge to save those who, as he saw it, were "lost," at this stage he still had everything to learn. Incredulous at first that God would speak through him "to the heart of any man," he presently concluded it might be so, and his success became a reassurance. Once, as he says, he had "set upon the work," and his countrymen understood, "they came in to hear the Word by hundreds, and that from all parts." After that, "neither guilt nor hell could take me off my work," he wrote. Thus he went on for the space of about two years, time enough for his own effectiveness to develop and his reputation to become an increasing threat to his safety. He was one of a queer and suspected company, all of whom would be condemned for the extravagances of the worst.

The same two years, 1657 to 1659, were years of unpredictable change on every level of English society. Nothing was as it had been, and still more far-reaching change might come again to-morrow. As John Aubrey, the antiquarian, two years older than John Bunyan, looked back on his life, "When I was a Boy (before the Civill Warres)," he remembered the Oxford scorn of newness, as he said, in the university, in agriculture, everywhere at that date. It had been "a Presumption," he wrote, to admit that anything could be better than what was already known and practiced. Now, by contrast, all was ferment, he said. With the death of the king, the unity of English culture was broken. A new age had begun. Bunyan had come in on the fringe of this newness. To be in the van of an age of cataclysmic change is to invite heavy blows if one is part of that change, and to be a spokesman of change, aged twenty-eight, is to have a chance to outlive opposition to a great cause. William Lloyd Garrison is reported to have said to young Whittier, aged fifteen,

> "My lad, if thou wouldst win success, join thyself early to some unpopular but noble cause."

It would be so for Bunyan likewise. The blows for him came early, and before long would cost him twelve years of his life, but he would also outlive the time when religious persecution could put any man behind prison bars in England. That he would have a share in dignifying the common lot by creating respect for individuality in religious experience has root in various conditions and personal characteristics, and in nothing more than in his own unassailable conviction that he preached the truth. Nothing he ever said comes nearer to revealing the secret of his place in religious history than his word,

76

"Methought I was more than sure, if it be lawful to express myself, that those things which then I asserted were true." [10]

Not sure, but "more than sure" spells the difference. The assurance
came early, and as he kept on asserting the same truths as he saw
them, he grew more heedless of warnings that became more vocal
with each new suspicion of wayside preaching. He lived in an angry
age, and that he could not continue to live safely was written in the
very stars.

During these crucial years 1656–1659, tension from one cause
was quickly followed by tension from another, each short-lived, but
each in turn adding to the general ferment. In 1656 one such tension
concerned the Quakers, who for their strange, boisterous behaviors,
as well as their doctrines, were in bad odor with civil as well as
ecclesiastical authority. Their numbers, thanks to the leadership of
George Fox, were increasing rapidly, and with his first imprisonment under the unfounded suspicion of plotting against the government, the loyalty of his followers became not only more vocal but
more militant as well. Report of hostility to Quakers in New England during this year, 1656, increased the zeal of leaders and followers alike. Meanwhile a group of Quaker itinerants, Francis Howgill,
Edward Burrough, George Whitehead, Richard Hubberthorne, as
well as George Fox, were making Quaker doctrine familiar throughout the country and providing local excitement by their market-
place disputations with itinerants of other persuasions. In almost
any village to which his travels brought him, an itinerant might
find himself contending for space on the green with a Quaker. No
sooner would he begin his own sermon than he would be interrupted
by another voice from the new arrival a few rods away. First he
would be heckled, contradicted, probably outvoiced, and then by
some noisier demonstration on the part of the intruder or his listeners, he would either be drowned out or see his congregation drawn
away by the other speaker. For a time each contender might try to
outpreach the other, but more often the next step was for the two
men to engage in a disputation before the combined crowd each
had attracted.

By engaging in one such controversy during this troubled year, John Bunyan found a new path for his young preaching energies, and a path which would determine many things in his future career. It was the path to the printing office. The occasion was a visit to Bedford by Edward Burrough, a recent convert to the Quaker faith. At this date he was only twenty-one, but his fiery eloquence and his personal gentleness had already earned for him the paradoxical epithet Son of Thunder and Consolation. He preached in the Bedford market place one day in May, 1656. John Bunyan was present, and challenged him on several of his statements. How extensive a debate followed and whether spirited or mild is not known, but apparently the encounter kindled Bunyan's combativeness and he immediately sat down to write a pamphlet in defense of his position. By late summer it was on the stands, the bookseller being Mathias Cowley, of Newport Pagnell, presumably Bunyan's friend of army days. It was entitled *Some Gospel Truths Opened, according to the Scriptures*. By September 6th Edward Burrough had answered it under the title *The True Faith of the Gospel of Peace*, and this pamphlet was also on the stands. Bunyan immediately answered in a second pamphlet, *A Vindication of the Book Called Some Gospel Truths*, and with equal haste and less courtesy, Burrough answered this answer in *Truth the Strongest of all, witnessed forth in the Spirit of Truth, against all Deceit*. This fourth pamphlet was published on May 5, 1657. Aged twenty-eight, John Bunyan had joined the army of controversialists of all causes, all faiths, on all levels of society, and by this initial skirmish he was on a path from which other and more important paths would open for him than for the "preaching tinker" alone.

This first book, *Some Gospel Truths Opened*, the first of the sixty he would write in the next thirty-two years, chiefly because it is the first, is an amazing performance. Amazement consists not in the doctrine marshaled to oppose doctrine, not in any originality of thought, felicity of style or expression. He is simply repeating somewhat clumsily what other Sectaries were saying against the Quaker doctrine of the "inner light," or a substitution of the Christ within, for the historic Jesus. This doctrine more than any other Quaker preachment inflamed their opponents, who had already hurled back

the argument Bunyan is presenting, and were doing it more force-
fully on many village greens, and in print. Bunyan adds nothing
to the barrage of argument in opposition. Amazement as to his performance consists in the fact of a printed pamphlet over his signature, bearing the date 1656.

Less than three years before he had been floundering in a morass
of doubt and perplexity, and was at times near to hopeless despair
as to what to believe, or whether to believe at all. His sense of alone-
ness had been well nigh complete. He was lost on the far side of
the high mountain, as he wrote later, and there was no way to get
through to the sunny spot where his believing friends sat refreshing
themselves in the sunlight. He was, as he put it, "shivering and
shrinking in the cold, afflicted with frost, snow and dark clouds."
No matter how sudden conversion to light and warmth may be,
there is a great deal more than one step between the high wall and
the blank vacancy of his condemned state while a sinner, and the
confidence with which he handled approved doctrine in this first
treatise, which ran to forty folio pages. He had learned volumes
during these three years, and learned it not only to recite verbatim
what he had learned, but to use it against other doctrines so slightly
different as somewhat to baffle a modern reader not able to recognize quickly the first faint signs of heretical divergence.

More than that, for a man without formal schooling to be able
to steer a fairly straight course, step by step to a known goal, means
and goal alike abstract, through a process of related statements, and
to sense when he had arrived, means that he had acquired something
of method as well as content. Naturally, it is the seventeenth century
preacher's method of division and subdivision, having a look of logic
in its numbered sequences, without inner logic, but it is orderliness
as opposed to hodgepodge. Most amazing of all are the knowledge
and use of Scripture which this pamphlet displays. The applications
are literal, as Bunyan intended them to be, but they apply on the
terms he announces, and he brings them forth in abundance, now
singly, now in mass, now comparing one with the other, and always
with a pertinence which is recognizable.

With this printed treatise accomplished, his life took on a new
dimension. Up to the time of his return from the army, the resump-

tion of the tinker's trade, his marriage, and the setting up of a household, his life is an understandable unit of human living, even with the devils that tormented him and the attacks of conscience under reproof. His conversion itself as the turning point in a life is understandable, considered for itself. His life after this first treatise, the books yet to be written, the sermons to be preached, the imprisonment, all that is also of a piece. It is the completeness with which the tinker's life had broken apart on that Sunday afternoon on the Elstow green which this dusty treatise against the Quakers represents. It amounts to a documentation of that severance. He was now on his life journey, as the world remembers him.

As he very quickly realized, controversy was not the realm in which he was happiest or most successful. Cross-fencing was not the best avenue for his intellectual or emotional energies.

"I never cared to meddle with things that were controverted," [11] he wrote later, and in this decision he was wise. That he had suffered from this first excursion into controversy is apparent in the prefatory address to his next pamphlet written by John Gibbs, another friend from Newport Pagnell days. John Gibbs is apologetic for Bunyan's lack of learning, but full of praise for his godliness, his preaching success, and his industry. "He is no drone," but "hath laid forth himself to the utmost of his strength. . . . I fear this is one reason why the archers have shot so sorely at him." Bunyan himself alludes to current criticism, and prays that "as the world rages, . . . stamp and shake their heads, . . ." he may take it all with patience and turn the other cheek.[12]

The year 1658 was not a good one for an itinerant preacher to be in the spotlight, either for his success or for the suspicion of officialdom. Hysteria, uncertainty, violence, bewilderment, real fears and groundless fears, restlessness, search for some stable authority —one can find them all in almost any diary for any month of this year. Ralph Josselin's single sentence entry for September 3rd is a comment on the times as well as a record. He wrote,

"Cromwell died, the people not much minding it."

John Evelyn wrote of the funeral day,

"The joyfullest funeral I ever saw, for there were none that cried but dogs." [13]

The title of Bunyan's treatise, announced in *The Commonwealth Mercury* immediately after the notice of Cromwell's death, provoked some grim witticism. Bunyan's title was *A Few Sighs from Hell, or the Groans of a Damned Soul.*

This 1658 pamphlet, presumably developed from a sermon, offers a sample of his early preaching, when popular thought as to the nearness of the last judgment made such a subject effective. By some computations it was only a matter of months away; by others it was overdue. "God's hand was up; the judgment was at hand," was believed by more than the Fifth Monarchists. Bunyan's desire in such preaching was of course to alarm sinners, and though he states that he has given only "a very short touch of the torments of hell," it would seem to be quite enough. He is ruthless. After he has tied his sinner to the stake, pinched off his flesh in little pieces for two or three years, filled his body with scalding lead and run him through with a red-hot spit, he announces that this is only flea-biting to the sorrows of one consigned to hell, and then goes on to other details, not forgetting to measure the length of his sufferings by the stars in heaven, drops in the sea and sands on the shore multiplied into years and centuries. His most vivid writing for these early years comes in this piece, with touches of originality in his imagery.

Parallels to such alarms as this on the same subject may be found wherever one turns during these last years of the decade. Church of England sermons, sermons to Commons, as well as the harangues of the lesser dissenting preachers ring the changes on these torments. The phrases of alarm were not yet worn out, the extravagant computing of misery in terms of eternity not yet commonplace. Bunyan was following a pattern, and had he kept on in this vein he would have had no lasting fame as a preacher. But as he said of himself, "Thus I went on for the space of about two years, crying out against men's sins, and their fearful state because of them, but after this I altered my preaching." His later publications bear evidence of this changed direction.

But that would be a long time later. During these crucial years, 1656–1660, he was moving by swift steps toward the prison cell that was awaiting him. For John Gibbs, an unimportant minister, to give him a good name in a pamphlet preface would avail nothing to officers of the law who were trying to quiet the noise that was rapidly turning English peace into unmanageable confusion. Bunyan's name was becoming known as that of a popular, stirring preacher, and also as a target of slander and abuse. Such attitudes lead to incidents, sometimes to mob violence.

In 1659, the year before his arrest, he went into print again, this time in connection with a shabby affair involving a Cambridge Quaker, accused of having bewitched Mary Philips, transforming her into a mare and riding her to a Quaker meeting in Cambridge. Such accusations were not uncommon at the time, most often advancing no further than vague neighborhood rumor, but this Cambridge affair got to the printing house in two surviving pamphlets, and with Bunyan's lost pamphlet to make three. The surviving titles are:

Strange and Terrible Newes from Cambridge Being a true Relation of the Quakers bewitching of Mary Philips, London, 1659.

and the other contradicting the truth of this story,

A Lying Wonder Discovered and The Strange and Terrible Newes from Cambridge proved false.[14]

Bunyan's pamphlet, alluded to in both of these pamphlets, has not come to light. He was addressed directly, as its author:

"And now to you John Bunion who goes up and down to preach and lookest upon thyself higher than the Prests and many others in that thou hast dispersed a paper abroad against the Quakers, . . . what, thou a preacher and so given over to believe lies, and false dreams which thou hast told, like the false prophets whom God was against!"

The implication that he believed the tale of the bewitching, as told to him by the alleged victim, has no support in anything that has come down to us over his own signature, but there would be nothing surprising about it. Such credulity was in high place and low, in print and out of it.

Another Cambridge treatise of the same year mentions Bunyan. This was *The Quaker No Papist* written by Henry Denne to Mr. Thomas Smith of Cambridge, who had disputed with George Whitehead and George Fox. Denne addresses Thomas Smith as "Antagonist to George Whitehead the Quaker and the preaching Tinker":

"You seem to be angry with the Tinker [he wrote] because he strives to mend Souls as well as Kettles and Pans; and you are so angry, that your passion clouded your reason, and made you forget what you have to do; the main drift of your Letter is to prove that none may preach except they be sent. . . ."

The tinker thinks so too, he adds, and so you contend with a shadow. Perhaps he has as good a Commission from the church at Bedford as you have from your church.

Bunyan also figures in Thomas Smith's reply to Henry Denne:

"Methinks he should not say this Tinker mends Soules: unless he mean that he mendeth them as he mends kettles, that is, stopping one hole and making many."

Thomas Smith also alludes to Bunyan, "whom his friends generally call the tinker," as "this ringleader, this famous preacher," and beseeches Mr. E. of Toft "not to think a tinker more infallible than the pure spouse of Christ."

The allusion "famous" is more properly interpreted as meaning in 1659 someone to watch, for he was "famous" for the wrong reasons and in the wrong places. At Christmas time of the same year he was invited by William Dell of Yielden to preach in his pulpit, and this invitation became one reason for the parishioners of William Dell to petition the House of Lords for his removal as their pastor. Dell's hospitality to Bunyan was in line with his printed accusations of university training as a qualification for the ministry, but this was a poor time to prove his assertions that

> "The bottom of Humane Learning is easily fathomed. Jesus and his disciples did not have it. Paul himself did not ascribe his success to his learning, but to the grace of God bestowed on him."

Both Bunyan and William Dell had counts against them for the Christmas-day invitation and sermon.

Bunyan's personal life during this troubled time was saddened by the death of his wife, leaving him with four small children: blind Mary, now aged eight, and the youngest, an infant. Fortunately his relation to the Bedford church would have meant helpfulness in this home crisis, and even without the authority of record, one may be sure that he had it. His assignments as an itinerant took him on foot or horseback to distant villages week by week, and his tinker's trade, when he had a chance to pursue it, also meant absence from home. He needed help. At some time in the following year, possibly early in 1659, he married again. All that we know of this second wife is her name, Elizabeth. She may have been a member of the Bedford congregation, but of that no record. Subsequently we know her for her courage, her resourcefulness and independence. She would need them all, for threats were gathering increasingly around Bunyan himself.

Conventicle Act not operative till 1664. An old Act from reign of Eliz. had to be revived to be used on. B. See p. 96

Chapter Five

Offender Before the Law

His arrest was inevitable. It was also purely routine in almost every detail. He was one of hundreds who dared to defy the law in a fevered time and in consequence paid for their boldness as civil authority had decreed. The law against conventicles had been duly announced, and itinerant preachers who continued to preach did so at their own risk. Penalties were sometimes inhumanly severe, but there was nothing illegal about the arrest itself. Bunyan was far more fortunate than an uncounted number for whom the rigors of prison life would mean speedy death or a more cruel and tortured lingering. Aged thirty-two, he had the physical stamina to survive what was immediately ahead for him.

Repressive measures in 1660 were not born of malice or bigotry, but rather fear of possible danger to the state. Since 1640 and the outcry against Samuel How, the attitude toward lay preachers had changed several times. Opposition to them as disqualified to interpret the Scriptures was now a thing of the past. Likewise the caution lest they broadcast heresy and corrupt the orthodox. There had been no stopping them on either count. In the sensitive first months of the Restoration era they were under the ban because of supposed seditious intent. Some few of them deserved the suspicion and were also disturbers of the peace. Most were not, however, but officialdom made no attempt to distinguish between noisy evangelism and the incitement of rebellion with intent to assassinate the king and overthrow the state. Hence all lay preachers, as potential leaders in such plots, were in line for arrest, and any ostensible religious assembly, aside from established parish worship, was strictly forbidden. Since John Bunyan was sponsored by a Baptist congregation, he was particularly in danger, as in civil thought Baptist and Anabaptist were identical, and Anabaptist had one connotation only, the riots of Münster. Why could they not break out in England also? Let us prevent such outrages at all cost. Disperse all crowds. Arrest all itinerants who attempt to assemble an audience anywhere, particularly in secret.

Had the constables who came to arrest the field preachers in most assemblies stayed to listen to what went on, they would not have heard a militant word. Repent and be saved was the usual theme. But they had not come to listen; they had warrants for arrest in their pockets; they produced them and led the preachers away. Even Quaker itinerants, boldest before magistrates, and sometimes guilty of misdemeanors in conduct, were not plotters against the state. It was the Fifth Monarchists, least of all in numbers, noisiest in demonstration, with their prophecies of the coming of King Jesus and the overthrow of all temporal power, who were chiefly responsible for the legal pursuit of all itinerants in this fateful year. The concern of magistrates with such prophesying is easily understandable, and would have foundation presently with the "insurrection" led by Thomas Venner in London.

Moreover, the scores of secret assemblies to which restless crowds were flocking were also justifiable reason for vigilance on the part of civil authority. Rumors were afoot that the regicides who had escaped to the Continent were planning a return, and the air was charged with anxiety on this account also. Conventicles are a risk. Arrest their leaders. It will be safer. Accordingly all constables were put on the alert.

Bunyan's offense in no way touched current reasons for this vigilance. He was guilty only of disobedience to a law he should have understood. In all his hundreds of printed pages, and presumably in the sermons upon which these were based, there is never a sentence which with a shadow of justice could be called sedition against the state. Years later in his *Forest of Lebanon* treatise he spoke directly of the Fifth Monarchy claims, and denied any share in them. Instead he wrote,

> "I confess myself an alien to these notions and believe and profess the quite contrary." [1]

He looked, he said, for the coming of Christ in final judgment, but before that day not with carnal weapons but only in spirit, and in the "power of his word to destroy Antichrist, to inform kings, and so to give quietness to his Church on earth." He believed in the last judgment as a scriptural certainty, personal to each man, but when it came the earth itself would be no more. To the Fifth Monarchists the coming they prophesied was an interim chapter, when Christ would sit in majesty on the throne of this world and all earthly kings would be overthrown. In so far as it can be reconstructed in its direction, Bunyan's preaching in 1660 had no prophetic strain, but was intended to meet the hunger for assurance of personal salvation on scriptural terms, undeserved and yet a free gift. Congregations met with their Bibles in their hands, and profited by the preacher's greater familiarity with chapter and verse, as they turned the pages together. These meetings were Bible study groups quite as literally as services of worship and preaching occasions. But in such troublous times, so simple and harmless a purpose was beyond the comprehension of constables searching for hidden arms and gunpowder.

Bunyan's behavior at the time of his arrest and trial makes it plain that he did not half understand the law he had defied. He felt only the desperate need of "saving souls" and his responsibility as one "called" to hold out hope for such as might repent under his preaching. In this single-minded obliviousness to all else he was most himself. This is the John Bunyan who wrote his name large in English religious history. He was a man of one purpose, driving straight ahead to that end and that end only, without so much as looking over his shoulder to see what might be following. Discretion was not in his books. Had he practiced it, as a sensible man would have done during this critical period, the world would never have heard of him.

Even when one recognizes this singleness of purpose for the

dynamic force it was in his life, however, his apparent unawareness of the spirit of the time is hard to understand. He had been a soldier in the Parliamentary army. How did he feel about the Restoration which would undo so much? Since Cromwell's death two years before, Bedfordshire had been one of the more restless areas, while Parliament and the army seesawed back and forth for power. Sir Samuel Luke, Governor of Newport Pagnell during Bunyan's army days, now M.P. from Bedford, had been the center of the local storm and had been excluded from Parliament because of his Presbyterianism. It would seem that a veteran half awake would have taken sides on such an issue. In February, 1660, the Freeholders and Inhabitants of Bedford County had sent a strong declaration to Parliament demanding the readmission of excluded members, else they would not pay the taxes imposed on them. As a resident of Bedford, Bunyan could not have failed to know not only the fact but also the intensity of resentment back of this formal declaration in this once Parliamentary stronghold.

Week after week also he would have heard the news brought by horseback messengers from London. On April 14th Parliament dissolved itself. The new Parliament recalled Charles II. On May 25th he landed at Dover, and was received by General Monk "with all imaginable love and respect."

"Infinite the crowd of people and the horsemen, citizens, and noblemen of all sorts. The shouting and joy expressed by all is past imagination." On his birthday, May 29th, he entered London. "All the world in merry mood," Pepys added. Parliament ordered this day to be "forever kept as a day of thanksgiving for our redemption from tyranny and the King's return to his Government." [2] In a divided England, which meant also a divided Bedford, there would have been echoes of both the joy and its opposite, but not a word from Bunyan as to any of this.

In the midst of all the mingled hope, enthusiasm bordering on hysteria, suppressed fears, the Fifth Monarchists kept on proclaiming the overthrow of all temporal power and the return, not of an earthly king, but of King Jesus. In part because of their noisy forecasts, the king's Declaration of Breda, that so long as he did not disturb the peace of the realm, no man would be molested for difference of religious opinion, was withdrawn, and henceforth all preachers who continued to assemble private groups merely awaited their turn to be arrested. Knowing ones among them would have desisted for a time, but not John Bunyan. His name was doubtless already on Justice Wingate's list, not for anything he had said or might say, but because he was known to be reckless and might disobey the order.

It is more than likely that a Fifth Monarchy meeting was mistakenly thought to be in prospect at Lower Samsell on that November day. The meeting place was a farmhouse where Bunyan had often preached, sometimes under the great elms, sometimes inside the house, as on this occasion. Word of the intended meeting had leaked out, and a strong watch had been set around the house in advance of the preacher's arrival, "as if we that were to meet together in that place did intend to do some fearful business to the destruction of the country," Bunyan wrote.[3] His friends did not disperse, but waited to warn him and to advise that the meeting be postponed.

He listened to their warnings and considered them with reference not to his own safety, but to the effect upon the cause in which they had met. He was not hasty, but first took time to walk alone among the trees in quiet meditation and no doubt prayer. He had an hour's grace and could easily have escaped, but he did not even try. When he returned to the house, it was

"With a full resolution to keep the meeting and not to go away . . . for I was resolved to see the utmost of what they could say or do unto me."

No small part in his resolution came from the sense of having been chosen by God himself, as he said,

"To be the first that should be opposed for the gospel. If I should fly, it might be a discouragement to the whole body that might follow after."

To an extent, this was exactly the reason the authorities had in mind. They needed an example, and Bunyan would serve their purpose better than someone less well known.

He was the *first* in a sense that boded him no good; on October

12th, just one month before this meeting, the Bedfordshire magistrates had issued an order restoring the body of the Liturgy in public worship. This order made the Book of Common Prayer once more a live issue with every parishioner. The consecration of Robert Lawrence as Bishop of Lincoln on October 24th did the same for the office of bishop, vacant in this see for some eighteen years. This fresh emphasis upon worship according to established practice, with ecclesiastical authority newly restored to enforce it, gave Bunyan's disobedience to civil order an importance it would not have had a month earlier, in spite of the standing order against conventicles. An affront to this new order would not be lightly passed over. Had he been less single-minded in the fulfillment of his own purpose, he might have sensed this new danger to the cause as well as to himself, but even so, he would not have taken cover. "To be the first that should be opposed for the gospel" was an honor he would in no sense forego. Therefore,

"No, by no means. I will not stir, neither will I have the meeting dismissed for this."

In Justice Wingate's view, for him to be the first was not a chance to be missed. Little did he know his man. Had Bunyan realized how ill-timed this particular act of boldness would be, he might even have gone out of his way to be arrested. He had fed too long on John Foxe's exhibit of martyrs and gloried in the triumphant inflexibility of their last words for any other answer to be possible, now that his turn had come. Therefore, "I will not stir."

This dismissal of all friendly warnings and the determination to proceed with the service as planned tells something fundamental to the understanding of Bunyan's whole life story. Call it blindness or courage, for it was both. It was also tenacity to the point of stubbornness. He had come to preach. He was innocent of any seditious purpose. Therefore it was the constable, not himself, who was out of order. The meeting would proceed. In response to the anxious fears of his fellow worshipers, he could only say,

"Come, be of good cheer; let us not be daunted; our cause is good. We need not be ashamed of it."

If we suffer for a good cause we shall be rewarded. As for himself, to be a coward in the face of danger was treason to the faith:

> "If I should now run and make an escape, it will be of a very ill savour in the country. For what will my weak and newly-converted brethren think of it, but that I was not so strong in deed as I was in word."

Also, if he should run, he might by so doing make them afraid to stand, "when great words only should be spoken to them."

The "great words" he might have said on this occasion were never spoken. He had intended to preach on the text "Dost thou believe on the Son of God?" but just as the meeting was called and the company stood, Bibles, not weapons, in their hands, "ready to speak and hear the word of God," and in the attitude of prayer, the constable entered. Nevertheless, the warrant was served, and then it was too late. Once again something had happened that would change the whole future course of Bunyan's life, as on that Sunday afternoon, long before, when he had heard, as he supposed, a voice speak to him out of the heavens. It was a moment of decision, of crisis, of swift, determining change for all the years yet to come. Once again, his life had broken apart, and a new chapter had begun.

Before he was led away, he took occasion to speak a few words of counsel to his congregation, assuring them that it was "a mercy to suffer on so good an account."

> "We suffer as Christians for well doing; and we had better be the persecuted than the persecutors."

Few dissenting congregations whose leaders similarly defied the ban on assembly during these turbulent months missed an experience like this one at Lower Samsell. Few also missed the sense of near martyrdom it gave them to be thus stopped by law from serving God according to their consciences. For the leader who was led away, probably to a prison term, and maybe to death, this sense of suffering for conscience' sake would mitigate his woes. For those left behind it would strengthen their resistance to what they felt was an unjust law. Bibles in hand, they would merely move to a more secret meeting place next time. Warrants in the hands of constables are mere scraps of paper, when a liberating idea begins to work in the minds of men who are ready for it.

Justice Francis Wingate being absent from home for the day, Bunyan was put in charge of a neighborhood friend for the night, upon the promise that he would be brought to the constable in the morning. There is a tradition, not authenticated, that he spent the night in a small room at the top of Harlington House, the home of Francis Wingate, before whom he appeared on the following morning, November 13th. Judge and accused had both been born in the same year, 1628, and were both young men, aged thirty-two. The examination, which took place in the paneled room known as the "parlour," was charged throughout with irony. This was Francis Wingate's first case in his new dignity as Justice, as well as the first case in the county against the new restriction as to conventicles. It was a test for the Justice, for the law, as well as for Bunyan. Margins were narrow, and not once but several times Bunyan was on the very fringe of going free.

Had the answer to Justice Wingate's first question been Yes, as was expected, everything would have been simple, but when he asked whether the members of the congregation were armed, and the constable reported only that he had found a few people come together to hear preaching, the Justice did not know what to say. He had been summoned home to this examination, and he must make his new office important. Besides, something about this culprit annoyed him. When asked why he did not follow his proper calling and let preaching alone, Bunyan answered somewhat wordily that he could do both "without confusion." This answer sounded impertinent, and put the Justice into such "a chafe" that he replied he would "break the neck" of these meetings. Another answer from Bunyan might have meant dismissal of the charge, but not now.

At this point Bunyan's sureties were brought in, and warned that if they did not keep him from preaching again, the bonds would be forfeit. Recklessly Bunyan spoke out of turn and said he would break them himself, that he would not leave off preaching. He was doing "a work that had no hurt in it, but was rather worthy of commendation than blame." As he might have known, the next step was the making of a mittimus, followed by an order to lie in jail until the next quarter sessions when he would stand trial.

While the mittimus was being prepared, he had two other conversations, intended to give him further chance to comply with the law and go free. The first was with Dr. Lindale, vicar of Harlington, "an old enemy of the truth," in Bunyan's view. Their brief parley was in the current controversial, even contentious, spirit of the time, and shows how far apart those who wore the cloth were from those who did not. Bunyan's tartness, even pertness, exhibited the manners of his class, and at one point had a spice of resentment felt by the poor man for those who were rich. He even used the word *rich*.

"But that Scripture coming into my mind, Answer not a fool according to his folly, I was as sparing of my speech as I could, without prejudice to truth."

Had he spoken in a different tone, he might have put himself in line for lenity.

Just as the constable was leading him from the room, he had still another chance. Lawyer Foster of Bedford entered, and in the presence of Justice Wingate, who had no doubt asked him to come, Foster placed the issue squarely before John Bunyan:

"If you will promise to call the people no more together, you shall have your liberty to go home, for my brother is very loath to send you to prison, if you will but be ruled,"

he said. Bunyan's answer was immediate and final. As he reported it,

"I durst not make any further promise, for my conscience would not suffer me to do it."

Foster tried argument, and he too was furnished with Scripture to support it. You have a calling; follow it, he began. Bunyan replied that he had two callings and would follow both. You are ignorant and not a fit preacher. That might be, but God had chosen the foolish to confound the wise. No one listens to you but ignorant, foolish people. If they are ignorant, the greater need that they be taught. God had called him and he could not leave off preaching.

There was no dealing with such a man, and Lawyer Foster agreed with Justice Wingate that prison was the answer for the culprit before them. The length of these two added interviews and the patience of both questioners suggest the reluctance with which the sentence of imprisonment was given. It might bring protest from a stratum of society that had best not be aroused to resentment at this moment. It might also deter other offenders, if a promise to leave off preaching could be exacted from one of the better known of the mechanick leaders. But it was of no use. "Thus we parted," Bunyan wrote:

"And verily as I was going forth of the doors, I had much ado to forbear saying to them that I carried the peace of God along with me. But I held my peace, and, blessed be the Lord, went away to prison with God's comfort in my poor soul."

From this initial hearing one may chart the whole future course of Bunyan's life, and also see more clearly than elsewhere the transparent simplicity of his mental processes. There had really been no decision to make. Given a single governing motive, everything fell into place. Other demands were disregarded. His imprisonment might be "an awakening to the saints of the country"; therefore, with a family to support, he went willingly to prison. He did "commit the thing to God and was satisfied it was His will and mind I should be there." That settled it, and he had peace in his soul.

One or two centuries earlier he would have been tied to the stake, and when the pyre was lighted he would have washed his hands in the flames and gone to his death with a Scripture verse on his lips. Of such singleness of purpose and unyielding tenacity to conviction are martyrs made in all generations. On November 13th, just before his birthday, Bedford County Gaol received him. In his trespass, his arrest, and his obstinate refusal to conform to law under questioning, his case was no different from that of scores of others soon to follow. His arrest had been legal. His behavior under examination was such as to make imprisonment prior to trial legal also.

Refused bail, in spite of his friends' entreaty, he lay in jail for seven weeks awaiting the quarter sessions. Had it not been for certain public happenings during these weeks, the issue of his trial might have been quite otherwise. Chief among these antecedent excitements was the affair of Thomas Venner. A wine cooper, and onetime freeman of Massachusetts Bay Colony, Venner had been, after his return to England, a prisoner in the Tower for certain desperate words as to murdering His Highness and a threat to blow up the Tower with powder. He had been released in 1659 and had returned to preaching in the Fifth Monarchy strain. On January 7, 1660/61, having first exhorted his congregation in his Coleman Street meetinghouse, he set forth with fifty of his people to overthrow the government and set up the monarchy of King Jesus. His watchword was "The King Jesus and the heads upon the gates."

After a skirmish with trained bands sent to meet him, he and his party retired to Highgate, and thence to Caen Wood. On January 9th they again appeared in the City, marched to Threadneedle Street, and put the king's soldiers to rout. Venner escaped, but was later repelled by the king's guards and captured in Wood Street. Most of his men were killed before surrender came. On January 17th he was tried at the Old Bailey before Chief Justice Foster, and sentenced to death. Two days later he was hanged in front of his meetinghouse in Coleman Street, and his body quartered.[4]

Naturally this sensational affair inflamed the public and put all nonconformists in new jeopardy. Baptists and Quakers alike denounced Venner's claims, and though nothing in their teachings matched his extravagant disloyalty, both suffered seriously because of him. According to a new proclamation of January 10th, not only all conventicles under pretense of religious worship, but assemblies of all sorts were under the ban. Apprentices on holiday, groups met in coffeehouses, guild members at their anniversary dinners—all were alike under suspicion. Watch them.

The Nayler affair of three years before came back into the public memory, and was given application to the suspicions of the moment. The cruelty of Nayler's punishment had owed much to Fifth Monarchy revolts also, although his offense, the blasphemous reënactment of the triumphant entry of Jesus into Jerusalem, had nothing to do with their prophesyings. He was a field preacher of extraordinary power, and the extravagant adulation of his followers had dramatized the danger of allowing such preachers to go free. One of his comrades in the army of the North, James Gough, had said of him,

"I was struck with more terror before the preaching of James Nayler than I was before the Battle of Dunbar, when we had nothing else to expect but to fall a prey to the swords of our enemies." [5]

Such men were better in jail in January, 1660/61. George Fox, also a man who could magnetize his hearers, was shut away. The "preaching tinker" was another of the same sort. His power in the pulpit had more to do with his treatment under arrest than any concern with what he had been saying. He moved his hearers too easily for such unsettled times.

His trial at the January quarter sessions in Bedford came at the peak of the new vigilance the Venner case had brought about. The scene was the Chapel of Herne, an ancient structure of uncertain history, standing close to the Grammar School. It was sometimes called Schoolhouse Chapel. Justice John Kelynge, who had been counsel to the Crown in the trial of the regicides, later to preside at the trial of Sir Harry Vane and later still to be Lord Chief Justice of England, at this time still a country magistrate, was chairman of the five magistrates who sat on the bench at this their first session. He was not a man likely to show mercy to a tinker who had refused to keep silence at a dangerous time. Later he would preside at the trial of Bunyan's Faithful under the name Lord Hate-Good. Sir Henry Chester and Sir William Beecher were both recently knighted and feeling their new dignities. Sir George Blundell of Cardington, an ardent persecutor of nonconformists, and Thomas Snagg of Milbrook were alike hostile. No one of the five was likely to be impressed with Bunyan's sense of dedication.

The charge was read. Since the Act of Conformity still lacked several months of being drawn up, legal accusation of Bunyan must invoke the sixty-eight-year-old act of the 35th of Elizabeth, when under different conditions entirely, private meetings had been de-

clared unlawful. Accordingly, in the language of this law, he was
accused of

"Devilishly and perniciously abstaining from coming to church
to hear divine service, and for being a common upholder of several
unlawful meetings and conventicles to the great disturbance and
distraction of the good subjects of the kingdom, contrary to the
laws of our sovereign lord the King." [6]

The little farmhouse group in Lower Samsell, standing Bibles in
hand, while their preacher prayed without the Book, was dignified
beyond their own humble thought of themselves by this high-
sounding accusation.

"What say you to this?" asked the clerk.

Bunyan confessed to the charge of not coming to church, giving
as his reason that he had not found it "commanded in the word of
God." The ensuing dialogue as to the use of the Book of Common
Prayer was inevitable, in view of its return to the pulpit desk, and
Bunyan's bluntness in saying that he could pray well enough without
it was no help to his case. "Take heed of speaking irreverently of
the Common Prayer Book," Judge Kelynge counseled, "for if you
do so, you bring great damage upon yourself." Bunyan had already
done just that.

His literalness of Scripture interpretation went so far as to require that if it were lawful, the Book of Common Prayer should be
mentioned by name in the Bible. Judge Kelynge took the hint, and
in his next question as to a tinker's fitness for preaching, asked for
scriptural warrant for such authority. Bunyan was ready with I
Peter, 4, 10:

"As every man hath received the gift, even so minister the same
one to another."

As he saw it, no other arguments were pertinent to his case. As for
the safety of the kingdom, nothing in his intent could harm it.
Therefore he was innocent of the charge. Prosecutor and condemned were poles apart. In Bunyan's thought, the kingdoms of

this world are transient. He was on his way to the kingdom of heaven. Even though he had been capable of understanding the turmoil of England in 1661, he would have dismissed present dangers as unimportant in the light of eternity.

Justice Kelynge soon tired of this futile parley, and proceeded to the sentence. Back to prison for three months, and at the next quarter sessions a chance to submit, go to church, leave off preaching; otherwise to be banished the realm, and if returning without license from the king, to stretch by the neck for it. No witnesses to his guilt had been heard. He had made no formal plea of guilty or not guilty. He had merely answered questions and talked back to the bench. He had not been condemned unheard, but by not promising to stop preaching, the indictment stood. The only illegality in the procedure was that his wordiness had been interpreted as amounting to a confession of guilt. Before he appeared again, Kelynge had seen to it that such an equivalent had been written into the law, but such was not true at this date. There had been nothing about the trial to feed spectacular interest, and had it not been for Bunyan's subsequent fame there would have been no reason to recall any of it.

Before he was taken back to prison, he was given one more chance to promise silence. No, said Bunyan,

"If I was out of prison today, I would preach the gospel again tomorrow, by the help of God."

There was only one answer to this announcement. "I was led home to prison again." In his own word he went away "sweetly refreshed."

During the ensuing twelve weeks of his sentence before the April assizes, he continued to hope for another trial, but it did not come. His disposition as to conformity was sounded out by Paul Cobb, the justice of the peace, who on April 3rd found him of the same mind, and so reported back to the court. If the detailed conversation with Cobb, as printed a century later, is indeed by Bunyan's hand, he was thinking clearly enough as to the intent of the law and judging equally clearly of his own innocence in line with that intent. Beyond that point his conscience was his law. The conversation with Cobb was not a legal occasion for a new sentence, and the first one had expired with the end of the three months, yet he was still held in jail, on the basis of this private conversation, without witnesses.

"I did thank him" [Bunyan wrote] "for his civil and meek discoursing with me, and so we parted."

On April 23rd the coronation of Charles II drove all else from the mind of England. Ordinary business could wait. Many prisoners were freed, as part of the coronation celebration, but Bunyan was passed by. He was to blame for this neglect in that not having sued for pardon, he was not in line for consideration. In this action also, his literalness was the reason. He was not guilty; therefore he could not ask for pardon, and on this point he was adamant.

Before the August assizes, however, his friends had persuaded him to submit a petition to be heard and judged in open trial. The bearer of the petition was his young wife, Elizabeth. Her performance of this office is one of the most moving chapters in Bunyan's story, and not of this occasion alone.[7] Young, apparently of his own humble class, she had the courage and the independence to go to London with the petition, to address herself first to Lord Barkwood of the House of Lords, and upon being told that her husband's release was in the hands of the judges of assizes, then to each of them in turn with her plea. Sir Matthew Hale received her kindly, and though offering no encouragement, promised to do what he could for her husband.

The next day she went to Judge Twisden, a passionate man, who being angry at her plea, treated her with discourtesy. "With abashed face and trembling heart," she returned to Sir Matthew Hale, as he sat on the bench at the Swan chamber in Bedford.

"My Lord, I make bold to come once again to your lordship, to know what may be done with my husband."

She had been well instructed by Bunyan's friends, and when she was told that his answer to the questions asked him at his examination had been taken for a legal confession, she replied that he had neither pleaded guilty to the indictment nor confessed guilt. Contradicted, she stood her ground, insisting that for a word of discourse to be taken for a confession was unlawful. In this distinction she was right, but the fact that since the examination, such words as he had spoken had been made lawfully equivalent to confession rendered her protest ineffectual. Justice Hale called for the statute book, and told her it was so recorded. Judge Chester, becoming impatient, repeated,

> "It is recorded, woman, it is recorded. He is convicted, and it is recorded."
> "If it be, it is false,"

she replied, whereupon Judge Chester offered the one hope left for him.

> "What, will your husband leave preaching? If he will do so, send for him."
> "My lord, he dares not leave preaching, as long as he can speak,"

and with this reply, all hope was gone.

> "Why talk any more about such a fellow,"

said Judge Twisden, and except for Sir Matthew Hale, all would have ended at this point. He asked what was his calling. When the reply was given, Elizabeth's outburst,

> "Yes, and because he is a tinker, and a poor man, therefore he is despised and cannot have justice,"

was spoken with a hint of the current resentment of her class. Judge Hale answered her outburst kindly, and explained that since her husband's words had been recorded as a confession, the conviction stood. Her quiet dignity throughout the ordeal became her. Only under Sir Matthew's explicit questioning did she tell of her own private sorrows, the premature birth and death of her child under the strain of her husband's arrest, and the needs of his four other small children, "that cannot help themselves and have nothing to live upon but the charity of good people."

The kindly concern of Sir Matthew is in line with everything history records of his life. In this painful scene his is the only kindness offered the woman before him. Carefully he stated the three courses now open to Bunyan under the provisions of law: to apply to the king, sue out a pardon of the indictment, or apply for a writ of error. Carefully he repeated them, suggesting that to procure a writ of error would be cheapest:

"I am sorry, woman, that I can do thee no good; thou must do one of these three things aforesaid." [8]

She pleaded to let Bunyan speak for himself but was refused. Tearfully she went away, weeping, as she said, not so much because they were so hardhearted against her husband, but "to think what a sad account such poor creatures will have to give at the coming of the Lord." Bunyan had at least one comfort, in her complete sharing of the conviction which motivated his own every action.

If Sir Matthew Hale could have conducted Bunyan's trial, he might have gone free of the indictment on the strength of his obvious innocence of seditious intent, but it would have been a brief freedom. He would have been quickly arrested again. Self-interest, even within the limits of good sense, was impossible to him. He would win on his own terms or not at all, and in 1660–1661, that such victory was impossible was as certain as a decree of fate.

Chapter Six

"The Lord's Free Prisoner"

Aged thirty-two, John Bunyan had become "a prisoner of hope," as he once styled himself, albeit a hope that would be twelve years deferred. Mercifully, in the first interminable days and nights, he did not know what was ahead, but confidently expected release at the next quarter sessions, only three months distant. When that session failed him, he continued to expect it at the next and the next. Hope would be punctuated by these time intervals, as the months slipped into years, but when the doors of Bedford County Gaol first closed upon him in November, 1660, he probably shared, with the hundreds of other prisoners for conscience' sake throughout England, the sense of being an honored initiate into the fellowship of near martyrdom for religion's sake. Nothing he ever said or wrote suggests that he was prideful of his sufferings, as was true for some of his fellow prisoners, but clearly he shared with them the sense of having been counted worthy to endure suffering. Evidence that he became a bigger man because of what imprisonment taught him is written large on many pages of his later history.

After what he called "above eleven years of imprisonment," he prefaced his *A Confession of My Faith, and a Reason of my Practice* [1] with a calm statement of peaceable intent at the time of his arrest, and as his continuing purpose now. He had examined, he said, "in cool blood, a thousand times," and as a "candid Christian," the grounds of that behavior which had put him behind prison bars, and after these eleven years, he believed himself able to judge of his own innocence.

"Let mine enemies themselves be judges," [he wrote] "if anything in these following doctrines, or if aught that any man hath heard me preach, doth or hath, according to the true intent of my words, savoured either of heresy or rebellion."

Had anything in either his writing or preaching justified almost twelve years of imprisonment, with the threat of exile and the gallows still hanging over him? Even if such a threat should become fact, he cannot consent that his soul should be "governed" in any of his "approaches to God, because commanded to the contrary."

"I have determined, the Almighty God being my help and shield, yet to suffer, if frail life might continue so long, even till the moss shall grow on mine eyebrows, rather than thus to violate my faith and principles."

It would have been easier to say this eleven years earlier, before he knew the toll the years would exact from him, but he was still able to say (and mean) it when the hope of release had been dimmed through eleven years of repeated denial.

"This tedious tract of time," as he called it, had brought perspective, until he had been able to write in his *Prison Meditations*,

> "This gaol to us is as a Hill
>   From whence we plainly see
> Beyond this World, and take our fill
>   Of things that lasting be."

Considered as rhymes, these 1665 verses are too easy perhaps, and hardly bear comparison, except for their sentiment, with the justly more famous seventeenth century lines on the "Iron bars" theme, but they express an experienced faith that knows its price. Bunyan's version continues:

> "For tho' men keep my outward Man
>   Within their Locks and Bars,
> Yet by the Faith of Christ I can
>   Mount higher than the Stars.
>
> Their Fetters cannot Spirits tame,
>   Nor tye up God from me;
> My Faith and Hope they cannot lame,
>   Above them I shall be." [2]

To have learned "Heart's Content, that like a Fountain springs," in such a straitened life was to have been teachable indeed. Rare souls among imprisoned ones in all ages have learned it, even in the concentration camps of our own century. They have also acquired a new sense of values which outward limitation may bring to those with only the top of a prison wall for a horizon. John Bunyan made a life not without richness for himself in Bedford County Gaol, and a life that permitted few successful impediments to the pursuance of his main business of living. In fact, prison life fostered achievement toward his main purpose in living, rather than jeopardized it.

In his hours of forced inactivity, his mind had been free, he said, "to study Christ," and his hundreds of printed pages for the prison years testify to the fruits of that study. For what he called recreation, he had John Foxe's *Actes and Monuments,* and to judge from the many references in his own writings to the printed pages of other men, various other books were brought to him by his visiting friends. For daily activity, instead of the charkha of Gandhi, he had materials for tagg'd shoelaces which he made by the many hundred gross, and possibly other small commodities for payment of his prison fees and the purchase of food for his family. He was deft with his hands, as his iron fiddle testifies, in one example, and if materials were available he probably achieved other triumphs in kind. Some prisoners made nets for boiling herbs; others, intellectuals and artisans alike, used their ingenuity and their hands in unaccustomed ways. There is no record that Bedford prisoners were obliged to beat hemp or engage in other forms of forced labor, as was true in some other prisons of the time.

For social exchange John Bunyan preached to his fellow prisoners

and counseled those who came to him from the various Bedfordshire
congregations to which he had formerly preached. It was not an
inactive life entirely, shut away as he was in this limited substitute
for an itinerant's scattered parish, back and forth from the common
day room to the common sleeping room or the courtyard, and no
minute of the twenty-four hours of the day in a square foot of
space that was his own in privacy.

Detailed knowledge of conditions in the Bedford County Gaol
for Bunyan's day are lacking, but there is no reason to think they
were greatly different from what prevailed elsewhere. All English
prisons were sadly overcrowded during these years, men and women
being all but herded together, without privacy or more than a
shadow of tolerable comfort. They slept on straw, usually without
frames to raise it from the floor. For this they paid the jailer five
pounds annually. There was no provision for baths. Water was no
nearer than the courtyard, and fresh air was scarcer than water.
Because of the window tax jailers had to pay, prison windows were
few. Some prisons had fireplaces and jailers granted coals on application, of course for a fee, but a century later Bedford Goal still
had no fireplaces, no infirmary, no baths. Many had died there of
jail fever.

To read John Howard's report of British prisons written more
than a century later is to wonder how Bunyan or any other prisoner
could have survived through twelve years of such physical restraint
and deprivation, particularly under such conditions as to cleanliness
and sanitation. His introductory chapter, "A General view of distress in prisons," is a sad, in fact, a revolting story.[3] One remembers
also Lord Bacon's remark, quoted by Howard,

> "The most pernicious infection next to the plague is the smell of a
> jail, whereof *we have had, in our time, experience once or thrice*,
> when both the judges that sat upon the jail, and members of
> those that attended the business, or were present, sickened and
> died."

Lord Bacon was one who had reason to know. John Howard was
pleading, some hundred and fifty years later, for the elimination of
jail fever and the payment of jailers by a salary instead of by prison-

ers' fees. There was a relation between the two. During his own examination of the English prisons, he wrote that he protected himself by "smelling to vinegar, while I was in those places, and changing my apparel afterwards." He reported his findings to the House of Commons, and had "the honour of their thanks" for the service he had rendered.

Allowance of food was also dependent on the fee paid the jailer. A quarter of a loaf daily was standard, to be supplemented by what a man's family and friends could provide. The tradition of the small jug of soup carried daily to John Bunyan by his blind daughter is not authenticated, but the short distance from the St. Cuthbert Street cottage to the prison would make the tradition plausible. The jug is still shown among the scant relics at the Bunyan Meeting Museum in Bedford.

A prisoner's measure of freedom, as well as the allowance of food and straw, was also at the whim of the jailer, and according to the amount paid him. In the beginning, that is, from the autumn assize of 1661 to the April session of 1662, Bunyan had a larger measure of freedom than he was to have again until near the end of his twelve-year term. He even preached to the "Christians at London" on one occasion, but the jailer, seeing that he would be run out of his place if he allowed this liberty again, recalled the privilege. After that, Bunyan was inside the walls by the month and year. The tradition that he was freed briefly in 1666 would seem to have no foundation in recorded fact, but it is entirely possible that there was an unofficial period of freedom at that time. This was the year of the Great Plague in London, and there are various records of services rendered by nonconforming ministers, not only in preaching to congregations deprived of their pastors but also in numerous services of comfort to the distressed and frightened ones who were unable to flee. In such a rôle Bunyan would be entirely himself.

So far as reliable testimony goes, there is nothing in his prison story to match the meaningless cruelty of certain jailers; for example, as reported by George Fox concerning his own eight imprisonments, totaling some six years. In Domesdale prison whence few came out alive, he spent one winter in a "smoaky tower" where the smoke from all the other rooms "stood as dew upon the walls," and was so thick he could sometimes not see a candle. "Ye winde being high and fierce," the rain came in. At the trial which had put him there, the judge had said, "All ye world cannot convince you," and it was even so. After these months of suffering as a half-starved prisoner, he was still not convinced. Some of his other experiences are too revolting to be described.

At Derby Prison, which he called "a shame to Christianity," he described his jailors as "like to two beare heards." One of them had beaten him with cudgels, "as if he had been beating a packe of wooll." Other prisoners here fared even worse. He tells of a young boy lodged in a hole in the wall, labeled "Little Ease," or better still, "The Oven." It was reached by a ladder within six feet of the hole, and beyond that point the boy climbed a rope. Obliged to descend for his food, which was left at the foot of the ladder, one day he fell to his death when the rope broke.[4]

Thomas Ellwood, a Quaker, was imprisoned at the time of the Venner uprising in the malt house behind Aylesbury Gaol. "Not fit for a doghouse," he said, but stowing him away there was meant as a compliment, as he later learned. The jailer knew that he could trust a "Friend" not to escape, and he needed space within the walls for a non-Friend, who could not be thus trusted. Later Thomas Ellwood was imprisoned in Newgate, which at that time was "very full of Friends." During the day the prisoners had "Liberty" of a first-floor room called the Hall, but at night they were lodged in a circular room having a central pillar from which three tiers of hammocks were swung, and fastened at the other end to the walls. Those sleeping in the two upper tiers had to climb up by standing in the hammocks below. There was no circulation of air. When investigation of these conditions was made after the death of one prisoner in his pallet, the foreman of the investigating jury is reported to have said,

"Lord bless me! What a Sight is here! I did not think there had been so much cruelty in the Hearts of Englishmen, to use Englishmen in this manner."

There was no need to question how the man had died, he added. "We may rather wonder that they are not all dead." He would see the king about it the next day, as he did. On the following day, one of the sheriffs summoned all prisoners to the courtyard, and spoke courteously to them,

"Gentlemen, I understand the Prison is very full, and I am sorry for it." [5]

They were all transferred to Bridewell, being allowed to go without guard, under condition that they get there before nightfall. At Bridewell they were allowed the freedom of a courtyard adjoining the workrooms where they beat hemp, and some of them were allowed to go home at night. This incident suggests that the rigors they had suffered at Newgate, and very probably those reported from other places, except for certain individuals among jailers, were traceable, not to intentional cruelty but to excessive crowding. Civil authorities were unwilling in such troublous times to risk the liberty of even one Quaker or Baptist who refused to keep silence. Too much was also at stake for those in high place, who deplored these rigors, to protest against them and to demand that arrests be made more discriminatingly. Samuel Pepys wrote in his *Diary* on August 7, 1664:

"While we were talking came by several poor creatures carried by constables for being at a conventicle. They go like lambs, without any resistance. I would to God they would either conform, or be more wise, and not be catched!" [6]

He was asking what seldom happened. Also he had seen what might be witnessed almost any day in country towns as well as in London. The meekness under affliction of these victims may be hard to understand for men and women of such spirit and courage, until one reads their reiteration of feeling "honoured" to be allowed to suffer for religion's sake. They meant it. Also, as Joseph Alleine, one of them, wrote, in prison they had liberty to sing hymns, to read the Bible openly, and to listen to sermons. No strangers could interrupt them there. They called it "freedom."

Joseph Alleine had been arrested and imprisoned at Taunton Castle for singing a hymn and instructing his family in his own house, others being present also. He was indicted as the "bell-wether of a naughtie flocke, and a ringleader of evil men." This was on the testimony of two witnesses, who were allegedly themselves threatened with jail if they did not take oath against him. Several of his letters to his flock during this first imprisonment suggest the spirit in which jail sentences were met, and also why jails were so overcrowded during this nervous time. Pastor Alleine's counsel was not only for courage under attack, but for recklessness in defying the law which forbade private meetings. He had apparently heard that some of his members had been timid about offering their houses for these outlawed gatherings.

"Is the communion of saints worth the venturing for? Shut not your doors against godly meetings. . . . What, shut out the word?
"Are you believers, and yet afraid you shall be losers by Christ?
"Away with that unbelief, that prefers the present safety before the future glory. . . .
"I desire and pray for your liberty; but if any of you be forced hither for the testimony of the Gospel, I shall embrace you with both arms." [7]

In Ilchester prison to which he was later committed, his aged father, seven other ministers, and forty private persons were also jailed for the same cause. He kept right on preaching, as one might have expected him to do. In every prison jailed ministers acted as unofficial chaplains, to the comfort of their fellow prisoners, and apparently were not molested in so doing.

John Torner, once a chaplain in the royal army, later the silenced minister of North Cricket, had attempted in his old age to evade the law against conventicles by sitting in the cellar door of Ford Abbey, ostensibly "teaching" his children and grandchildren on a Sunday morning. The windows above him were all open and in each room sat a silent company listening, as he raised his amazing voice beyond the needs of the small group gathered around him or hidden in the shrubbery. Discovered by the officers, he was committed to Ilchester

Prison, where on Sunday morning he would preach through the
bars to a crowd his voice had assembled outside. Shot at by one
whom tradition identifies as the jailer, he turned his head in time
for the bullet to miss him, and kept on preaching. He was imprisoned
for five years and lived to be ninety-four.

The few extracts preserved from Joseph Alleine's letters to his
flock make one wonder why, for its doctrines, such preaching
could have been thought dangerous by the civil authorities or worth
the risk of those who dared to come to listen. No allusion to prison
sufferings, no resentment against those who had caused them, merely
accepted evangelical doctrine: confess Christ and be saved, have a
care for the welfare of others. There is no party spirit, no insubordi-
nation to all things lawful. But in a matter of conscience, stand your
ground.

There was likewise no resentment in Bunyan's spirit.

> "This prison very sweet to me
> Hath been, since I came here," [8]

he wrote after eleven years of confinement. He meant literally just
that. Here dwells good conscience, also peace, and he had both.

> "The answer of a good conscience will carry a man through hell
> to heaven. . . . But if thou be guilty, look to thyself: I am no
> comforter of such,"

he wrote, and meant that literally also.

No quarter-sessions records survive for the period of his imprisonment, except for sixteen lists of prisoners at the bar. Five of these
lists contain Bunyan's name as in jail at the time. Again and again
he tried to get his name into the calendar for the next quarter sessions, in order to state his case openly in a new trial, but each time
he failed, one of "my greatest opposers," as he thought, being the
clerk of the peace, to whom he had appealed and to whom he had
paid the fee. Presumably, the clerk had merely pocketed the fee,
knowing, as John Bunyan should also have known, that such procedure was wrong. At his trial in 1661, he had refused each of the

three methods by which a new hearing could be granted, and since his lengthy explanation offered at the trial instead of a direct plea of guilty or not guilty had been made, by statute, equivalent to a confession, getting his name into the calendar was impossible.

The saving grace of his sad situation during his long imprisonment is purely hypothetical, but with the succession of repressive measures which had quickly followed his 1661 sentence, and his own stoutly announced determination to keep on preaching regardless of statute, it would seem that had any freedom been secured for him, it would have been short-lived indeed. Also, a second offense under the statute he had defied (the 35th of Elizabeth) would have meant exile beyond the seas, and death by hanging if he dared to return. Accordingly, prison for him during these twelve years amounted to a refuge, extending his life to nearly twice its length at the time of his imprisonment. In 1660, when he was arrested, he would still have twenty-eight years to live, thanks to prison, and in 1660 he had as yet done nothing for which posterity remembers him. Bedford County Gaol gave him his chance.

His energy and capacity for being a "ringleader" wherever he was, suggest directions of activity despite his limitations during these years thirty-two to forty-four. One cannot think of him as passive under external conditions or dispirited because of them. Despairs for him concerned invisible chains, not prison locks. His energies would have found channels of friendliness and cheer for his associates, most of whom, like himself, were there for nonconformity. Whether felons were separated from religious prisoners in Bedford Gaol is not recorded, but at this date Dissenters would have been in the majority in any English prison, so that religious exercise and conversation would have been a natural expression of group desire. There would probably have been daily gathering for prayer, singing, or Bible reading, and possibly sermons more often than on Sunday.

One of his prison publications, *The Holy City*, in 1665, was developed, as Bunyan himself says, from a sermon preached one Sunday in "our prison chamber." His prefatory note to the published treatise indicates that he had not known, on that Sunday, that it would be his turn to speak, and had come unprepared, feeling "so empty, spiritless, and barren," that when he was called upon, he thought he "should not have been able to speak among them so much as five words of truth with life and evidence." In his helplessness, he opened his Bible, where his eye "providentially" fell upon Revelation 21, 11, a verse picturing the New Jerusalem as

"Having the glory of God: and her light was like unto a stone most precious, even like a jasper stone, clear as crystal."

He bowed his head and pondered the verse before him, until presently he thought he perceived "something of that jasper" in whose light the Holy City would descend. He began to speak, and as he spoke, the subject opened up until his thought grew to a "full basketful," which he distributed to the satisfaction of all.[9] One cannot read this prefatory note without summoning the picture. It would be a dimly lighted interior room, too small for the huddled company that sat silent on the floor, listening to the man who faced them, a book in his hand, his voice echoing down the dark corridor, where a guard doubtless stood on duty, the only one unmoved by the speaker's words.

How much of the printed treatise, which he said was first written, then rewritten and then written again, was part of the prison sermon on that Sunday morning, there is no knowing, for the treatise as printed is of book length, but whatever the specific details included, the theme is significant as suggesting a realm of thought in which Bunyan was sufficiently at home to be able to speak extemporaneously on it. It was not the present, or whatever in the past had brought them together in this sad place, that inspired his thought to a "full basketful" that morning. It was not the frustrations of their lives as men and women or as Christians. He had nothing to say as to the amelioration of their sufferings in the life to come. The Holy City of this sermon was not the city to which Christian set out from the City of Destruction. Bunyan is using the apocalyptic vision of John to symbolize the Church of the Christian fellowship returned from captivity and restored to her true dignity. Gone will be the divisions, the bickerings. Once again Christ's followers will be one in doctrine and in Christian grace. This restoration was the intense concern of Bunyan and his hearers, and it is the preëminence of their hope in something beyond their own condition that gives the scene and Bunyan's words a significance that is arresting.

"Blessed is he whose lot it will be to see this holy city descending and lighting upon the place that shall be prepared for her situation and rest! Then will be a golden world. . . . It will then be always summer, always sunshine, always pleasant, green, fruitful, and beautiful to the sons of God.

"Never was fair weather after foul, nor warm weather after cold, nor a sweet and beautiful spring after a heavy, and nipping, and terrible winter, so comfortable, sweet, desirable, and welcome to the poor birds and beasts of the field, as this day will be to the church of God." [10]

All religions of the world in all ages have held out hope for the fulfillment of life in some far future, and in ways as various as the imaginations of men. On that Sunday in Bedford Gaol Bunyan and his companions found some sparkle of new hope in this step-by-step, verse-by-verse elucidation of what his mind saw in the jasper of John's vision. He expressed it literally, but what he saw in this verse was worthy of poetry. The overtones of this prison scene, as this sermon suggests them, are memorable.

It is apparent throughout the long printed treatise developed from this extemporaneous sermon that Bunyan was closely familiar with current millenarian thought. He uses many of the phrases which others were using. There is knowledge, as well as individual interpretation, back of his verse-by-verse commentary on the symbolism of John. Yet he is concerned not at all to predict an earthly rule of Christ, with the consequent ending of the rule of the Beast and the overthrow of Antichrist. In so far as this is Fifth Monarchy language at all, he is using it for a different purpose. As the Holy City descends,

"She meddleth not with any man's matters but her own; . . . the governors of this world need not at all to fear a disturbance from her, or a diminishing of aught they have; . . . She is not for meddling with any thing that is theirs, from a thread, even to a shoelace. Her glory is spiritual and heavenly, and she is satisfied with what is her own." [11]

In expressing what he repeatedly declares to be spiritual, not temporal, Bunyan's own insistence upon the first, secondly, and so on down to the twelfthly of it, puts clogs on his own flow of thought. He could never resist the impulse to explain, not realizing that some things are clear only when one does not try to explain them. His troublement over the blotting out of the invisible names in the Book of Life might have been spared him.

Hints of probable release came unexpectedly, and immediately after one of the darkest periods for the nonconformist cause. Between the spring of 1670 and that of 1672, Bedfordshire Dissenters, as all others, were hunted down systematically by spies organized and directed by local magistrates, who knew both the secret places of meeting and those who attended these conventicles. Heavy fines had been collected, the loyalty of nonconformists had been severely tested, and in some cases whole congregations had abandoned the attempt to meet. Then in 1671 had come the first hints that better times were ahead. Parliament was suddenly prorogued. The king, temporarily left free of interference, and for reasons of his own, was minded to relax the severity which the Act of Uniformity had imposed, and though his motives were under suspicion by Protestants, temporarily, the Dissenters among them profited by this relaxation.

In anticipation of the royal proclamation, during the later months of 1671, Bunyan was allowed to leave the prison occasionally, and the Bedford church began to think of him as the most likely candidate for pastor. After years given to Bible study, to the writing of religious treatises, to acting as unofficial chaplain in the prison, and also in numerous services as scribe for the church of Bedford, he was now more in line for a settled pastorate than for resumption of the itinerant's calling.

Natural choice though he was, however, the brethren of the Bedford church took nothing for granted. A matter of such importance would call for much counsel, much deliberation, and more prayer.

Therefore, they proceeded to "seeke God about the choice of Brother Bunyan to the office of an Elder that their way in that respect may be cleared up to them." Finally, after various meetings for this purpose, the principal brethren met at Brother Fenne's. Other meetings of the associated congregations were also held, and on January 21, 1672, "At a full Assembly of the church" at Bedford,

"After much seeking God by prayer, and sober conference formerly had, the Congregation did at this meeting with joynt consent (signified by solemne lifting up of their hands) call forth and appoint our brother John Bunyan to the pastorall office or eldership." [12]

Bunyan was present at this meeting, and formally accepted the appointment by "receiving of the Elders the right hand of fellowship" and giving himself up to "serve Christ and his church in that charge." Legally he was still a prisoner, but he had already taken steps for his release to be made official.

Release might have been delayed much longer, or not have come at all, except for the kindly offices of the Quakers, against whose doctrines he had inveighed so bitterly years before and would do so again. The Quaker concern for the freedom of religion beyond their own borders is a pleasant story of human friendliness, born of a long-continued common experience of hardship. As George Whitehead wrote it down in his *Christian Progress*, he tells of William Carter's request that certain Dissenters besides Quakers might have their names in the same *Instrument* and be discharged with them. "He earnestly requested my Advice, or Assistance, which I was very willing to give in Compassion to them," Whitehead wrote, "and accordingly I advised them to Petition the King (with the names of the Prisoners in it) for his Warrant, to have them inserted in the same Patent with the Quakers." This was done. The names were inserted, Bunyan's among them. The king signed one copy of the Instrument; it was engrossed in the Patent Office, and passed under the Great Seal of England. Eleven copies were then made on vellum of the four hundred names included, each name written eleven times, so that the parcel was "swelled to that Bigness." Messengers were then sent, George Whitehead and William Carter among them, riding on horseback to all the prisons of England and Wales where Friends were confined. The jailers released those whose names were included. The king's pardon was of May 17, 1672. Bunyan's name in the original Patent, but not in the list, is written in Latin, *Johanni Bunnian.*

There is one sentence in George Whitehead's account of this procedure which should be remembered. It is,

"Our being of different Judgments, and Societies, did not abate my Compassion, or Charity, even toward those who have been my Opposers." [13]

Bunyan was one of that number. He was one of six released in Bedford.

It remained to secure a license to preach, and Bunyan had already taken action toward this end also. His application, as preserved in the Public Record Office, is in his handwriting and includes the request for twenty-five other preachers as for himself, all under the heading *Congregational.* His is the sixth name on the page. Beside each name is the name of the place for which the license is requested.[14] For Bunyan it is for Josias Ruffhead's "house in his orchard in Bedford." The license was granted May 9, 1672, and is signed "By his Majesty's Command, ARLINGTON."

Thus equipped, with a king's pardon, an appointment to the pastorate of the church of Bedford, and a royal license to preach in a place prepared for him, John Bunyan walked out of Bedford Gaol a free man. Prison doors would close on him again, ere three years had passed, but in 1672 one lived a day at a time, and as he walked the short way to his St. Cuthbert Street cottage, he might well have felt that he was born again in that hour. One may be sure he would have found a Scripture verse to match such a return to life.

The prison years had been fruitful in more ways than in his growth in grace, which would have been his own measuring rod, possibly the only one. He had sent manuscripts to the printing house more than a dozen times, and more were in preparation or in his thought. It is highly probable that among the small possessions he was allowed to carry home with him from the prison, there was a parcel of manuscript some day to be entitled *The Pilgrim's Progress,* and that in it Christian's story had been set down as far as his meeting with the shepherds of the Delectable Mountains. The fourth shepherd had just bidden him and his companion Hopeful "Godspeed," when Bunyan wrote, "So I awoke from my dream." Whether his awakening was the release which had opened the prison door for him we shall never know, but the conjecture bears pondering.

As for the tiny volume *Grace Abounding,* it had been a fact since 1666, and was already in its third edition. One may be sure that every member of his church had read it and that it was probably among the recommendations for his election as pastor. The year 1672 would have been too late. The decade of the sixties had called forth many such recitals from men of Bunyan's age and previous experience. Other impulses were back of the expression demanded in the 1670's. Bunyan had told the story of his conversion when both he and his reading audience had been ready to receive it. To understand both the story and its writer, it is best to consider it in its own time and place, and also as a book written in the gloom of a prison chamber.

Chapter Seven

"The Head of Goliath in My Hand"

One thinks of a remark of Prime Minister Nehru, whose prison years somewhat exceed John Bunyan's in number. When he was asked, aged sixty-six, what were the landmarks of his life, he replied that he would have to go back to prison and stay for a long term in order to think back. In prison, he said, there is no present, only the past, and there the past comes back in "a deep and continuous way," hardly possible in active life.[1] As a mature man, John Bunyan would have understood what he meant, and though he would not have been likely to make the observation, his two prison books are evidence of its truth for him also. Had he written the first of these, *Grace Abounding to the Chief of Sinners*, some eighteen or nineteen years sooner, while he was still in the midst of the tortures and ecstasies which are its content, the result would have been a quite different book. Chiefly, the experience would have lacked horizons in the telling.

Instead, when he sat down in his prison chamber to write it, aged thirty-seven, clamors above, beneath, and around him, and some five years of monotonous days and nights blotting out what had come before, he recollected the great battle of his life with detachment, if not tranquillity. He was able now to see it as a whole and in the perspective of a mature assurance that it had ended in victory. On every page it is a young man's battle, but the teller is not so young now, and he sees significances in the struggle which go beyond its meaning for himself. The experience is still his own, but as he recalls both the struggle and the victory, it might also be Everyman's.

He was not writing for posterity, but for his own friends and fellow members of the Bedford church. Some of them had heard him tell his conversion story for the first time, when, perhaps falteringly, he was applying for membership among them. Since that time they had heard him preach, perhaps many times, and probably some among them were already cherishing the hope that someday he might be their pastor. During the long, bleak period of the Conventicle Act, when public services had been forbidden, some of the members had suffered hardship for their secret meetings, some had fallen away. Bunyan had had news of this from those who visited him in the prison. He was writing to hearten those who had stood fast, and possibly to reclaim some who had grown fearsome. The Church Book is silent for these years, but when the record is resumed two years later, it is apparent that some had not dared to risk the danger. It is with this small band of fellow members, his friends and neighbors for some thirteen years now, that he chose to share this "unfolding of my secret things." By so doing he paid this little group a rare tribute.

"It is something of a relation of the work of God upon my own soul," he wrote, "even from the very first till now." [2] That is precisely what it is, an intimate account, written to those whose relation to him is suggested by the pastoral salute, "Children, grace be with you, Amen," of his preface. It is not to be wondered at that he did not fill out his own earlier story in more detail, as he might have done, had he been writing for strangers.

The impulse to tell the conversion story had been born with the experience, particularly at moments of victory. As he wrote for one such moment,

"I was now so taken with the love and mercy of God, that I remember I could not tell how to contain till I got home; I thought

I could have spoken of His love, and told of His mercy to me, even to the very crows that sat upon the ploughed land before me, had they been capable to have understood me." [3]

This lyric note is what we miss by not having had the story told two decades earlier, but for the story's sake, it is better so. When he "could scarcely feel the ground I trod on," was not the time to try to put such an experience into words, even if one be a poet, as Bunyan was not. In 1666, when the pen he had wished for was in his hand, he was a preacher, writing in the hope that other "sinners" might be "saved" by his recital. The preacher's purpose does not spoil the high drama of the battle, but unconsciously it shapes it at times. Also it shows itself too plainly for art sometimes, although art was none of Bunyan's purpose. Unconsciously there is art, however, as there is in Newman's quite different *Apologia*.

"I will draw out, as far as may be," Newman wrote, "the history of my mind,"

and that is what Bunyan is doing, as he recalls his own panorama of struggle, punctuated so sparingly with gleams of hope and brief release from tension. Even after some twelve or fifteen years, he remembered the acuteness of his distress and the alternating relief of the brief transports of joy, as though days, not years, had passed. His anguish of spirit was as definite as his childhood nightmares and the clutch of the devil at his coat.

Tension in the telling is increased somewhat by the first-person narration, but not by any heightening of style or language:

"I may not play in my relating . . . but be plain and simple, and lay down the thing as it was,"

he wrote in his Preface, with the result that in the story itself is the power of it. Tension is also increased by the fact that his memory was emotional, even physical. He felt the experience, he saw it, he heard it, as Ezekiel heard the voice and the great rushing noise of the wings of the living creatures and the wheels over against them.

That which was abstract had size and shape and weight and color. States of mind could be apprehended directly by sight and hearing and touch. Texts "bolted" into his mind, "spangled" in his eyes, voices spoke over his shoulder, hands clapped him on the back; in fighting temptation with his mind, his body responded. He pushed and thrust with his hands and elbows. He strove mentally until he was out of breath with striving. In a tug with Satan over a word of Scripture,

"I pulled and he pulled, but God be praised, I got the better of him."

For the literary medium he would choose for his greater book, this faculty would serve him well. He could use the ability to see the tempter "leer and steal away," and "the God of grace follow with a pardon in his hand"; to hear tumultuous thoughts roaring and bellowing like "masterless hell hounds"; to feel a sudden rushing wind "as if an angel had come upon me," commanding "a great calm in my soul." [4]

His story was not unique. In the 1650's and 1660's conversion accounts poured out from London presses by the score. No other kind of religious book was so likely to bring immediate demand for a second printing. Preacher and layman alike wrote them, and everybody read them. Naturally the more extravagant, the greater the general interest, but all were eagerly read. For a preacher to write of a dramatic conversion after a wicked life not only meant added interest, but amounted to a credential, increasing his prestige in the pulpit. To have been a sinner was not enough; therefore to be "the chief of sinners" was a coveted distinction, claimed among others by Oliver Cromwell. Bunyan's "Jerusalem Sinner" was superlative in sin. To compare the *Grace Abounding* with any one of the more popular conversion accounts of the decade is to understand at once why it did not attain an equally current popularity, and also why it is still printed almost three centuries further on. Except for *The Holy War*, it is the only one of Bunyan's sixty books which still shares that distinction with *The Pilgrim's Progress*. Its individual cast, however, is increased rather than lessened, when it is put beside those whose popularity went well past it in the 1650's and '60's.

Quaker itinerants were prolific in this sort of tale. Among such accounts, that of Vavasor Powell, a Welsh itinerant, with Baptist and also Fifth Monarchy leanings, as well as Quaker loyalties, very nearly resembles Bunyan's story in its main outline.[5] Until he was twenty, he was, as he said, very "active and forward in the pursuit of the pleasures and vanities of this wicked world." Like Bunyan, he all but boasted that he had been "a Captain or Leader in all Evil" except drunkenness. He had read romances, profaned the Sabbath Day by sports, prayed without the Book and not known the Scriptures. Then came a sermon by a godly minister, and later Richard Sibbes' *The Bruised Reede* and an earnest talk with a "sober mortified Christian," but not until God "visited him with the toothache" was he really aroused. If the toothache, he thought, can be so bad for a matter of days, what will hell be? This same "How much more" argument seemed ultimate logic to many a sinner in these conversion stories. When the pain had almost deprived him of his senses, he came on one of William Perkins' books, which further enlightened him. More sermons followed, more books, diligent Bible reading, discipline while eating and drinking which permitted only twelve bites to a meal and that of only the coarsest food, prayer half the night with his bare knees on the stone floor, until presently he reached a state calm enough to enable him to preach. Even then, like John Bunyan, he lived with doubt, and felt, as he expressed it, that there was a wall between God and his soul. Remembered as a powerful preacher, he suffered prison for eleven years, and died at fifty-three.

Various of Bunyan's experiences can also be matched against those of George Whitehead, whose story is that of a sane, thoughtful, well-bred man, not given to extravagance in any dimension, and also one of the most powerful of the Quaker itinerants. After he had been in prison for a year, he wrote under the title *Jacob Found in a Desert Land*. He was dead shortly thereafter. From one story to another during these turbulent years, sensitive young men were suffering the same tortures, as they made the same all but desperate search for assurance that all was well with their souls, and when they had attained a measure of peace, the same urge to proclaim both the sufferings and the release, that others might have the same inner testimony of what they called salvation. Even for Puritans, these men were hard on themselves, and in the same breath, they were prideful of the depths from which they had risen. The deeper the pit, the more blessed the grace, runs like a theme through these gloomy recitals. Bunyan himself observed, "The best saints are most sensible of their sins, and most apt to make mountains of their own mole-hills." [6]

Richard Hubberthorne, another Quaker, admitted that he had yielded obedience to his own will and been "a man pleaser" until awakened by the "light of God." In his own word, his flesh had wasted off his bones and his bones had smote against one another. Like George Fox,

"In my trouble I cryed in the evening would God it were morning, and in the morning would God it were evening." [7]

In this state God called him from the vineyard he was tending, as he had called the husbandman Elisha and the herdsman Amos. For obeying the call which had placed him, in his own thought, with the prophets, he was now in West Chester Prison, where he wrote his story. Most of these conversion accounts, like Bunyan's, are prison books.

Nearly every call was matched pridefully with its biblical parallel: Saul blinded by the great light, Ezekiel smitten to the ground by a mighty blow, Moses and the burning bush. Angels with flaming swords appeared to these young men on the shop-board, pillars of cloud came in at the window, as the voice of God spoke to recalcitrant sinners. It was not quite enough for some of them to match the biblical drama; they must needs exceed it at some point, for the brighter the light and the louder the sound of the mighty rushing wind, the more authentic the call. In their preoccupation with their inner selves, these men were true sons of their seventeenth century day. Hamlet might well have been their exemplar, although most of them had never heard of him, nor would they have recognized the slightest kinship with him and his imponderable problem, had they seen him on the boards. It was an age of introspection for thoughtful men, whether in religion, politics, art. To keep a diary was standard practice, not only for telling the day's events, but for recording one's dawn-to-dusk emotions, shortcomings, perhaps sins. For those of religious leanings, the daily entry amounted to a confessional, and doubtless afforded some passing relief, even comfort.

Some of the more sensational of the conversion stories had been news items before they were in print as autobiography. There was, for example, William Franklin, a ropemaker of Stepney, who announced himself as the son of God, and claimed to have been crucified two and a half years before.[8] It was he who had "seduced" Mary Gadbury, who followed him and in her turn "seduced" others. She called herself "the spouse of Christ," had "revelations," and was visited by "multitudes of people from divers places." The fact that she was illiterate was interpreted as a recommendation, God having chosen the foolish things of the world to confound the wise, a verse much overquoted. There was also Anna Trapnel, daughter of a shipwright, who announced that she had received "the Seal of the Spirit." In her trances she uttered or sang words too low to be heard, and spoke prayers in rhyme which were written down as she spoke them. She was heard in Whitehall for eight days, and the account of her raptures when "earth was gone and heaven came," widely published. Throngs came to catch a glimpse or hear a syllable. Excerpts of her verse, as taken down at the time, were later printed under the title *The Cry of a Stone*.[9] Similarly, what Sarah Wight said in her trances attracted the attention of ministers, physicians, ladies of quality, and throngs of those seeking either light for themselves or one more novelty in the name of religion. Despairing souls were entreated to take comfort through her experience.[10] No wonder the restless extravagance went on, fomenting the hostility of those who were not impressed by it.

As might have been expected, interest passed, as extravagance overreached itself in such examples as that of Nicholas Smith, a shoemaker, whose "wonderful Prophecies," under strict scrutiny, were judged a delusion; of William Claxton, of Lancastershire, who on his title page called himself "the only true converted messenger of Christ Jesus, Creator of Heaven and Earth." His book is a chaos of extravagance, its only importance being to illustrate the extremes to which those lacking anchor could be blown in a time of religious confusion.[11]

Except for the Quakers, most of these extremists belonged to no sect, but tried them all in succession and usually rejected them all, striking out for themselves in the end. Some, particularly the Ranters, were prosecuted for blasphemy, some were imprisoned, and died in prison. Most of the authors of the fervid confessions dropped out of sight after their books were printed. Their heyday had been brief, but while it had lasted it gave a bad name to those who had a story of religious exaltation to tell. Angry outbursts against all such enthusiasts were frequent, but unless their excesses went beyond decency no law could touch them.

It is easy enough to understand how excessive emotionalism of the sort these books display could get an equally emotional hearing in the market place or at Paul's Cross. Strange behaviors, deviations from the normal, get a hearing in any age. It is harder to see why a book like Richard Alleine's *Vindiciae Pietatis, A Soliloquie*, which has slight relation to anything tangible, could have been refused a license as dangerous.[12] The printer, seeing its sales value, printed it without a license. It was rapidly bought, and "did much to mend this bad world." Aroused by its popularity, Roger Norton, the king's printer, seized the unsold portion and sent it to the royal kitchen to be burned. On second thought, reflecting that it was "holy and saleable," he corrupted the cook, bought back the unburned sheets, bound them and sold them in his own shop. His disloyalty being discovered, he begged pardon on his knees before the Council. The remaining copies were ordered to be "rubbed over with an inky brush," and sent back to the kitchen fire, but even that was not all. The book was illegally reissued, and went on being a best seller. A story persisted that a Yorkshire man who stole a copy from a bookstall for the binding read the text, was converted, and brought the book back to the owner he had robbed.

To understand why these twenty-one pages could be considered dangerous enough to fit these details is to understand something that in John Bunyan's day called for no explanation. For pages Alleine's words gush forth in the manner of this sample.

"O happy Soul, how rich art thou! What a booty I have gotten! It is all mine own. I have the promises of this life, and of that which is to come. Oh what can I wish more! How full a Charter is here. . . . Rejoice ye Heavens, strike up ye Celestial Quires, Help Heaven and Earth, Sing unto the Lord. . . . Oh my soul, if thou couldest wear out thy fingers upon the Harp, and wear thy tongue to the roots, thou couldest never sufficiently praise thy Redeemer." [13]

What harm in this? Indeed, what profit in it? From first to last, there is no hold on reality, no help in daily living. It is an emotional outflow focused on an ecstatic state of bliss not here but hereafter. "To mend this bad world" by such means is to mend it rather easily. By contrast, in Bunyan's *Grace Abounding* one meets a living, suffering human being, not a mere gush of words.

Partly for this reason, his book was not greatly popular in its own day. After he became known as the author of *Pilgrim's Progress*, it became somewhat better known. Three editions had been published before his release from prison in 1672, and before 1698 there had been seven. He himself corrected and enlarged the edition of 1680. The fact that there were no trances, no contortions, no forty-day fastings, no prophecies in rhyme, no revelations as to current personages in high place, or to events to come, puts it in a different category from the greater number of the itinerant accounts. There is not a news item worthy a broadside issue in the whole book. Even today, a few items such as the boyhood nightmares, the small-boy profanity, the tipcat game, the bell-ringing, are almost the total of remembered detail for his admirers who have done him the honor of reading one more of his books, and these are pale items indeed in comparison with the common stock of the 1650's and 1660's.

For the student of his life story, however, the importance of this book is major. In it he sat for his portrait as in nothing else he was ever to write, just as Pepys in his *Diary*, Rousseau in his *Confessions*, Montaigne in his *Essays*. In discovering themselves to themselves these men laid bare their minds and made their innermost secrets public property. *Anatomy* was a word of the time in Bunyan's day, and in its specialized seventeenth century sense it is a word not amiss for this book, which embraces the whole circumference of

Bunyan's soul in its youthful confusion and desperation of search. It also embraces more, for in his ruthless self-examination and insistence on completeness of self-knowledge, whatever the cost, and his acceptance of what he finds without apology, Bunyan is in truth wrestling with the problem of the individual man's place in the vastness of the universe.

Such an "exact diary" written with such scrupulous honesty is, in Thomas Fuller's luminous word, "a window into the heart of him that maketh it." The *Grace Abounding* is precisely that for John Bunyan. The picture given back is not that of a saint. Far from it. Nor is it that of a man who touched the highest heights or looked into the profoundest depths of religious experience, as some others who have tried to make their glimpse articulate. One thinks again and often of St. Augustine, of St. John of the Cross, of Jacob Boehme, of St. Teresa of Avila, of Richard Rolle of Hampole, perhaps of William Blake. By comparison with these who for want of a better term we call mystics, Bunyan was limited by the utter literalness of his concept of what he called salvation and also by his own capacities. Perforce he set limits, made equations, fitted his experience to a system, and unconsciously stayed within the pattern. Nothing in his pages touches the state of grace as St. Augustine expressed it in the scene with Monica at the window, or of certain moments in George Fox's story:

> "Now was I come up in Spirit through the flaming sword into the paradise of God. . . . Great things did the Lord lead me into, and wonderful depths were opened unto me, beyond what can by words be declared; . . . I came to know the hidden unity in the Eternal Being." [14]

One thinks also of the implications of T. S. Eliot's phrase,

> "But to apprehend
> The point of intersection of the timeless
> With time, is an occupation for the saint." [15]

This was not Bunyan's world. He had taken a narrow path into self-knowledge, and had gone unsparingly to the very end. Only a man capable of ruthless sincerity could have put himself through such an ordeal of honesty with himself. Like St. Augustine he demanded to be as certain of things unseen as he was that three and seven make ten, and he would not deceive himself by a hairsbreadth until he had the inner evidence it was even so. He differed from Augustine and other great saints in the kind of evidence he demanded. The difference goes deeper than language, but he was one with them in the intensity of his desiring, and the willingness to give all he had in exchange for what he sought.

His *Grace Abounding* is still raising perennial questions, as it is subjected to modern psychological analysis. Can a personal experience be taken at its face value after lying in a man's memory nearly twenty years, particularly a man who had used it countless times to dramatize his own preachments? Does dramatic exaggeration suitable to evangelical sermons unconsciously write itself into the story? Is an experience invalidated by being shaped to theological niceties and made to illustrate scriptural texts? [16] The answer to all such questions is a qualified Yes. Recalled in the perspective of maturity, particularly a maturity hastened and deepened by the hardships Bunyan knew, and with prison as his foreground, the experience might understandably have taken on darker colors. Particularly his story might have become exaggerated in the impression it gives of unrelieved distress, as though the five or six years of struggle were lived on the level of its climaxes of tension. If so, life would have been unendurable to human flesh and blood. The mature narrative is also given an orderliness that would not have been possible in so passionate a struggle. That the orderliness would be shaped by the doctrines he was preaching was inevitable, but there is no reason the experience itself should be less accurate because he believed the doctrine. The terms "conviction," "repentance," "divine grace" are mere labels which belong to human experience in the first century or earlier, as well as after Calvin had fitted them into his own symmetrical structure of belief. Bunyan's language is that of the seventeenth century preacher, but the experience he recounts is that of every man who by any system of theology achieves peace of conscience through humility and faith.

Chapter Eight

Pastor of Bunyan Meeting

The first Sunday of the life that had now been given back to him by his release in 1672 was memorable to more residents of Bedford than John Bunyan and his family. As the members of the church to which he had been appointed pastor, and many of their friends, made their way to Josias Ruffhead's barn that Sunday morning, they were anticipating a privilege long withheld. Twelve years before, the hospitality of St. John's Church, where they had met in Pastor Gifford's days, had been withdrawn, and since that time they had had neither a regular place of meeting nor regular preaching. The members who dared to take the risk had met in one another's houses, under the direction of one of their number, to read the Bible together and to counsel one another. This morning they walked openly and without fear to their duly licensed place of meeting, a barn, standing in an orchard in what is now Mill Street.

After the appointment of Bunyan as their pastor, Josias Ruffhead, a shoemaker, and one of the members, had purchased the barn and the orchard in which it stood from Justice Crompton of Elstow. Under date of August 20, 1672, this property had been legally conveyed by Indenture for the sum of £50 to "John Bunyan, of the Towne of Bedford, Brasier; John Fenn, Samuel Fenn, of the said Towne, Haberdashers; Thomas Crocker of Kimbolton in the County of Huntingdon, Linen Draper; Thomas Cooper of the Towne of

Bedford, Last Maker; and Samuel Hensman of the same Towne, Draper." These men were leading members of the congregation. John Fenne had been newly appointed a deacon. To have a pastor, a place of meeting, and to be able to walk to it, even under the eye of the constable, was something more than a threefold blessing.

All that we have of detail as to that first Sunday service is the word of an anonymous friend, who was probably not present. His statement that the meeting place had been newly built by subscription of the church members is an error, and the report that it was "so thronged that many were constrained to stay without," could easily be imagined without his word for it.[1] For such occasions one would wish a word from John Bunyan himself or of someone who was an eyewitness. With Bunyan's feeling for texts in their literal applicability, one may be sure he would have chosen one not likely to be forgotten by anyone present. This day marked a new era in the group life of this small flock. They would meet in this barn, referred to as Meeting Barn, for the next thirty-five years, when a new building, later referred to as the Old Meeting House, would be built on the same site. Today, as one walks through the impressive bronze doors,[2] depicting scenes from *Pilgrim's Progress*, it is pleasant to know that underneath the present structure also is a portion of the "small parcel" of orchard once bought by Josias Ruffhead.

Detailed knowledge of Bunyan's sixteen-year pastorate to follow, interrupted as it would be by the second imprisonment three years later, is limited to the few entries in the Church Book, some of them in Bunyan's handwriting. These entries tell very little, and as is true for all such records, they report too often that which is out of line with the purpose of the fellowship. Disciplinary action against those who have failed to "walk orderly" takes up a large share of the space in seventeenth century church records on both sides of the Atlantic. Cases against members guilty of breaking the Sabbath, not paying their debts, neglecting preaching, slandering each other, brawling with their neighbors, using unseemly language, countenancing card playing, guilty of immodest company keeping—the list is long, and individual only occasionally as in one later item against one brother for "abuseing his wife and beateing hir often for light matters."[3]

"Holy walking" was achieved only after many missteps. Any church book in any communion, in which discipline lay in the hands of the membership, would show entries in all these categories, and to assume (as some have done) that Bunyan was more diligent in reproof or more severe in censure than other dissenting pastors is to misread the record. A member's conduct was under constant scrutiny by his fellow members, as well as by the pastor, and the vote of the whole congregation was necessary to give admonition, exact confession, impose penalty, or to excommunicate those who failed to "walk orderly" after censure. The congregational way of government prevailed in Bunyan's church, as in most Baptist churches at this date.

The Church Book also provides entries throwing light on the admitting of members. To study these for the entire period of Bunyan's pastorate is to see him continuing the liberal policy of John Gifford, who had gathered the original twelve members into a church, and welcomed them to the "communion of saints with saints" without rigid adherence to the usual Baptist requirement of "believers' baptism" by immersion. Such administration was in line with Bunyan's own clear-cut and lifelong principle that an inner experience rather than adherence to an outward form should be the basis for church membership, a liberality in which most other Baptist churches of his own time did not follow him. According to seventeenth century terminology, the Church of Bunyan Meeting belonged to the Open Communion branch of the Particular Baptists. During his lifetime the pulpits of the Strict Communion branch were shut to him, and he was the target of much harsh criticism from other Baptist preachers because of his liberal view. He did not oppose adult baptism, and as an applicant for membership, he may have been rebaptized himself, but as pastor he welcomed to the church fellowship those who had been baptized as infants and did not wish to repeat the rite.

For the Bedford church to have taken this position originally, when John Gifford united the original twelve into a church body, was natural enough. As Church of England communicants, they had all been baptized in infancy, and presumably so had John Gifford, who, so far as we know, had no special Baptist leanings. In his final letter to the members, written shortly before his death, he had particularly enjoined them not to let themselves be divided over the matter of baptism. "I charge every one of you, . . . that none of you be found guilty of this great evil." [4] That was in 1655. In 1653, when Bunyan became a member, his thought was strongly on his own inner experience, and in the light of his own later pronouncements, one may wonder whether the outer rite was important to him at that time. At any rate he was silent about it. He had come to the Bedford church, not because of sectarian sympathy, but because of the helpfulness of John Gifford and the four women members to whom he felt so deeply indebted. He accepted the membership basis as he found it, and throughout his pastorate held to the liberal view of John Gifford.

In his *A Confession of my Faith*, written immediately before his release from prison, and in his answers to the criticism it provoked, he made his position clear enough. In brief:

"I own Water-Baptism to be God's Ordinance, but I make no Idol of it.

"I will not let Water-Baptism be the rule, the door, the bolt, the bar, the wall of division between the righteous and the unrighteous.

"I am for communion of saints with saints, because they are saints; I shut none of the brethren out of the churches, nor forbid them that would receive them.

"I am not against every man though by your abusive language you would set everyone against me; but I am for union, concord and communion with saints as saints, and for that cause I wrote my book." [5]

To this position restated in his three treatises in this controversy, he brings abundant scriptural proof, which his opponents strove to demolish. They made short work of his pleas for union and accord, and berated him for "Egregious Ignorance," calling him "one of Machiavel's scholars," and "topful of ignorance and prejudice." "How he hath darkened counsel by words without knowledge." To men like William Kiffin, Henry Jessey, Henry D'Anvers, and

Thomas Paul, Bunyan was an exasperating opponent, for though all of them argued with Scripture literally, Bunyan's applications were not specific enough to suit, and he slipped too easily into generalization, as in his phrase "communion with saints as saints," which seemed to them meaningless.

Bunyan was also indifferent to the label *Baptist.* Asked directly what name he went by, he replied, in his *Peaceable Principles:*

"And since you would know by what name I would be distinguished from others, I tell you, I would be, and hope I am, a Christian, a believer, or other such name which is approved by the Holy Ghost. And as for those factious titles of Anabaptists, Independents, Presbyterians, or the like, I conclude that they came neither from Jerusalem, nor Antioch, but rather from hell and Babylon, for they naturally tend to divisions."

In his *Heavenly Footman* he urged Christians to have a care of Quakers, Ranters, Freewillers, and "also do not have too much company with some Anabaptists, though I go under that name myself." [6] Throughout his life, the word Anabaptist was a word of reproof even in Baptist circles, and since in popular usage the two names were often confused, in this passage he may be referring to the derogatory application, for he would have hardly taken the label willingly. In all such controversies, he came persistently back to the reality of religion as an inner experience, as the one thing needful.

In this connection much inquiry and considerable ingenuity has centered on the baptism of his own infant son Joseph in St. Cuthbert's Church, November 16, 1672, at the very time he was engaged in answering D'Anvers and Paul on this baptism issue. One of the more recent theories is that this Joseph was not his son but his grandson.[7] This record will doubtless continue to invite argument for those to whom sectarian lines are more sharply drawn than Bunyan cared to draw them. He spoke not once, but often, and spoke bravely in a day when all roads led to separation, not to union, as in our own.

Immediately after his release from prison, Bunyan had engaged in a less important and more rancorous dispute with Edward Fowler, rector of Northill, a neighboring town of Bedfordshire. Bunyan's book was apparently written in prison. It was an attack on Fowler's *Design of Christianity*, and had the title, *A Defence of the Doctrine of Justification by Faith*.[8] The faith-works issue was always a subject to arouse Bunyan to a pitch of zeal, and in this somewhat carelessly written treatise he is once again insisting on inner rather than outer change. Both men indulged in personal abuse, and a bad situation was made worse in Fowler's reply to Bunyan's treatise under the title *Dirt Wip't Off*. Characteristically, Bunyan was not given to abuse in controversy, but this time was an exception.

In addition to being drawn into such contentions, which were not to his taste or his talents, the new chapter of freedom had other dark pages. He had his enemies for other than sectarian reasons, as one of his forthright speech and action might expect to have. Also, like any other public figure in a small community, he lived in a glass house. The slander he suffered during this return to freedom because of Agnes Beaumont, a young girl of twenty-one who at her brother's insistent request rode on a pillion behind Bunyan to a church meeting at Gamblingay, would no doubt have been forgotten as it deserved, had not Agnes herself written down the story, and had the manuscript not been preserved. Also, Bunyan himself had seen fit to deny the implications of the tale in a later edition of his *Grace Abounding*. He did so with spirit and finality, thus:

"My foes have missed their mark in this their shooting at me. I am not the man. I wish that they themselves be guiltless. If all the fornicators and adulterers in England were hanged by the neck till they be dead, *John Bunyan*, the object of their envy, would be still alive and well." [9]

Richard Baxter likewise had suffered from a situation almost parallel to the one which called forth this denial from Bunyan. Baxter had taken refuge under a tree during a heavy rainstorm, when a woman, a beggar of low repute, had also taken refuge under the same tree, on the other side of the hedge. Neither saw the other, but a passerby saw them both, and a shabby story was spread abroad forthwith.

Agnes Beaumont, who figured in Bunyan's accusation, was a resident of Edworth, and a member of the Gamblingay group, one of the congregations under Bunyan's supervision. He was on his way to preach at Gamblingay, when the brother of Agnes importuned him to let his sister ride on the pillion, as she had no other way to get to the meeting. This was the day when her brother was to be received into the membership. He had only one horse, and his wife was on the pillion behind him. At first Bunyan refused, then gave way to the tears of the disappointed young girl. Back at home that night, on foot most of the way, for Bunyan had gone back by another road, she found herself locked out by her angry father, who had heard what had happened and who bore a grudge against Brother Bunyan. After being implored for several days, to the knowledge of the whole village, he opened the door, but only on the promise that Agnes would attend no more meetings without his consent. But the strain of his long-continued anger was too much for his strength and he died that night. At that point scandal overreached itself in the tale that Agnes had poisoned him and that Bunyan had furnished the poison. At her trial, she was eventually cleared, but only after the affair had caused such a neighborhood upheaval as may be imagined.

Her manuscript account of this whole affair,[10] regrettable as the details reveal it to have been, is a social document of importance in Bunyan's story. The extravagant emotionalism of the young girl, who could write,

"It was like death to me to be kept from such A meeting";

the shocked rebuke of her brother, when he heard that she had promised not to go to meeting again without her father's consent,

"Oh, sister, what have you done?"

the share of a brother minister in publishing the scandal against Bunyan; the sympathy and kindness of the villagers with the accused girl; the intense partisanship which Bunyan's preaching aroused— the whole story opens a window into the stratum of English life which his preaching reached. These were the people to whom what he had to say had almost a life-and-death importance. Four years hence, those of them who could read, and many could not, would read *Pilgrim's Progress*, and except for the Bible it would be the only book they would ever read. What did his preaching mean to them, and how important was its importance to them in the long English record? The answer is many-faceted, and goes straight to the heart of one aspect of what we call Puritanism, considered as a great tide of change in English culture. One current of that change was toward individualism, and that too is many-faceted. Bunyan's preaching and that of many of his fellow dissenting preachers made religion a personal matter to a degree not hitherto preached from the Sunday pulpit. By this personal interpretation, the lives of simple people were dignified and given a dimension beyond the humdrum of the weekday round of hard work and small village concerns.

Bunyan was not an emotional preacher. On the printed page the treatises developed from sermons do not evaporate into emotional extravagance, as is often true for fervid evangelism, once it hardens into print. He gave his hearers credit for having minds and being able to understand the doctrine he preached. He sent them away with a sense not only that religion mattered, as they already believed, but that they mattered, as individual men and women, and to God Himself. In his own religious struggle in youth, he had wanted some special sign of acceptance from Christ Himself. He had taken the Scripture personally, and had agonized to know that he, John Bunyan, a tinker of Elstow, was the one to whom the promises had been made. Whole areas of his *Grace Abounding* express the intensity of this yearning for an individual assurance that he was accepted. In his preaching he made the scriptural promises as personal to the Agnes Beaumonts before him as he had desired them to be for himself. The sequel was that it was "like Death to miss a meeting."

The importance of such religious leadership as Bunyan's in his own day is to be found mainly on the village level. Over two generations the Quaker itinerants and Baptist lay preachers had gone a long way toward leavening the area to which most of these preachers themselves belonged. They had gotten the ear of thousands of those to whom the solemnities of worship had hitherto been external to their lives. Ordinary men and women? Yes. Individually of limited importance beyond their own village limits? Yes, but let them become impelled by faith in a great cause, or emboldened by a great idea, and they can put a force behind it which can change many things. The significance of Bunyan's leadership was that to a degree greater than that of many of his fellow preachers, he could get the ear of these people and move them to action. It was a signal gift.

In the midst of this busy life at the writing desk and the encouragement of success as pastor and preacher came a blow which once more threatened to end it all. This was the king's Proclamation of February 3, 1675, suppressing all conventicles and ordering that the names of all those failing to appear for communion in their parish churches be listed by the bishops for ecclesiastical action. As a dissenting preacher who would not comply with the order against preaching, no matter how well he might remember what a former disobedience had cost him, and who also would continue to absent himself from St. Cuthbert's on communion day, Bunyan was once more in line for civil, and this time also for ecclesiastical, action against him. It came promptly. On March 4th, exactly a month and a day since the king's Proclamation, he was served with a warrant charging that within the month he had several times

"preached or taught at a conventicle meeting or assembly under colour or pretence of exercise of Religion in other manner than according to the Liturgie or Practice of the Church of England."

He could not have been surprised. The Act of Indulgence three years before had been a royal decree, not a constitutional act, and this reversal was also by royal prerogative. Two years earlier the king in anger had torn the seal from the Act of Indulgence and canceled all licenses issued under it, but since the immediate passing of the Test Act had served the purpose of expelling all Catholics from office, Dissenters had temporarily not been molested. Leaders among them, however, had not at any time since 1672 been easy in their minds about their freedom, for the feeling for constitutional government in Commons was too strong not to triumph sooner or later, and the king, not Commons, had issued the Act of Indulgence. Now their uneasiness was justified.

What they could not know when this second proclamation was issued was that after three years of freedom to preach and listen regularly to dissenting interpretations of faith and practice, there could be no effective silencing of preachers or restraining of listeners. Not only had the seeds of the new doctrine been too widely blown to be gathered up again, where they had fallen, but the boldness of those who for three years had walked freely to their places of meeting was not now to be restained. When they refused to comply with either order, they were not acting in the spirit of Thomas Venner or other insurrectionists; they were self-respecting Englishmen, law-respecting, not only convinced in their own way of thinking, but also convinced that they had a rightful share in the making of the laws they lived under. They could hold on until they found a way to gain their freedom lawfully. Temporarily the restraints were severe, and many suffered for them. The wise ones used discretion, but not John Bunyan. He was one who would again suffer.

The offense for which he was served the warrant did not call for immediate imprisonment. Rather a fine of £20 for the first offense, £40 for the second, and imprisonment if the fines were not paid. The sum would have been too large for him to raise, or for the brethren of the church to assume. Besides, very quickly, he would have offended again. He may have gone into hiding for a time. In the prefatory letter to his congregation, printed with his pamphlet *Instruction for the Ignorant*, issued at this time, he wrote that although his treatise was intended "for public and common benefit" he could do no less, "being driven from you in presence, not affection, but first present you with this little book. Accept it therefore, as a token of my Christian remembrance of you." He ends the letter,

"Yours to serve you, by my ministry, when I can, to your edification and consolation." [11]

The treatise itself is a brief catechism, labeled as "fitted to the capacity of the weakest," as though it were intended for those newly of the company or for children.

The next document in his story clearly does not belong to the offense of preaching at a conventicle, but for failure to appear at

St. Cuthbert's to take communion. It is a bond dated June, 1677, and signed by two Londoners, Thomas Kelsey and Robert Blaney, who gave themselves as sureties for John Bunyan who stands excommunicated:

"John Bunnion, tinckar, for continued absence from communion at St. Cuthbert's Church."

The signatures of these two men which made them responsible for his conforming to the king's command within six months indicates that Bunyan was in prison for an ecclesiastical, not a civil offense.[12] Sir William Foster of Bedford with whom he had had a wordy exchange at the time of his 1660 arrest and examination, was now Chancellor of the Diocese of Lincoln, and very probably he had been in part responsible for seeing that Bunyan's offense did not pass unnoticed.

There was no ecclesiastical prison in Bedford, so that offenders would have been committed to the county jail, where Bunyan had already spent twelve years, lacking some six months. The discovery of this cautionary bond therefore settles the long dispute as to the place of the second imprisonment, and establishes, against long tradition, the unlikelihood of the jail under the bridge as the place where *Pilgrim's Progress* was written. This tradition dies hard, but it would seem that even the town order to repair the prison early in 1675 cannot turn what many regard as a picturesque story into fact. There might conceivably, though improbably, have been a brief incarceration there during the period of legal procedures incident to his trial and sentence, but if the law worked according to usual practice, the king's writ would have been executed by the county sheriff and he would have been conducted back to Bedford County Gaol.

Chapter Nine

Pilgrim's Progress

"This Book will make a Traveller of thee"

Accordingly, aged forty-eight, he found himself again behind prison bars. After these three and a half years of blessed freedom, and the dignity of a village pastorate, he was back in Bedford County Gaol. The same clamors around him, the same harsh commands and scant comforts, the noisome odors, pale faces, moans from the suffering ones, fewer Christians; more felons, as his companions now, possibly fewer request sermons from his fellow prisoners, occasional visits from his friends of the parish, bringing news, books, encouragement; otherwise the same unending monotony. For a man of Bunyan's energetic zeal, and a man in the full maturity of his powers, with abundant pastoral and preaching success immediately behind him, this sudden paralysis of all his active endeavors would seem to have been harder to face than his first prison term, when he was still hopeful of speedy release. Remembering that he had hoped unavailingly for nearly twelve years, he would be more realistic now. Nevertheless, we may believe that his buoyancy of spirit was still sufficient unto the day.

Had he known what he could never know, that out of this dreary six-month return to privation and forced inactivity would come leisure to complete a book that would make the name of John

Bunyan familiar to many thousands three centuries hence, and had he been given choice of such remembrance or the chance to keep on "saving souls" by his preaching, unquestionably he would have chosen to preach and to die forgotten. His name would then have been preserved only in the baptismal register of Elstow church, on the muster rolls of Newport Pagnell, on his several title pages to date, and in various official lists in the Bedfordshire Archives. Nor would anyone have cared to search for them even there. Choice not being his, however, he was led back to the jail where he had dreamed his dream, and where the genius of a tinker would make it into a book to be read in many languages the world over.

The Pilgrim's Progress was entered in the Stationer's Register on December 22, 1677. It was licensed by the printer on February 18, 1677/78, and published by Nathaniel Ponder at the sign of the Peacock in the Poultry shortly thereafter. Bunyan had been released from prison in late June or early July, 1677, only five months before the book was offered for license action. It was his twenty-third publication. That it was a prison book is a safe-enough assumption, the evidence beginning with the gloss opposite the word *denn* of the first sentence: [1]

"As I walked through the Wilderness of this World I lighted on a certain place where there was a Denn, and laid me down in that place to sleep; and, as I slept, I dreamed a Dream."

In the margin of the third edition, the word *denne* is glossed as the *gaol*, presumably by Bunyan himself, as he added certain other details to this 1679 edition.

From this gloss various questions start. In which of his prison terms did he dream the dream? When did it "fall into an allegory" under his hand? When was it "in black and white" for "length and breadth" in such "bigness" as we now know? Speculation has been voluminous on all these queries, but there is no certain answer to any of them. Unfortunately so, since various stages in Bunyan's development as man and artist are implicit in the conception and execution of this his greatest work. Even the slight changes and additions in the second and third editions are revealing as to his taste, care in

141

revision, and sense of narrative interest. More insistently still, what does this book tell us about the creative process at work in a mind unaware and unsuspecting of its own originality and power? That the book was very probably completed during the six-month imprisonment of 1676–1677, or very shortly thereafter, would seem to be clearly indicated by the Stationer's Registry entry. But how long before had the idea teased Bunyan's mind? Probably a very long time. Likewise the writing itself had demanded time, much time. Such apparently spontaneous ease and energy of creation, as makes these pages memorable, is no result dashed off in quick haste and never touched thereafter. Maturity is written all over *Pilgrim's Progress*, maturity of thought and workmanship. However instant may have been (and probably was) the first flash of inspiration which lighted up the landscape from the City of Destruction to the gate of heaven, and pricked out the figure of Christian caught in the toils of the fateful journey, even though maturity is not altogether a matter of time, it would seem that many months, perhaps stretching into several years, went into putting the dream in such "bigness" as Nathaniel Ponder sent forth in the early summer of 1678.

The interruption of the story after the meeting with the shepherds of the Delectable Mountains, in Bunyan's word, "So I awoke from my dream," and its resumption in the following sentence, "And I slept and dreamed again," need not have so literal an interpretation as the pardon of 1672, although return to the very active life of the Bedfordshire pastorate would understandably have put completion out of probability for some time. The delayed publication date makes it seem likely that completion would have been accomplished three years later, during the less active life of the second imprisonment, but of this assumption no certain evidence exists. There is no break in the story, either in its thread or in its spirit, as he sees the same two pilgrims going down the mountains where he saw them a moment before.

Conjecture of the first stirrings of the pilgrim idea in Bunyan's mind are guided somewhat vaguely by himself. In his prefatory *Apology* he tells us that while writing another book, which he identifies only as "the Way and race of Saints in this our Gospel-day," he "fell suddenly into an Allegory," and that as he tried to continue the saints' journey to heaven, the allegorical ideas multiplied in his mind so fast, that "Like sparks that from the coals of Fire do flie," they threatened "to eat out

The Book that I already am about."

To prevent this "eating out," and also not to lose these fast-breeding ideas, he says that he put them by themselves for a time until he could finish the book in hand.

No one of his titles fits this interrupted treatise of the "race of Saints" exactly, although a good case can be made out for *The Heavenly Footman*, presumably written in the late sixties, and with less warrant, for *The Strait Gate*, published in 1676. It is of course possible that he referred to some title that has not come down to us.

The Heavenly Footman is a sermon-shaped treatise on the Christian journey to heaven considered as a foot race. The text, "So run that you may obtain," is clarified by directions and cautions toward winning the prize, which is of course heaven. It is only one step, and a short one, from this array of dangers and obstacles in the runner's way to the story of the runner himself, but in this treatise Bunyan remains the preacher, clarifying doctrine only. There are a few details which suggest Christian's journey, as, for example, in the Sixth Direction:

"Take heed that you have not an ear open to any one that calleth after you as you are in your journey. . . . I give thee notice of this betimes, knowing that thou shalt have enough call after thee, . . . one crying, Stay for me, the other saying, Do not leave me behind, a third crying, and take me along with you." [2]

The picture of Christian comes to mind, putting his fingers in his ears so as not to hear the pleadings of his wife and children; his neighbors thronging out to see him run, some mocking, some threatening, some crying after him to return, and Obstinate and Pliable resolving to fetch him back by force. But so slight a suggestion of parallel proves nothing as to whether or not this was the interrupted book. Similarly the cautions as to bypaths the runner must avoid, the crosses in his path, the briars, the quagmire. Given the idea of a foot race which demands speed, and a pilgrim journey over unknown terrain, such parallels are inevitable. The strongest suggestion that this is the book Bunyan referred to is the title itself, announcing that the footman's goal, like the pilgrim's, is heaven itself, but salvation being the goal of all Bunyan's preaching and writing, it need not be made especially important in this one example.

The Strait Gate, or the Great Difficulty of Getting to Heaven, is concerned not with the whole journey but only with the gate itself. Little objectivity is permitted. "The straitness of the gate is not to be understood carnally," but "mystically," Bunyan wrote. You must not think of the entrance into heaven as "some little pinching wicket." It is wide enough to admit all "truly gracious and sincere lovers of Jesus Christ," and narrow enough to keep all others out.[3] Mention of the gate as a wicket is a minor detail and a very natural one for Bunyan who knew wicket gates by scores in Bedfordshire pastures. The word "pinching" makes it English unmistakably. For his readers, particularly non-English ones, it means one gate only, as we see Christian straining his eyes over the space of a very wide field to follow the pointing of Evangelist's finger.

"Do you see yonder wicket-gate?" says Evangelist.

"No," says Christian.

"Do you see yonder shining light?"

"I think I do," Christian answers.

"Keep that light in your eye, and go up directly thereto, so shalt thou see the gate, at which, when thou knockest, it shall be told thee what thou shalt do." [4]

Bunyan may have seen the light and the gate too, as the allegory broke into his thought.

There are other incidental reminders of Christian's journey as the treatise proceeds: the porters at the gate, the fact that one may miss heaven by ignorance (not yet personified), the man later to be called Talkative, "whose religion lies in the tip of his tongue," the legalist and the formalist, the professor who can be anything for any company and can cast stones with both hands. But these are attitudes and qualities, not individual human beings, and there is no reason to think that they are on the way to be human beings. Why should they be? Artistic creation does not proceed logically, step by step in an orderly progression; at least not often. All we can say of such incidental reminders is that a "carnal" interpretation of the way to heaven seems to be tempting Bunyan, and that probably, given time, he would yield. Inevitably, instinctively, his mind forced him to objectify his concepts. Doctrine must needs express itself in characteristic behaviors, take on tones of voice and theology clarify itself visibly and tangibly.

Mozart is credited with saying that he did not hear the parts of his musical compositions in succession, but as it were, "all at once," and unforgettably. When his mind was fired with a musical idea, the subject enlarged itself in his thought until it stood almost complete and finished before him. He could survey it at a glance, as he would a picture or a statue. Committing it to paper was merely a reporting of what had been finished before he began to write. Bunyan gives no such hint of the creative process for himself, only in this case the memory of crowding allegorical ideas interrupting another work, a dual activity of mind which could probably be matched many times over in the experience of other artists, whatever their medium.

In the absence of all clues save Bunyan's own words, which are too vague for certainty, one is shut up to conjecture as to the beginning of the pilgrim idea in Bunyan's mind. Conjecture will doubtless still invite suggestion, for the query has its importance. The imaginative zest back of the creation of this book would seem plausibly to argue for an earlier rather than a later date, for surely it was written years before the *Life and Death of Mr. Badman* or *Pilgrim's Progress*, Part II. There is youth in it, a verve and fecundity of thought and expression to which Bunyan did not attain in later years. It is reasonable to suppose that with his emotions stirred and his mind plowed up in the effort to put his own conversion experience into words, the urge to translate the experience into story might have possessed him soon after 1666, when the *Grace Abound-*

ing left his hand. The "very apt similitude to set before the saints of the Lord," as he said of the *Footman* treatise, may have provided the spur, for this book is a succession of pictures: the lazy ones stopped in their running, the misguided ones running the wrong way, others weighted down with stones in their pockets, "great lumpish shoes on their feet." There is talk in it too, in the reasons given by those who do not choose to go: I have married a wife, I have a farm, I shall offend my landlord, I shall lose my trading, I will stay until I am older. In such details it is easy to see the allegory breaking uninvited into the sermon, and with an insistence that might claim the preacher.

In any case these crowding allegorical ideas were only the initial impulse, and an impulse that may have had a long maturing. Bunyan's phrase, "that little time I have been a professor," in the *Footman* treatise [5] establishes only the limit of 1653, when *professing* for him had a public beginning. When *Grace Abounding* was published in 1666, his conversion was already thirteen years behind him, and before he wrote *The Pilgrim's Progress* he had traveled a long way further; perhaps not a much longer way toward heaven, but far more deeply into himself. The *Grace Abounding* is the tale of John Bunyan, the great sinner of Elstow, on his tortured way to eternal salvation, an individual experience, told as he remembered it; *Pilgrim's Progress* is Everyman's journey, and not to the celestial city only. It is the universal quest of man to the goal of his supreme desiring, his passionate search for an unseen perfection, unattainable on earth. It is a universal quest, realized individually. With the generations the perils change, the landmarks change, the goal changes, together with the theology or philosophy which interprets them, but as long as human records exist for this journey of the spirit, man, the pilgrim, has undertaken search past the here and now of his life. Bunyan's own caution is pertinent:

> "Take heed, also that thou be not extream,
> In playing with the outside of my Dream;
> Nor let my figure, or similitude,
> Put thee into a laughter, or a feud.

Yet Christian is somewhat in dividualized (margin note)

Leave this for Boys and Fools; but as for thee,
Do thou the substance of my matter see." [6]

It is the outside of the dream that changes. The substance remains constant. In Kafka's *Castle* there is no city whose foundations are framed higher than the clouds. There are no Shining Ones who come out to meet the pilgrims. There is no salute by the King's Trumpeters, with ten thousand welcomes of joy; there are no bells ringing. There is no glimpse beyond the gates, such a glimpse as made Bunyan, the Dreamer, who stood on the other side of all this glory, write the most haunting sentence in the whole book:

"And after that, they shut up the gates: which when I had seen, I wished myself among them." [7]

The representation of man's life on earth as a pilgrimage is an idea anyone can understand. Man the wayfarer is an inevitable metaphor, and one of the oldest on record. There is something romantic about a journey whether one has never made one, or whether one has sailed all seas and gazed on a myriad of wonders. Variety, endless change are implicit in the very fact of setting forth. The wayfaring man meets seemingly impassable barriers, makes unwise tarryings, misses the signposts, loses his way, meets strangers who prove friends, encounters dangers of man and beast, experiences delights for which words fail. Whether he seeks adventure, searches for lost treasure, discovers new worlds, is an exile trying to find his way home, there is always a goal which steadies his thought and strengthens his arm.

In Western literature the journey story is everywhere. It is both Jewish and Christian, ancient, modern, and of all times in between. One thinks easily of Moses and the Promised Land, of Ulysses and the ten-year sea journey, of Attar's *Colloquy of the Birds,* of the quest for the Grail, of the otherworld journeys of Irish myth, in which the traveler disappears through a little mound in the hillside, is gone for a thousand years that pass as one day, of *The Rubáiyát,* of Dante led by Vergil, of the journey of the Red Cross Knight, and in these later days, of various journeys of the mind, of Kafka, of

Joyce, of Proust and, one may hope, of others yet to come. Every country, every century has made man a wayfarer on journey.

"The days of my pilgrimage are an hundred and thirty years," said Jacob to Pharaoh. He spoke literally, as men may, but ever since poets first wrote on clay tablets or parchment with stylus and pen, the pilgrim idea in every generation has escaped the literal and carried men's thought forward to some far country, some house not made with hands, eternal in the heavens, and at least in their dreams, other men have set out to find it.

The persistent effort to derive Bunyan's pilgrim from one of the many early renderings of this journey story is bootless and unprofitable. Except for the Bible, Bunyan was not a man of such books as we call literature, and there is the scantest of reasons to think that Spenser's *Faerie Queene* or Guillaume de Guilleville's *Le Pèlerinage de la vie humaine* or any other memorable version had ever been in his hand. His friends brought books to him in prison, but not these books. They brought current religious treatises, collections of sermon materials, controversial pieces. That he had seen Richard Bernard's *Isle of Man* is not to be doubted; also Benjamin Keach's *The Glorious Lover* and that in its turn he would see Keach's *War with the Devil* and various imitators of Spenser, whom we gladly forget. The authors of contemporary allegory learned from him and he learned from them, but comparison of their works with Bunyan's is limited to details such as a trial scene, a council in hell, a battle, the storming of a castle. These men all drew from a common stock of materials, but they drew differently and used what they drew differently.

Not all, in fact not many, current allegories, or even the earlier ones, take the traveler from earth to heaven. More commonly, as in *The Travalyed Pilgrim* [8] of a century earlier, the scope of the story is the life span of the pilgrim from birth to death. In this book, Man, the Traveller, bids Infancy farewell, mounts his horse Will, rides through the Field of Pleasure, the Pomp and Glory of the World, and comes at last to the Chamber of Pain, where life ends. His is no flight from sin to bliss. It is the human journey of a valiant man, counseled by Reason and defeated by Death alone. In such analogues of the pilgrim tale, there are pleasant valleys, high mountains, a

House Beautiful, always something to lift the story and suggest a plane other than the literal.

Had Bunyan been a man of books beyond the narrow limits of his itinerant preacher's calling, it would be logical to suppose that he had seen a 1670 translation into English of the Theban *Tablet of Cebes*,[9] one of the earliest known analogues of the pilgrim tale. Here is Man the wayfarer, as conceived five centuries B.C. by a Theban disciple of Socrates. Here is the Court, or Inclosure, where mortals range, crowding toward the gate which admits them to Life. He who is called the Superintending Spirit gives instructions as to which road to take, if they would come safely to the end of the journey. There are three gates to pass through, three concentric circles to traverse. At the first gate, Fortune, a blind woman, tosses out gifts: Wealth, Fame, Children, Crowns. The Pilgrim chooses unwisely, snatches greedily, and then wastes what he has chosen. At the second gate False Learning waylays him. He drinks of the proffered cup of Error and Ignorance, is enslaved by Profligacy, Flattery, and Incontinence and thrown into the House of Woe. But Repentance comes to show him the way to True Learning, a way narrow, steep and hard, and few there be that find it. At the third gate True Learning, standing high up on a firm, square stone, seemingly inaccessible, helps him to reach it. He drinks a purifying drink, is welcomed by Courage, Self-Control, Temperance, Gentleness, Liberty, and their sister virtues, who conduct him to their mother, Happiness, in the Seat and Mansion of the Blest. But this is not all. He is then taken back to the place from which he started, but now having a true sense of things, and being safe from all corruption, he engages himself in helping others to make the right choices as they set forth on the long journey.

The 1670 readers of this little book, written nearly twenty-two centuries before, were not of Bunyan's stratum of English society, and it is entirely safe to say that he had never heard of it. Had he seen it, the diagram which the text elucidates might have caught his attention. There is design in it and originality. Certain details might have pleased him: the little copse of wood, the delightful meadows, the three gates, but he would have had no sympathy at all with the Socratic philosophy of the good life which is its content. This is no chart to salvation through divine mediation, with eternal bliss as its goal. It is the path to a good life on earth and nothing beyond. Trust not Fortune, Cebes is saying. She bestows gifts blindly. Take from False Learning what is valuable, but stay not long. Haste away to True Learning, whose gift is Knowledge that changeth not. There is nothing Good but Wisdom; nothing evil but Folly.

On all levels of English society at this date, allegory, as a mode of thought, still spoke clearly. For the next generation, the beginnings of a scientific approach to truth would lessen its hold, as respect for concrete fact gained ground. But not yet. The ability to comprehend abstract meaning when clothed in concrete pictures was part of the English heritage from medieval times. Allegory did not require translation or exposition. It was even clearer than straightforward statement. Separation of symbol from meaning was not necessary. The image did not stand for the idea. It was the idea. Allegory was not a puzzle to be put together piece by piece. It must be perceived as a whole. Back of this singleness in duality was the assumption that the universe itself was charged with meaning. Every part and parcel of it spoke of something beyond what the eye could see.

Unquestionably Bunyan owed something to his contemporaries who were also writing allegory in the 1660's and 1670's, but in the deepest, truest sense *Pilgrim's Progress* was not born of any prototype from the pen of any other writer. The source underneath this tale of Christian, the pilgrim, with a burden on his back and a far goal in his eye, was a whole stratum of English culture, stretching far back into the centuries. Of this indebtedness to a long tradition Bunyan himself was completely unconscious. Layer on layer and generation by generation, one strand of this tradition had grown up around the village church as a center and the village pastor as a spokesman. Another had survived in folk tale. To leave out of account in any day of history that which does not appear on the printed page is to miss one of the most enlightening clues to man's way of thinking his thoughts. Ideas and symbols filter down from generation to generation, losing the signature of those who first uttered them. Words, phrases, images, coined in a speech, a sermon, a song, survive in contexts other than the first to catch them in print.

During the Middle Ages, when few Englishmen could read or write, the Sunday sermon was the one avenue of intellectual stimulus and satisfaction to the average village man or woman. What they heard during a lifetime, fifty-two Sundays in the year, and what their fathers had heard before them and their children would hear after, left a deposit in the folk mind from which the groundwork of a literary tradition was presently made for Chaucer, Spenser, Shakespeare, Milton to inherit, and for each in his turn, to add to, render articulate, and also to make permanent in print. Some of this tradition in the Middle Ages was revealing itself week by week in the voice of the parish preacher.

On thousands of manuscript pages it was written down in the painstaking script of the thirteenth and fourteenth centuries. Of these pages a few remain to give hints of what the preacher was saying before the tradition lost its clerical signature. To explore a fair number of these extant homilies and sermons in their manuscript survivals is to meet Bunyan's pilgrim in scattered items unexpectedly. For the initial spur to such investigation, scholars are indebted to Gerald R. Owst, the first in our time to give extensive study to these medieval preachments and to suggest the light they might throw on literary monuments.[10]

Not once but again and yet again in these homilies one finds the pattern for a pilgrim story. Man sets forth from some City of Destruction "to the place where he shall dwelle ay withoute ende." He is a wayfarer in a strange land. The world is not his country. He bids farewell to his household and neighbors, who will not be persuaded to go with him. He carries a burden on his back. Thieves and robbers beset him. Dangers multiply. He is clothed with armor to withstand them. Good companions overtake and counsel him. Eventually, after many dangers, many victories, he arrives at the gates of Paradise, which open to receive him.

There is one homily, unfinished, presumably of the fourteenth century, which may stand as a specific example of this pilgrim journey to the promised land. It is entitled "The Weye to Paradys." It was found by Mr. Owst in a Harleian MS. collection. The parallel to Bunyan's pilgrim at the Slough of Despond is startling. The incident is pictured by a crude drawing, showing the pilgrim, burdened by what the text calls "a sack of synne," attempting to cross on a narrow plank a perilous ditch, called "the Slough of Hell." "No man may put down this sack of sinne but oonly by confession," the preacher is saying, in the text below the picture.[11]

This is not an isolated example. Scattered items throughout various volumes of these MS. homilies suggest the central plot of the journey story allegorically interpreted. Later in this same fourteenth century homily the pilgrim journeys on horseback. There is of course not the slightest likelihood that Bunyan had any knowledge of such manuscript materials or any acquaintance with them. What came down to him as a boy, listening to sermons from the Elstow pulpit, is not on the record, but it is reasonable to suppose that in the village sermons of Bedfordshire in his day something survived of the allegorical framework of the religious life considered as a journey and as a warfare. In fact, it survives in any Christian pulpit today, with the Bible as its source. Unknown to himself, Bunyan's dream also tapped resources of folk memory, as well as the resources of his own boy reading of romance, an area of immense proportions and richness. In the spirit of his allegory, as well as in the parallels of incident from homily and romance, *Pilgrim's Progress* is in line with the medieval time, not with the last quarter of the seventeenth century, when both religion and the world of faery were beginning to be successfully challenged by materialistic values and scientific inquiry. In both spirit and letter this book was on the verge of being outdated before it was even conceived in a tinker's brain.

Bunyan's first sentence projects the reader into a world where anything can happen. The familiar is made immediately strange. The man has no name. The place has no geography. It is in a "certain place," no more definite than "the wilderness of this world." The teller of the story is sleeping "in a denne." In two sentences Bunyan has created a setting in which whatever happens will be accepted without challenge. The picture comes with the words, the man in rags, the scene outside his own house, the book in his hand, the burden on his back. Joseph Conrad said that he did not begin a story with an idea but with an image, and so it would seem Bunyan does likewise. He thought in pictures; he wrote in pictures.

Christian opened his book. He read. He wept. He trembled, and then he asked the question, "What shall I do?" The whole book is the answer. In some of the long disquisitions to follow, a multitude of words drown the memory, but not here.

Nor in Dante's beginning,

"In the middle of the journey of our life I came to myself in a dark wood."

Nor in Langland's,

"In a summer season when soft was the sun
    I was weary forwandered and went me to rest
    Under a broad bank by a burnside
    And as I lay and leaned and looked in the waters,
    I slumbered in a sleeping."

Nor in *Everyman*,

"I will show you how it is,
    Commanded I am to go a journey,
    A long way, hard and dangerous."

In Guillaume de Guilleville's *Le Pèlerinage de la vie humaine*, action begins at line 10,244, when Grâce Dieu, the pilgrim's guide, leaves him to go on alone. All that precedes has been direction, questions, answers, and most of what follows is also dialogue. In Simon Patrick's *Parable of the Pilgrim*, published in 1663, the journey begins in Chapter XX. There is no story value at all. This is a book of devotion. By contrast, from the first sentence *Pilgrim's Progress* is a story of action. Something happens on nearly every page.

To read Bunyan's book as a whole is to be freshly astonished throughout at the familiarity of person and place, action and speech. Whether recognition stems from childhood acquaintance or literary allusion, no matter; we are in a terrain we know; these are people we have met; men and women whose voices we can hear speaking. It all comes back in pictures and sounds: the land of Beulah, whose air is very sweet and pleasant; the meadow curiously beautified with lilies; the Valley of the Shadow, a very solitary place; Vanity Fair, laid out in streets, as the Elstow green had been at fair time in Bunyan's childhood; "a lusty fair" it was; the Hill Difficulty, where Christian fell from running to going, and from going to clambering; Bypath Meadow, where the going was easier; the delicate plain called Ease; the view through the perspective glass at the top of the hill called Clear; the Enchanted Ground, where the Shining Ones commonly walked.

The names fit their owners: Talkative, the son of Saywell; all that he hath is in his tongue; Little Faith, a good man, but why did he not pluck up a greater heart? Hategood and his wicked jury, made of Bunyan's own memory of his trial in the Chapel of Herne; the verdict of each against Faithful is what one might expect from one so named:

"I could never indure him," says Mr. Love-Lust.
"I hate the very look of him," says Mr. Malice.
"A sorry Scrub," says Mr. High-mind.
"My heart riseth against him," says Mr. Enmity.
"Hanging is too good for him," says Mr. Cruelty.[12]

Pickthank is sworn in not to tell the truth, but to witness against the prisoner.

In the town of Fair Speech live By-Ends, Mr. Two-Tongues, the parson, Mr. Smoothman and Mr. Facing-both Ways, Mr. Anything; one could trust no one of them. Mr. Hold-the World, Mr. Money-Love, Mr. Save-All have all gone to school to Mr. Gripe-man, a schoolmaster in Love Gain, a market town in Coveting. Atheist talks like one of the Ranters. He falls into a great rage and then into a great laughter. Ignorance is a brisk lad; it goes hard with him at the last. Giant Despair with his crabtree cudgel, and what a choice he made in a wife, Mrs. Diffidence, who kept him under her thumb with nagging. She looked ugly on the prisoners. Bunyan's economy of words in these portraits is a triumph.

The sound of everyday speech is on these pages in short cut, quip, epigram, homely comparison. One might have heard it on any Bedfordshire street corner:

> You are not yet out of gunshot of the devil.
> Then it came burning hot into my mind.
> They are for hazarding all for God at a clap.
> Why art thou so tart, my brother?
> He might, methinks, have stood one brush with them.
> They seem to be hot for heaven.
> He was of the weak, and therefore went to the wall.
> Besides, the king is at his whistle.
> His house was as empty of religion as the white of an egg is of savour.
> Here will I spill thy soul.

Strange things happen in this journey, and we see strange wonders: the huge parlor full of dust at the Interpreter's House; the fire against the wall that water cannot quench; the shoes that will not wear out; the man in the iron cage; Christian's burden tumbling into the sepulcher at the foot of the cross; the lions that did not harm Christian; he did not see the chains; Apollyon straddling over the whole breadth of the way; the lock of the dungeon that went damnable hard, but the Key did open it; the chariot and horses waiting for Faithful; Evangelist always conveniently near when his help was needed. He reminds one of Dante's Vergil.

To list once more the merits of this tale would be as impertinent as to retell the familiar story from Christian's setting forth, through its marvels, its near disasters, its friendly meetings, and its victorious ending. To object to the verdict of many generations, as to its right to be called literature would not unseat Bunyan; at least not yet. To attempt a wholly virgin estimate is perhaps impossible for a book that has itself contributed to one's notion of excellence for its kind. Perhaps the fact that it is no longer often reread in the twentieth century is itself a verdict. That which we call classic English literature has many titles honored by all, and yet read by few.

Bunyan has his detractors, however, now as when he lived and

wrote. When Alfred Noyes in 1928 took part in a symposium com-
memorating the three hundredth anniversary of Bunyan's birth, he
called the book a pathetic revelation of the man himself, finding it
of little interest except as a "human document," almost as complete
in its own sphere as the diary of Samuel Pepys in his very different
world. In Alfred Noyes' thought, it has lived on for that reason, not
because it transcends its own age.[13] Strong dissent to this view was
voiced at the time, but doubtless many who did not reply in print
to this verdict readjusted their thought of the book as literature
because of it. The challenge to the accepted view and the comment
it aroused were healthy.

In 1956 M. Esther Harding, an analyst, examined the book as a
dream experience in accordance with the laws of Jung. She called
it "a rather fusty old book, which contains, besides the immediate
human experience, many boring pages and many banal-seeming allegorical characters." [14] She discussed the "human experience" of it
(with particular reference to what happens at the Interpreter's
House) as case material, and concluded that Bunyan's material "was
not just contrived allegory," but that it came from "a deep level of
the unconscious, which rings true even when subjected to a scientific
scrutiny." This investigation also was healthy. Literary evaluation
was no part of her purpose.

To test the book for the altitude of its religious aspiration is, probably for most inquirers, to find limits to Bunyan's reach as well as
his grasp. Its concreteness is a limitation to those whose satisfaction is God Himself, not heavenly bliss. Thomas à Kempis would be
a better choice for such readers. This is not the mystic's vision of the
Ineffable. Its goal is not a moment's realization of the divine and
human in unity. Christian was on his way to heaven, and so was
Bunyan. Heaven was a goal of security, of happiness, of an end to
all woe. It assured a final escape from the just punishment for the
sin to which man, by his nature, is prone. Heaven was salvation,
undeserved, a free gift, and yet demanding unwearied, lifelong
search. For Christian the search was only a means, not, as for Lessing,
a pursuit that was of itself sufficient reward. For Christian and for
Bunyan it was a stiff climb to a certain and final paradise.

But so to say is not to forget that, after all, the scope of Bunyan's vision takes us beyond the limits of life, and puts Christian's journey in relation to an eternal order of being which takes in all men. Such a vision enlarges the mind of one capable of receiving it. Bunyan not only had the vision but he was able to hold it in focus, and give it depth through imaginative expression. His allegory of Christian takes us only to the threshold. We do the rest ourselves, as we are capable.

Circumscribed as it may be by the theology of a time, there is something in this book larger than the ideas we call Puritan. It is Puritan chiefly in the intensity of religious passion with which it is infused. This intensity escapes the seventeenth century; it escapes, or rather transcends, Puritanism, Calvinism, sectarianism, in the feverish loyalties of them all. It would fit the fifth century B.C. or those who were first called Christians at Antioch, as well as those of the twentieth century. Christian, the pilgrim, is not of any century, ancient, medieval, renaissance, modern; he is a member of the human race. Moreover, there is an amplitude in this book which fits religious aspiration wherever one may choose to name a locale for it. Religious experience is hard to communicate in words. In Bunyan's handling, it is the dream itself that communicates. In this allegorical foot journey over rough terrain, up hills, through pastures, Bedfordshire locale though it may recognizably be, an epic of the inner life unrolls before us. The Valley of the Shadow of Bunyan's description was a real place and has been photographed, but for the discerning reader's sake it need not be. It leads one's thought beyond what the camera can catch. The negative limits the view. "Words fitly chosen, apples of gold in pictures of silver," invite the imagination, and we walk in a place of the mind and spirit, not in Bedfordshire.

But that is not all. Perhaps Bunyan comes closest to literature in his power, at moments, to bring to birth, as it were, something of the creative impulse of the writer himself. We forget Bunyan, as he forgot himself while he wrote, and Christian's experience becomes our own. There is no higher tribute to be paid the imaginative writer than thus to transform the reader into the actor, whose story unfolds before him. Words that can do this are powerful words. Simple words they were, in Bunyan's coinage, and at his best, not too many of them.

Bunyan's vision has root in a tragic sense of life, yet it is a supreme affirmation. It interprets reality through a vehicle closer to fairy tale than to fact, and yet the sense of truth is stronger than fact can convey. Something is here that is not lost when the story is translated into the dialect of a Kaffir tribe. There is something universal and something permanent in this book. It defies analysis; fortunately so.

Perhaps not many modern readers, like Dr. Johnson, would wish it longer than Bunyan made it, but perhaps some who might be willing to give themselves to it for an evening may come back to the ringing of the telephone and the sound of their own voices with a sense not only of having been very far away indeed, but also of having lived once again an experience of their own.

The dream finished, and the dreamer broad awake, John Bunyan looked at what he had written and asked advice of his friends. Fiction was as yet hardly to be dared.

> "Some said, John, print it; others said, not so;
> Some said, it might be good; others said, No."

"In a strait between them,"

> "At last, I thought, since you are thus divided
> I print it will, and so the case decided."

Meanwhile, whether with or without forecast, the cautionary bond offered by his two friends was accepted, apparently without question or investigation, and *Pilgrim's Progress* must wait only a little longer before going to print.

Chapter Ten

Bishop Bunyan

Once more he walked out of Bedford County Gaol a free man. He had eleven more years to live, and these would all be years of freedom. Prison rigors were over for him, although not the fear of still more of them, for Dissent was still a perilous way of life. Midway in the next decade there would be a veritable reign of terror for all nonconformists, whatever the sect. Nevertheless, fear was not in Bunyan's thought, in June, 1677, and straightway he threw himself into the duties of pulpit and pastorate with the vigor of a young man who was just beginning.

The eleven years left to him were to be the most active of his whole life, not only in the Bedford pulpit and parish, at his writing desk in the St. Cuthbert Street cottage, but also in the saddle, as week by week he answered urgent entreaty for a sermon at some distant Bedfordshire or Cambridgeshire point, or for a special service in some brother minister's parish. Brother Bunyan's talent for handling difficult human tangles had become matter of report, and during these years it would cost him many a long, hard journey afield. In the end it would cost him his life, but even had he known, he would still have gone willingly and with a sense of duty laid on him by God Himself.

These extra-Bedford pastoral journeys were itinerancy with a difference. He was no longer the tinker by trade and the preacher on Sundays. The forge beside the door and the tinker's cart were now the property of his son John, who was carrying on his father's trade. Bunyan was now "Bishop Bunyan," a label first bestowed in derision by those to whom nonconformists were targets for scorn, but accepted by those of the faith as a deserved honor. Although in the beginning it may have had reference to his supervision of outlying parishes associated with the Bedford church, strictly it had no authorized meaning. The label stuck, however, and in time lost some of the ridicule intended by his detractors.

The pages of the Bedford Church Book for these years attest the increasing labors of the pastorate, in sequel to the growth persecution itself had fostered. No figures are recorded for the membership, but if it be estimated from the one in ten nonconformists in Bedford town and one in twelve for the county, or four times what it had been in 1660,[1] Josias Ruffhead's barn must have been exceedingly well filled on Sunday mornings. The recall of licenses for nonconforming preachers in 1675 had ended nothing but the public expression of their purpose, which had been strengthened in proportion as it had been forced to operate underground. More severe measures were still to come, but they too would be ineffectual. There was no stopping the tide. The membership of the associated congregations in outlying villages was also growing past the point where one man could exercise the supervision required. Bunyan faced days and nights on horseback, and often the preaching of sermons on weekdays, as well as in his own Bedford pulpit on Sunday.

Of his personal life, except for his journeys, his sermons, his publications, in this period we know very little. For this important decade, 1677 forward, as indeed for his whole life, his best biography, and for long stretches his only record, is in his own printed words. He continued to live in the St. Cuthbert Street cottage, and to enjoy the affection and respect of his parish flock; possibly also an added respect from his fellow townsmen, but that is a conjecture only. It was still not a time of safety for Dissenters, and despite his legal freedom he still lived in danger of losing it any day.

As a preacher during these years, he was at the peak of his popular success. Charles Doe, the combmaker of Southwark, who spoke as an eyewitness, wrote under his title *The Struggler*, after Bunyan's death, that when he preached in London,

> "If there were but one day's notice given, there would be more people come together to hear him preach, than the Meeting-house would hold."

He had seen as many as twelve hundred at a seven o'clock morning lecture in wintertime. He also computed that "about three thousand came to hear him one Lord's Day at London at a Towne-end meetinghouse, so that more than half were fain to go back again for want of room, and then himself was fain, at a back door, to be pulled almost over people to get upstairs to his Pulpit."

> "What hath the devil or his agents gotten by putting our great gospel-minister Bunyan in prison?"

he asked.[2] The answer is that prison had helped his preaching fame. Also, the publication of *Pilgrim's Progress* in 1678 had helped it still more, and would continue to do so increasingly during all the years he had yet to live. He had had friends in London during the early preaching years, when his activities were chiefly in Bedfordshire, but during the last decade of his life the number had increased markedly, and he seems to have been well enough known, at least in nonconformist circles, to deserve to be called to some degree popular.

Occasionally he was invited to preach at Pinner's Hall, leading meeting place for London Dissenters. In 1682 a group of London merchants had set up a Tuesday lecture here, naming six ministers to preach on these weekly occasions to a mixed assembly of various sects. Richard Baxter, one of the original six, withdrew after preaching four times, because of objections to what he had said.

> "All the City did ring of their back-bitings and false accusations,"

he wrote. In fact, so persistently did it ring, that he went into print against their accusations. But Baxter was looking far ahead in his margins of difference with certain nonconformist doctrines, which it was still too early to announce publicly. Bunyan was not, and there is no record of opposition to his opinions from nonconforming hearers. Other London congregations received him eagerly also, among them the members of what became the Zoar Chapel group, in Gravel Lane, Southwark. Their meetinghouse was not yet built, but Bunyan was well known in this neighborhood, having often preached in an alley near the site of the chapel.

Except for the treatises published during these years, there is no indication of the themes and content of the sermons he was preaching, but very probably there was a correspondence in his thought at the desk and in the pulpit. Like his earlier publications, those of the late 1670's and 1680's are expanded sermons, with a text, and all the scaffolding of reasons for the doctrine, objections to it, applications and uses. For the most part, controversy had been left behind. He was more concerned now with fundamentals, affirmations rather than quibbling on disputed points. His own conversion was no longer the main theme. He was rarely personal now. What Christian grace could do in a man's life was a frequent theme, although he still warned sinners with what he had once called "an awakening word." Hardly if ever did he let a congregation go without at some point in the sermon reminding them that every act of our life here on earth has eternal consequences. He had lived his own daily life from dawn to dusk in this assumption, and it is everywhere in his teaching.

The treatise *Saved By Grace*, published just before his second imprisonment in 1675, although longer than of sermon length, in outline and substance may have been preached almost as it appears in print. It is developed by the question-and-answer method, so frequent with him: five questions and five answers, with subdivisions within subdivisions in each section. To read this piece aloud is to gather some hints of its effectiveness, as it was heard by such an eager, crowded auditory, as Charles Doe reports for this later period of Bunyan's preaching.

The effectiveness goes deeper than voice and gesture of the vigorous, evangelistic sort. It begins, as effective speaking in any age must begin, with what already exists in the minds of the hearers. Bunyan's hearers, saints and sinners alike, brought with them a knowledge of the Bible greater than has existed since for any typical congregation in England or America, and also a greater respect for, and even awe of it, as ultimate authority. Nearly every verse that the preacher quoted could have been repeated with him by a goodly number of the congregation, and in their thought the word was final. Until the last decade of the century, the average man and woman still held to a few unassailable certainties: the existence of God, a hereafter determined by the life lived on earth, a heaven of bliss, a hell of torture, a means of salvation, and a fixed scheme by which it might be attained. The preacher need not waste a minute trying to prove these assumptions. He merely reminded those before him of what they already knew and doubted not a hair. The sermon message began at this point.

Bunyan's individual way of making his preachment effective, as nearly as can be judged from the printed page, had not changed greatly since his earlier days in the pulpit. He knew how to give the impression that the whole sermon was a conversation with each hearer individually. In his persistent questioning, he uses the second person and seldom implies the plural. *You* is always one hearer only. In the answer which the question demanded, each man could hear himself replying. In this sermon treatise, the reasons for a sinner's despair take in everyone, in turn:

My sins are of the worst sort.
I have a stout and rebellious heart, a heart that is far from good.
I am as blind as a beetle; I cannot understand any thing of the gospel.
I cannot believe in Christ for mercy.
I cannot pray to God for mercy.
I cannot repent.[3]

For each of these typical responses, there was an appropriate quota of Scripture promises, each one striking home with the finality of a divine decree.

His illustrative material was likewise familiar to those before him. Let us come down to martyrs, he said, and the pew knew them all, as pews today would not. The story of stonings, burnings, last words, came with the names, and many could call up the pictures accompanying them in Foxe's *Actes and Monuments:* Stephen, Ignatius, Romanus, Menas, Athanasius, Constantine, Marcus, Eulaliah, Agnes, Julietta, all are called to witness the faith of a saint. Bunyan knew them better than his audience, for he had lived with them, page by page, in his prison chamber, but all were familiar enough to a Pinner's Hall audience for the names alone to summon the heroic tale.

Bunyan continually interrupts himself by such passages as

"O sinner! What sayest thou? How dost thou like being saved? Doth not thy mouth water? Doth not thy heart twitter at being saved? Why, come then . . ." [4]

Delivered with spirit, with warmth, to those who did not doubt the truth of the doctrine, and by a preacher who preached what he felt, as he put it, what he "smartingly" did feel, such directness would be effective in the 1680's and on occasion might be powerful.

Such a barrage of quoted Scripture, such a recall of long-past martyrdoms, would leave a modern audience entirely cold, and no knowing evangelist would dare it. There would be too faint an echo of the familiar in any of it, and no lure toward the kind of a hereafter it promised, also less sense of the inexorable certainty of its truth. Bunyan spoke as any preacher must speak in any age, as a man of his own day, sharing the convictions of his hearers, and basing his appeal on a shared sense of their certainty. Bunyan's sermons were not made of novelty, but of accepted doctrine, and he could make it as powerful as though it were being heard for the first time. It was his genius, and nothing less than genius, to be able to communicate with those to whom he spoke. Of all the gifts the angel who presided at his birth had granted, this ability to communicate was the best gift of all for one who would stand before men. His pulpit fame during the last decade of his life proved not only that he possessed it in generous measure but that he had developed it to a point of high effectiveness. It is a gift not easily analyzable, and one that differs with each person who possesses it.

Stated differently, it is a way of meeting people where they live.

With Bunyan, it had something to do with simplicity of speech, something with homely figures drawn from daily life:

> "Discouraging thoughts are like cold weather, they benumb the senses, and make us go ungainly about our business."
> "Poor coming soul, thou art like the man who would ride full gallop, whose horse will hardly trot."
> "The temporizing Latitudinarian [they knew the word] his Religion is like the Times, turning this way and that way, like the cock on the steeple."
> "A *desire* will take a man on his back, and carry him away to God, if ten Thousand Men stand by and oppose it, . . . without the desire, all is like rain upon Stones, or favours bestowed on a dead dog."

Figurative language was a natural idiom of speech for him. Pictures came without summons, and he thought in metaphor.

Even when the blackness of sin or the certainty of eternal doom was his theme, he still kept the conversational tone, persuading rather than frightening his hearers. There is no counterpart in his pages of the violent denunciations and threatenings which identify Savonarola in characteristic voice:

> "I am the hailstorm that will break the heads of those who do not take shelter."

Bunyan did not indulge in such thunders. He preached the fires of hell just as he preached the bliss of heaven. Both were incontrovertible certainties, and to read the corresponding passages aloud calls for no more raising of the voice in one than in the other. The power back of his words was the authority he could invoke for their utter truth. It was the authority of God Himself, and also his own unshakable conviction. He was trying to convince those before him, and he spoke to their minds, not to their emotions. In response they did not faint, or cling to the pillars of the building in a frenzy of terror. They went home, looked in their Bibles for the proofs he had assembled, and came back for more of such teaching.

John Bunyan

When Charles Doe spoke of his readiness of speech and "Gift of Utterance" such as confounded the "Wisdom of his Adversaries" that heard him or heard of him, he may have been recognizing what one senses on the printed page, perhaps expressed as a fullness and richness back of what he said, as though he were tapping resources plentiful beyond the moment's need. It was a richness that had come at a price, not only of thought and study, but also of depth in his own private religious experience.

Making due allowance for the fact that current verdicts of his successful preaching, during this last decade of his life particularly, were the verdicts of friends and brother ministers who wrote prefatory notices to his books, it seems fair to accept their praise at almost its face value. It was the verdict of a time, for preaching which belongs to that time, not to ours. His sermon thought does not possess contemporaneity for later times. Such is more likely to be the word of those skeptical enough to look beyond their own day and its beliefs. Bunyan did not pose the unanswered questions that tease the mind afresh from one generation to the next. He preached approved doctrine in its contemporary expression. His *Grace Abounding* tells more about personal religious experience in its unchanging nature over the centuries than any sermon he ever preached, and the *Pilgrim's Progress* does what no sermon could very well do toward making religion a way of life. Its power is the power of a hundred sermons. At the same time the current impact of his sermon thought should not be undervalued. There was life in it for those who heard, and there is still life in it for those who read it imaginatively.

One should ponder it, as though listening from a pew in Pinner's Hall in the tenseness of the 1680's when at any minute soldiers might "rush in upon" the preacher at the desk, as they did one morning when Francis Bampfield was preaching in 1680. He was "dragged away" at the point of rusty halberds, served with a warrant of arrest, and carried before the mayor. Released after examination, he was "dragged away" again, when he came back to finish the sermon. "Multitudes were in the streets," he wrote. A few days later, he tried again, with the same result. "I carried my Bible openly in my hand through the street," he wrote. "Great flockings after us." Im-

Bishop Bunyan

prisoned, he died in Newgate two years later.[5] Thomas Jolly, pastor
of Altham Chapel, once more took to his trick pulpit in his own
house, when secret meetings elsewhere became too dangerous. A
divided door at the bottom of the stairway, from which the upper
part, which was on hinges, fell away to make a platform, provided
a way to escape detection. When the alarm was given by a guard
stationed outside, a string was pulled, the pulpit disappeared, the
divided door came together, and the preacher escaped upstairs. The
entries Thomas Jolly was making in his *Notebook* in the 1680's
would have fitted the 1660's quite as well, and yet he kept on
preaching, sometimes, as he wrote, ten times in eight days, "besett
by the constable" at break of day, not being able to find bondsmen
for sureties, and thanking God for what safety still permitted preaching.

"Marvellous how God prevented drowsiness and weariness in
secret meetings in the dead of the night," [6]

he wrote. These men were nearer a clear day of freedom than they
might have guessed, but in the mid-eighties it hardly seemed so.

Early in the decade, after King Charles II had dissolved six Par-
liaments and had begun to rule without check, he attempted to win
the favor of the increasing number of nonconformists by blaming
Parliament for the previous persecutions. Bunyan was not deceived
by this propaganda, and in his *Holy War*, under the devices of
Diabolus, he veiled very thinly the casting out of Robert Audley,
Recorder of the Bedford Corporation, the recall of the Town
Charter, the execution of beloved Lord Russell, and the reorganiza-
tion of the Corporation [7] in line with the king's wish. Six years
later, when King James offered him a post in the reorganized Corporation, through his agent Lord Aylesbury, he ignored the bid.
He may have been so advised by members of his congregation,
several of whom he apparently suggested for similar posts at the
time, or he may only, as was in line with his singleness of pastoral
effort, have wanted to be free of civil responsibility. He may also
have been shrewdly aware that by accepting the post he might be
tricked. He would not be caught. Some recognition of his promi-

167

nence as a nonconforming preacher is suggested by the overtures made to him by Lord Aylesbury.

In 1685 the brief and tragic affair known as Monmouth's rebellion, and the Reign of Terror for Dissenters which followed, once more threatened the freedom of all who did not wear the cloth. In anticipation of another prison sentence, Bunyan at this time made over the St. Cuthbert Street cottage and all his personal property to his "well-beloved wife Elizabeth," who in the event of imprisonment for him would have been left destitute. His property would have been seized. Since he escaped a third imprisonment, the Deed of Gift was never produced. At the time of his death in 1688, Elizabeth apparently did not know of its hiding place, for his estate was administered in the Archdeacon's Court, as that of one who had died intestate. The Deed of Gift, hidden in the wall of the St. Cuthbert Street cottage, was found two centuries later, when the cottage was demolished in 1838.[8] The interest of this record, still bearing some of the wax which held the two-penny silver piece to it, is his designation of himself as "John Bunyan Brazier," suggesting, possibly, that he still occasionally served his Bedford neighbors at his trade, or, as is more likely, that with complete naturalness he thought of himself as belonging where his birth had placed him, not on the higher rung where preaching success and authorship had put him through many years.

His power as a preacher, while he went to and fro as "Bishop Bunyan," owed something, perhaps a great deal, to the fact that he considered himself on the same level as those whom his preaching attracted. As a tradesman, a worker with his hands by the day, sharing the lives of his congregation, he possessed something which the established clergyman missed, and there was power in it. By this shared life on their level, he also lost something which set-apartness conferred, but the gain outweighed the loss. He not only could speak to them in their own language, but he knew the need of those who listened, for he too shared it.

Chapter Eleven

"Our Author Bunyan"

This last decade of Bunyan's life was not only the decade of his greatest triumphs in the pulpit, but it was also the period of greatest fruitfulness at his writing desk. Twenty-one separate publications appeared during this time, and at his death in 1688 he left ten more in manuscript which were published in 1692.[1] Partly in recognition of the number and frequency of these publications, but more because of the fact that *Pilgrim's Progress*, published at the beginning of this last decade, 1678, had proved "acceptable to many in this nation," "Bunyan, the famous preacher" became also "Bunyan the famed author." In contemporary thought this new designation had special reference, not to the sort of religious treatise, developed from a sermon, such as he had been writing for twenty years, but to four books which might not have been expected of a pulpit man. The first of these appeared in 1680, and was entitled *The Life and Death of Mr. Badman*.

THE LIFE AND DEATH OF MR. BADMAN

"I have put fire to the pan"

The title tells us what to expect. Also, as Bunyan states in his preface, through this tale of a wicked life, he set out to mirror for sinners, as in a glass, "the steps that take hold of Hell." In *Pilgrim's Progress* he had shown Christian's step-by-step way to Paradise; now it has come into his mind to write of the ungodly on journey from this world to hell.

"The Butt therefore, that at this time I shoot at, is wide,"

he announced, and clearly his aim was to leave nothing out, with the result that his book became almost an encyclopedia of sin, as he had observed it in village terms. His picture of evil is unrelieved. From birth to death Badman is consistently evil, lacking even in impulses toward better things. He wages no battles with his conscience, makes no decisions, but merely sins in continuing sequence, piling evil deed on evil deed, until he becomes an exhibit, hardly an individual at all. Christian, by contrast, in his waverings, his mistakes and stumblings, had been real enough to be believed. He is by turns each of ourselves. Badman is not drawn from life, but is rather a sermon illustration, or a bundle of them, and in consequence he is sometimes repetitious and tiresome. That is, to a modern reader.

To readers of 1680, however, it would have been far otherwise, particularly in Bedford and Elstow, or wherever else in the county Bunyan came and went as a preacher. This book is truly a mirror. It would have been opened in trepidation and read with excited suspense from page to page by those who feared to find themselves somewhere in it, as well they might. Badman's catalogue of evil doings has a local cast. Bunyan's prefatory remark that he had gone "as little as may be out of the road of my own observation of things" would have put readers on the alert. He makes the danger of identification even more definite:

"I think I may truly say, that to the best of my remembrance, all the things that here I discourse of, I mean as to matter of fact, have been acted upon the stage of this world, even many times before mine eyes." [2]

It was the stage of Bedfordshire in particular. Badman, we are told, had left many relatives behind him, so that there is scarcely a family or household in a town where he has not a brother, a nephew, a

friend. Sometimes, as in the case of William Swinton of Bedford,
sexton of St. Cuthbert's Church, Bunyan uses the initials W. S.
These escaped no one, but even without them Swinton would have
been identified. For a fee, he had turned informer to the authorities,
had climbed trees to watch unseen, stolen into secret wooded places,
and spied out those meetings by night during the period of forbidden conventicles.

Some of the discipline cases in the Bedford Church Book can also
be matched against Badman's excesses, and found to fit too neatly
for comfort to the accused. There was one escapade to fit John
Rush, who, "for being drunk after a very beastly and filthy manner,
that is above the ordenery rate of drunkerds," had needed three men
to carry him home from the Swan, and when they arrived, they
"could not present him as one alive to his familie he was so dead
drunke." There was one to fit Sister Landy, John Stanton, one for
the railing wife of Brother Witt, one for John Wildman, that "abom-
inable lyer and slanderer of our beloved brother Bunyan," and others
whose frailties had been written down in superlatives.[3] Badman
"swarmed with sins," and could provide example, particularly for
the impenitent ones who had been "cast out" of the fellowship.
Bunyan said he could call names if he wished, but he would not
make the offenders public for the sake of the relatives who survive.
No one in Bedford would read that sentence with long-lived relief,
however, after they had seen the initials W. S. for William Swinton.
With or without initials, Bedford was too small a theater of sin
for anonymity.

To a reader from another century, the interest of this highly
colored panorama of village evil lies less in the bald preachment
these landmarks to hell were intended to serve than in the vivid-
ness of the narrative, for there is powerful writing at times in this
book. Also, the fact that it is a narrative unified by one idea, sustained throughout, is arresting. More probably, however, interest
will lie in these pages as a chapter in Restoration social history at
the class level of the village tradesman. Unintentionally and unaware,
Bunyan has written precisely that chapter. For the twentieth century reader the interest is similar to that one may take in Thomas
Dekker's *The Bel-Man of London*, "bringing to light the most notorious villanies that are now practiced in the Kingdome." That was

in 1608; or in the sequel the following year, *Lanthorne and Candle-light*, or *The Bell-man's second Nights-walke*, "In which he brings to light, a Brood of more strange villanies than ever were till this yeare discovered." *The Seven Deadly Sinnes of London* is still another exhibit of sin according to Elizabethan patterns. As Dekker in these books conducts us through the unlighted streets and crooked alleys of his own London, the Elizabethan city reveals itself with unmistakable features of itself at a particular time and no other. The "most notorious villanies" with which he entertains us are of the hardy perennial sort, of course, changeless through the centuries, and yet as he pictures them, they take on the recognizable accent of a particular time.

Bunyan's *Badman* is not so notable a panorama as Dekker's. It lacks selectivity, and the exaggeration is too uniform. Badman's sins are all major. He needed some little sins for variety. But quite unwittingly, through his birth-to-death excesses, the picture Bunyan has drawn for him fits a Midland country town at a particular time in the seventeenth century. This is not quite the England of pre-Restoration days. It shows the more reckless, bolder corruption of the 1670's, and after the long insulation of prison walls, Bunyan felt the shock of difference from the day the prison doors had closed against him. In 1672 he walked forth into an England that to him seemed to be "shaking and tottering" by reason of the burden Mr. Badman and his friends had wickedly laid upon it. Indeed, what has made him publish this book is that "wickedness like a flood is like to drown our English world. It begins already to be above the tops of the mountains." The accent of shock is everywhere in Bunyan's account of Badman's career of wickedness. All that the preacher can do is to cry the alarm, not knowing how many the shot "will kill to Mr. Badman's course, and make alive to the Pilgrim's Progress, that is not in me to determine. . . .

> However, I have put fire to the Pan, and doubt not but the report will quickly be heard." [4]

The tale of Badman's evil awakens no suspense in its ending, for we are told at the outset that he is already dead. As the hours pass before his funeral, two lay figures, Wiseman and Attentive, sit down under a tree, and talk over his evil life. This is the same setting as Arthur Dent made popular in *The Plaine Man's Pathway*, one of the two books Bunyan had read in the dark hours of his own floundering in the Slough of Despond. He develops his thought by the same method as Dent, that of dialogue, chosen, as he says, for greater ease to himself and greater pleasure to the reader. For himself, the ease is self-evident. Question and answer ask little of the writer except clarity and directness. Bunyan is not developing a character. He is merely attaching sins to a robot, and the dialogue method permits adding details easily, in answer to the adept questionings of Attentive. Such dialogue is a short cut to the full composite of evil, which is Badman. The reader's pleasure may be flattered by the brevity of the direct answers, and also by long familiarity with the dialogue method. Even those who were not brought up on Dent's *Plaine Pathway* had listened (in books) to men talking under a tree from school-days forward.

In thus setting forth the drama of sin and punishment in personal rather than in abstract terms, Bunyan was following a fashion, rather than inventing one. For a long generation preachers had been enlivening their sermons by borrowing from Samuel Clarke's *Mirrour or Looking-Glasse Both for Saints and Sinners* or from Thomas Beard's *Theatre of God's Judgments*, the latter being a collection intended to show, as the author announces, that "God has woolen feet but iron hands." Bunyan was familiar with these collections, and in *Badman* uses seven tales from Clarke's collection, which had come out in a new and enlarged edition in 1671.[5]

Broadside imprints "adorned with lively cuts" were also making such examples of sinners current in this decade. There is an imprint of 1672 which lists forty-four examples of notorious sinners. The four cuts show among Sabbath breakers who met death because of disobedience to the fourth commandment, the profane Israelite who gathered sticks on the Sabbath and was stoned to death, several young men who played football on the ice, broke through and were drowned, and a woman and her daughter who pilled and dried flax and were burned, and also a miller. In the following year another imprint, entitled *A Timely Warning to Drunkards, or the Drunk-*

ard's Looking Glass, lists twenty-one examples of God's judgments against drunkards. Like Badman, these sinners in coming home late from the alehouse, fall off their horses. Unlike him, they usually break their necks in the fall and their story ends abruptly; Badman breaks only his leg, and lives to sin again. Another imprint (undated), entitled *A Dreadful Warning to Lewd Livers,* showed twenty visible judgments upon drunkards, eleven upon swearers, five against whoremongers and adulterers, and sixteen against profaners of the Sabbath. This broadside gives places, dates, sometimes names of offenders, and makes much of the "authentic Information" or "Approved Histories" which are its source. Bunyan was late in contributing to this sort of preachment, but familiarity with these paragons of vice had apparently not dimmed their popularity by 1680. Pulpit and press borrowed freely from Clarke's *Who's Who,* usually without acknowledgment, and also from his *Generall Martyrologie,* containing the "greatest Persecutions which have befallen the Church of Christ." He had also issued the *Lives of Ten Eminent Divines,* in 1662, and had enlarged the book to include thirty-two in 1677.

Bunyan's picture of Badman differs from the picture of sinners in the *Looking Glass* collections and the broadsides, which usually make him into a sottish wretch in the sin of his choice. Bunyan's Badman is not revolting in spite of the fact that his sins run the full gamut of the Seven Deadlies and the biblical *Thou Shalt Nots.* Bunyan still keeps him within the village shopkeeper's status, moderately prosperous, outwardly almost respectable, yet such a master of deceit as repeatedly to blindfold his neighbors to his falseness, dishonesty, and manifold evil practices by day and by night. His wickedness, black as it is, is seldom extravagantly sensational. Nevertheless, it is as nearly complete as Bunyan can make it. Badman has not a single redeeming feature.

His evil career began early. He was a "master-sinner from a child," robbing orchards, telling lies, inventing bad words, sleeping in meeting, violating the Sabbath. In fact, he was the very ringleading sinner or the master of mischief among other children. Lying was his arch sin. Under the very rod of correction by his godly parents, he would "stand to his lie as steadfastly as if it had been the biggest of truths." In swearing he was Bunyan's own rival. To

swear was as "common with him as it was to eat when he was an
hungered, or to go to bed when it was night." "He stuffed his words
full of the sin of swearing." In desperate hope for his improvement,
Badman's father put him to one of his friends as apprentice, but
"nothing took hold of his heart." He disregarded the good books in
his master's house, laughed at the good example set before him,
profited nothing at all from the good sermons to which he was
taken on Sabbath. On this path he soon fell into bad company, went
deeper into sin, and ran away from his master. So it was also with
his second master, a hard man, but Badman would not be ruled.
He joined himself with a wicked man of his own trade, and served
out his time. Set up in business by his father, he became a shopkeeper, sold poor goods for high price, "hoisted his price to match
the best"; "mingled his commodity," diluting good merchandise
with bad; used false weights, having one weight for his own buying
and another for selling. Even so, he did not prosper, and was like
to go to prison for his debts, but by marrying a rich wife under pretense of religion, he saved himself from his creditors.

The sequel to this "wonderful deceitful doings" was that, his
debts paid with her money, he "hangs his religion on the hedge,"
pulled off his vizard, and was religious no longer. When dangerous
illness came to him, and he thought his end had truly claimed him,
he once again indulged groans for his vile life, and donned religion
as before, but, recovering, he allowed atheism to triumph even more.
Repentance "passed away like a mist or a vapour." The only grain
of surprise in this monotonous recital comes at the end when Badman dies quiet as a lamb. It is almost an artistic touch. Every expec-
tation would have pointed toward violence of panic and roaring.

To Bunyan's readers, escape from a sense of monotony in the
tale might have come from the wealth of anecdote the book supplies
by way of analogue to Badman's evil doings. In between his successive sins Attentive asks leading questions which Wiseman answers by supplying anecdotes of other sinners, who in one direction
or another exceed Badman in blackness of iniquity. Some of these
anecdotes are taken from Beard or from Clarke, giving hearers the
pleasure of the familiar. Bunyan tells them better than Beard or
Clarke, but even a spirited telling or the brisk narrative of Badman
himself cannot make this story into a powerful book.

At the same time one can learn much about Bunyan from these pages. He put much of himself into this book, but it is not the Bunyan the world has remembered for three hundred years. In it he is the country preacher, catching the conscience of the country listener of his own class. The tradesman's world belonged to him. He had been born to it, and except for the prison years it was the world in which he was at home. There was much good in it, as well as mediocrity and falseness, and it is understood only as both are included.

We are still a long way from Defoe in these pages, despite what the more generous of Bunyan's critics have liked to think. In his realistic observation of low life he was creating an appetite for what someone else, not a preacher, would begin to satisfy. He had the intimate familiarity with this area of experience. He had the imagination and the knowledge of human nature as a mixture of good and evil, but in this book he was intent on showing a contrast to goodness, and he was content to let two lay figures offer incidents all in one key to show Christian's opposite.

Pilgrim's Progress did not need this contrasting picture. Had Christian's journey been all comfort and joy, victory and glory, his story too would have missed the mark. Instead Bunyan wrote it out of a deep understanding of human nature as it is, neither all one nor the other, and the truth of his Pilgrim has the very bedrock of life under it. In *Badman* he is the collector of data of one sort only, and instead of being overwhelming and powerful, the result is flat and unprofitable. Probably the best commentary on this spirited portrayal of evil is that the book has not been translated into the languages of the world and reprinted all but countless times. The country preacher, not the Dreamer, wrote it.

THE HOLY WAR

"Mansoul it was the very seat of war"

For one who thought allegorically, the battle between the body and the soul was an inevitable choice, and Bunyan could hardly

have missed it. For those more nearly in touch with their own day
in 1682, the vogue of allegory was fast passing. Men's thought was
turning into new directions, and as the spirit of scientific inquiry
gave fresh importance to fact as fact, the duality of meaning lost
its hold on the imagination. It was enough to probe into the nature
of the thing itself, and ignore its shadowed significance. The swan
on still St. Mary's lake, no longer floated double, swan and shadow.
For a new and more realistic generation, the swan alone was sufficient. But not for John Bunyan.

In his own Preface to the Reader of this book, he pays passing
reference to contemporary interest in the heavenly bodies, and declares his own interest to be elsewhere:

> "Count me not then with them that to amaze
> The people, set them on the stars to gaze,
> Insinuating with much confidence,
> That each of them is now the residence
> Of some brave Creatures; yea, a world they will
> Have in each star, . . ."

Some forty years earlier Bishop John Wilkins had set all England
gazing at moon and stars, particularly the moon, reminding them
that both ancients and moderns have thought there might be a
world there, a world of earth, water, mountains, valleys. Our posterity, if not ourselves, Wilkins had said, might find out a convey-
ance to this world, and if so, the perfecting of such an invention
will surely make a man famous and also the age wherein he lives.
" 'Tis not impossible," he dared to think, that man might apply
wings to his body, "As Angels are pictured," or teach great birds,
such as Marco Polo wrote of, to carry him thither. Better still, it
might be possible, "to make a flying Chariot, In which a man may
sit, and give such a motion unto it, as shall convey him through
the aire." It might even "bee made large enough to carry divers men
at the same time, together with food for their viaticum, and commodities for traffique." [6]

To all such probabilities Bunyan speaks a quick dismissal; they

are alien to all reason. He promises instead no such filmy speculations or vain stories, but what is here in view,

"Of mine own knowledge, I dare say is true."

Hearken to the tale of Mansoul.

The story begins much in the manner of the current Utopias, as
the traveler-storyteller, in wandering through many regions and
countries, comes upon the famous continent of Universe, a gallant
country, in which lieth a fair and delicate town called Mansoul. It
is the "top-piece" of the Almighty Shaddai, built for his own delight.
In its center is a stately palace, called Heart, which he has given
into the keeping of the men of the town.

We soon know that this is no Utopia to which we have come.
Though the town is invincible for situation, set between two worlds,
and impregnable as to its walls, there are five gates, admitting those
to whom the townsmen give consent: Eye-Gate, Ear-Gate, Mouth-
Gate, Nose-Gate, Feel-Gate. Outside, an enemy, Diabolus, awaits
his chance to enter. Once high exalted in Shaddai's kingdom, but
now cast out for treason to Shaddai's son, he plots in revenge to
secure Mansoul for himself. He calls a council of other fallen angels,
and plans are made. There is no siege. The citizens of Mansoul are
led to believe themselves in blind bondage to Shaddai, and the town
is taken thus subtly by deceit. The two incorruptible leaders, Captain
Resistance and Lord Innocent, are slain. The citizens willingly yield
obedience to Diabolus, and become his vassals. He quickly New-
models the town, installs his own officers, and demands an oath of
allegiance from all the townsmen.

The title, *The Holy War*, concerns the main action of the story,
which is the counterbesieging of the town by Emmanuel, son of
Shaddai, and his eventual victory. To the recounting of this siege,
Bunyan brings all his powers. Shaddai's "stout and rough-hewn
men" advance to the gates: Captain Boanerges, bearing the black
colors, ten thousand men at his feet, his ensign Mr. Thunder and
his escutcheon three burning thunderbolts; Captain Conviction,
bearing the pale colors, ten thousand men at his feet, his escutcheon
the Book of the Law from which issued a flame of fire; Captain

Judgment of the red colors, ten thousand men at his feet, his ensign Mr. Terror and the escutcheon a burning fiery furnace; Captain Execution, also bearing the red colors, his ensign Mr. Justice, his escutcheon a fruitless tree with an ax at the root.

The summoning of the townsmen, the speeches of the captains, the refusal of the townsmen to all entreaties, and then the tumult and confusion of the battle are detailed with spirit and compelling interest, in spite of the familiar outline and the predestined victory. After the town's rebellion against Diabolus and the sending to Shaddai of a petition for pardon and mercy, the great moment of Emmanuel's triumphant entry into the surrendered town is Bunyan at his best. The Prince came clad in golden armor, riding in his royal chariot, the trumpets sounding, the colors waving, the ten thousands at his feet. It was a magnificent sight. The elders of Mansoul danced before him. The casements, windows, balconies, roofs of the houses, were crowded with those who came to see how the town would be filled with good. Once again Mansoul was New-modeled; all were in a glorious state, and their cup did indeed run over.

The story should end here, but it does not. Diabolus still lived, and he was powerful. When he heard that those still loyal to him were to be tried, imprisoned, and perhaps put to death,

"He snuffed up the wind like a dragon, and made the sky to look dark with his roaring."

His wiles were many and various. Once more he "sugared his lips" and deceived the townsmen. It was not so easy as before, but Carnal Security was full of devices, and Unbelief was a "nimble jack." An army of Doubters was raised and the town was again corrupted, but not entirely. The loyal ones sent petitions to Shaddai. Diabolus raised an army of Bloodmen, but they were routed. After many petitions and much remorse, Mansoul again won the forgiveness of Shaddai. Emmanuel came again, but not to stay. He enjoined the townsmen to watch, fight, pray, make war against their enemies, and hold fast until he came again.

No mere summary of the action, no matter how detailed, can give a fair idea of the merits of this book, often confusing in its

richness and intricacy of texture. Bunyan had given more than two
years to the writing of it; at least he had published nothing else
since 1680. It is the most ambitious of all his books and the most
elaborate. In it he tells once more the great story of his conversion,
with his long struggle toward the light, only this time under the
figure of military movements, sieges, costly battles, minor skir-
mishes, retreats, gains, and eventual victory, first on one side and then
on the other. His own reminiscences of soldier days are here; Cal-
vinistic theology as he preached it, is here, in its whole scheme of
man's redemption. So also are stretches of English history, and
local incidents of Bedford town affairs, more recognizably detailed
than in anything else he ever wrote. The millennial hopes of his own
day are here, often lifting the story to poetry.

But for all its richness of texture, its dignity and depth of significance, *The Holy War* is not a great book. It topples over by the
sheer weight of what the story is asked to carry. The web is too
close woven, the pattern too intricate, the multiplicity of detail too
abundant. On many pages it is Bunyan at his best, but its excellence
is obscured by the elaborateness of design, the crossing and re-
crossing of the various themes. The high pitch of excitement is
never relaxed, creating something of a strain on the reader. By
contrast, the steadfast purpose behind Christian's journey, no matter
how many wrong turnings he made, or how long the sermon inter-
ludes, gave a singleness to the story to which Bunyan's genius responded. There was a natural flow to it, which one misses in this
complicated action in which the story does not seem to be telling
itself. Allegories, and also books that are not allegories, have a right
to various layers of meaning, of course, and in this richness may be
their greatness, but in this book the layers are all on the same level,
not one below the other, and the richness is sometimes confusing.

The wealth of these pages, however, illuminates Bunyan's own
personal story in ways not found elsewhere in his work. Most literally, there are reminders of his soldier days in the garrison of Newport Pagnell. He speaks with the confidence of firsthand knowledge
when he describes a stronghold besieged, soldiers under attack, in
defeat, in victory, wounded, fearful. In the New-modeling of Mansoul, first by Diabolus, and then by Emmanuel, when he wins it

back again, there are details of Cromwell's organization of the Parliamentary army. The oft-quoted passage describing the exhibition commanded by the Prince, when among other "outward ceremonies of his joy" he showed Mansoul some military feats, is "marvellous taking" to any soldiers among the readers, as it was to the citizens of Mansoul who looked on from windows, balconies, and rooftops:

> "They marched, they counter-marched, they opened to the right and left, they divided, and subdivided, they closed, they wheeled, made good their front and rear with their right and left wings, and twenty things more, with that aptness, and then were all as they were again, that they took, yea ravished the hearts that were in Mansoul to behold it. But add to this, the handling of their arms, the managing of their weapons of war, were marvellous taking to Mansoul and me." [7]

The passage carries with it suggestions of more than a remembered picture, rather of remembered movements from Bunyan's own drilling days. He is back in the ranks and feels himself marching and countermarching. His muscles respond to the orders, as he wheels, opens, closes, handles the pike and stave.

The eloquence of the many speeches is not that of sermons. It is the rhetoric of partisan speeches. Bunyan had heard them: the Recorder's loud words, "as if they were loud claps of thunder," Lord Will-be-Will's "big and ruffling words" to the trumpeter of Captain Boanerges, Diabolus in his speech to the town, setting the alternatives before them, and sometimes speaking in epigram,

> "Liberty you have, if you know how to use it,"

the speech of Apollyon, President of the Council, of Beelzebub who opposes, and of Lucifer, who seconds him and spoke "the very master-piece of hell." There are echoes in these last speeches of Milton's Council in hell, which Bunyan may possibly have seen, although other models were numerous.[8]

Emmanuel's captains have in spirit and sometimes in appearance stepped out of the Apocalypse rather than out of Cromwell's army:

Captain Credence in the red colors, Captain Goodhope in the blue, Captain Charity in the green, Captain Innocent in the white, and Captain Patience in the black, with three arrows through the golden heart for his escutcheon. Newport Pagnell reality is so deeply overlaid with scriptural pageantry that at times the impression is as much Old Testament and New Jerusalem as it is Cromwellian New Model. The blend is appropriate to Bunyan's purpose, and in separate incidents sometimes powerful. The approach to garrison reality in the management of so vast a theme, however, particularly in the earthiness, the humor, the colloquialism of the human exchanges, is out of line with the loftiness of the subject. The recalled life of a "centinel" in the ranks, the village and the garrison setting, tell much of remembered youth and also the current Bedfordshire turmoil, but much of this is hardly appropriate for a subject of epic dignity, with the Son of God as protagonist.

One of the most persistent details in Bunyan's own reminiscence, and also one suitable to epic story is that of sound: the battering rams against the walls, the stones "whizzing by mine ears," the captains shouting orders, the trumpet peal above all, and in moments of victory, always the ringing of bells. When the captains heard that Shaddai was sending his Son, they "gave a shout that made the earth rent at the sound thereof." "Yea, the Mountains did answer again by Echo, and Diabolus himself did totter and shake." It is made even better, when Bunyan writes without a word of description, "You cannot think unless you had been there, as I was, what a shout there was."

Once he leaves the literal warfare, with its details of movement, color, sound, the going is harder. For the retelling of his own religious experience the warfare analogy serves him well in the more intense struggles, just as it served the medieval allegorist, but in the long periods of doubt and dumb despair, martial imagery is hardly appropriate. Dialogue might have served him better, as in the long (too long) example of Christian and Hopeful, as they walk through the Enchanted Ground. One of the most memorable versions of the battle of the spirit from medieval times is the *Debate of the Body and the Soul*,[9] when in utter silence, the silence of death itself, the soul pauses for a moment just as it leaves the body and accuses it of having been so poor a place to dwell. Why did you not make it a better place? the Body replies, and as the debate goes on, all of life is recalled, and the hereafter summoned. To read this poem, slowly, quietly, as it requires, is an unforgettable experience, perhaps in proof that inner states of mind can be better represented by voice than by the clash of arms, whether at the *Castle of Perseverance* or at Newport Pagnell.

But so to say is not to miss the glories of this book. Bunyan's vivacity of imagination is tireless. He enjoyed writing this tale; the evidence is on every page. Perhaps he tried too hard; he included too much; in his own experience too many sermons were behind him.

PILGRIM'S PROGRESS Part II

"I slept and dreamed again"

Many years and "the multiplicity of business," preventing him from his "wonted travels," would make this second dream very different from the first. This time apparently no crowding ideas, coming uninvited and insistent, to interrupt another kind of writing, perhaps not such eager setting pen to paper "with delight," as when the pilgrim journey first took possession of his thought. Other compulsions stirred him now, among them a reading public clamoring for more and yet more of the pilgrim story, and other men assuming to dream it for him, a threat that had already become fact in other Part II's from other pens. There would be more of them.[10]

Most insistent of all, however, his own compelling necessity for completeness turned his thought back to Christian's wife and sons who remained in the City of Destruction. They too must be "saved" and on their way to the Celestial City. Not the head of the house only, but the whole family, must be gathered into the church body, for Bunyan is the pastor now, not the individual Christian, setting out alone. After years as pastor of the Bedford fellowship, he now sees the journey to heaven as a different path for each traveler. Not every pilgrim, like himself and Christian, need flounder so desperately in the Slough of Despond, carry so heavy a burden of sin, or find the Hill Difficulty such hard going. That "God breaketh not all hearts alike" would be clear to any pastor after years of counseling with beginners.

In *Mr. Badman* he had painted a wicked man on journey in the opposite direction, and had the satisfaction of completing his idea by what contrast could suggest. In Part II of *Pilgrim's Progress* he approached completeness by sending women and children on the journey to Paradise, and with pastoral gentleness accommodating its rigors to their frailer strength and greater need for guidance and support. Such a story will perforce lack heroic overtones but it need not lack truth according to life.

From the day Christiana, together with Mercy, who "has fallen in love with her own salvation," and her own four sons set forth "on a sunshiny morning," they have "the weather very comfortable to them." Along the way inns and great houses for rest and shelter provide protection, food, entertainment, gifts at departure. They are expected guests, remaining for long periods. Whenever danger, discouragement, bewilderment come, there is always Mr. Greatheart, a doughty soldier with his sword, and more pastor than soldier, to guide and cheer them. He will deal with the footpads, slay Giant Maul and Bloody Man, lend a hand over rough ways, admonish, comfort, instruct them. There will be no loneliness in this journey, for they are traveling in a company. This is a Christian fellowship, not the solitary journey of one man, staggering under a burden too heavy to be borne, sometimes lost, sometimes wounded in combat, sometimes locked in a dungeon. Instead, it is a smiling journey, as at the Interpreter's House when

"one smiled, and another smiled, and they all smiled, for joy that Christiana had become a pilgrim."

Not only at this comfortable way station, but all the way it is a friendly passage. There are such in life, Bunyan had discovered, as he did not know, when he dreamed of Christian's setting forth.

Christiana is not a dream woman. She is a believable wife, tardily awake to an understanding of her husband's quest, and on second thought, impelled to follow him, partly for love, and also because, after "guilt took hold of her mind," she is earnestly desirous of grace for herself. She has been a dutiful mother, concerned to train up her sons in the way they should go. Through their catechism answers, correct to the last syllable, and their own wise questionings, we catch a glimpse inside a Puritan home. It might have been Bunyan's own.

"Good boy, Joseph," says Prudence, "thy mother has taught thee well," and she had.

A considerable part of the reader's pleasure in her milder adventures comes in the familiarity with the country through which she passes. We have been here before, and as is often true of a second visit to difficult terrain, the hills are never so steep, the path not quite so rough or the waters so deep as when we did not know how steep, or rough, or deep they would be. The recognition is pleasant, and minor differences enhance the pleasure. In the arbor where Christian lost his roll, Christiana leaves her bottle of spirits behind. "I think this is a losing place," says Mercy. The Valley of Humiliation is beautiful with lilies; it is "a fat land," and "as fruitful a place as any crow flies over." The Lord Himself formerly had his country home here, we are told. He chose well, for it is a spot free from noise and the "hurryings of this life." Mercy finds that it suits with her spirit to be "where there is no rattling with coaches, nor rumbling with wheels."

At the Interpreter's House we see what Christian saw, the man in the cage, the man that cut his way through his enemies, and "the picture of the biggest of them all." We also see new exhibits. At the moment Christiana enters, she sees the angels ascending on Jacob's ladder. A moment later and she would have missed them. She sees the golden anchor, the sheep that took her death patiently, the great spider on the wall. It is hardly a scriptural spider, but Christiana recognizes the significance. We shall see this spider again in the *Country Rhimes* and also the hen with the brooding note. Most significant of all, she sees the man with the muckrake in his hand. He could look no way but downward, as he "raked to himself the straws, the small sticks, and the dust of the floor." Over his head was a celestial crown, which he saw not. The hint of such a man had stayed in Bunyan's thought since the day he read Arthur Dent's *The Plaine Man's Pathway* in the Elstow cottage, but it is Bunyan, not Dent, who made this figure memorable even down to the twentieth century. As a concession to sectarian thought in this later decade, this notable stopping place affords a ceremonial bath (of course baptism) as further preparation for their journey.

As they continue on their way, it is Christiana's pleasure to discover that all the country "rings of Christian." In lieu of direct combat for herself, everywhere she meets reports of her husband's brave encounters, his dire sufferings, hard-fought victory over temptations, giants, or whatever overtook him of discouragement or disaster. She discovers monuments left to him, memories, and just beyond Forgetful Green where he vanquished Apollyon, she sees his blood upon the stones, and finds some of the shivers of Apollyon's darts. Something of richness is imparted to this gentler journey by these echoes of what he endured. In the Valley of the Shadow, which has only hints of the dangers he met, she exclaims:

"Now I see what my poor husband went through. Poor man! he went here all alone in the night. . . . To be here is a fearful thing."

As befits Christiana's easier way, Bunyan dares a lightness of touch which was suitably more sparingly used in Christian's harassing adventures. This note is struck at the very beginning, in the gossipy household exchange of Mrs. Timorous, Mrs. Light-mind, Mrs. Bat's Eyes, Mrs. Inconsiderate, Mrs. Know-Nothing. With Bunyan's genius for coloring the least important remark with some tint of the speaker's personality, each one introduces herself in her true character. Said Mrs. Timorous,

"While we are out of danger, we are out; but when we are in, we are in."

Said Mrs. Bat's Eyes,

"Oh, this blind and foolish woman."

Said Mrs. Inconsiderate,

"A good riddance, for my part, I say of her."

Such talk is all too deep for Mrs. Light-Mind, who changes the subject with report of yesterday at Madam Wanton's where they were all "as merry as the maids."

The light touch comes admirably in the mention of the "young woman whose name was Dull"; she speaks not at all, but lives unfadingly in her name alone. It is in every line of Mr. Brisk's courtship of Mercy, and his quick departure after she cooled his courage by telling him she sewed for the poor, not for domestic prosperity. Bunyan once insisted that he was shy with women, and he probably was, but he had listened to them well enough to put a very feminine remark in Mercy's mouth, when as she reminisced about her former suitors, she remarked that though they "did not like my conditions, never did any of them find fault with my person."

One of Bunyan's best creations, also in a few words, is Madam Bubble:

"Did she not speak very smoothly and give you a smile at the end of a sentence?
"Doth she not wear a great purse by her side, and is not her hand often in it, fingering her money, as if that was her heart's delight?"

There is a quality about such characterization which reminds one of lines of Dickens, such as "In came Mrs. Fezziwig, one vast substantial smile." Bunyan could do it too, and in a single detail. He had a cartoonist's eyes for the choice of a single feature: a high forehead, a double row of teeth, a lock of hair, busy eyebrows, a slightly too firm chin.

In this comfortable journey there is feasting, dancing, guessing riddles, and on all occasions music.

"Wonderful," says Mercy, who often acts as a chorus. "Music in the house, music in the heart, and music in heaven for joy that we are here."

John Bunyan

It would be difficult to find anything Bunyan ever wrote that did not somewhere make a place for music. In this journey minstrels play at supper. Prudence plays on the virginals, Christiana on the viol. As the pilgrims cross the river, there is music of trumpeters, pipers, singers, and players on stringed instruments. As Christiana crosses over, Mr. Greatheart and Mr. Valiant-for-Truth play on the well-tuned cymbal and harp for joy.

The continuation of a successful story, particularly after the writer has lived years in between the successive parts, is always a risk. For this and other reasons, the continuing of this pilgrim tale lacks the compelling interest, the first freshness, the richness of the unspoken, the inevitability of idea and symbolic action of Part I. This is not a universal myth. It is a story about real people. Instead of the magic a dream quality gave to Christian's adventures, there is maturity of thought, a widened human sympathy, a mellowness that experience has brought to the writer. There are still rich imaginative resources back of the figure of Greatheart, agile in mind as well as with his sword; also back of Mr. Honest, the old pilgrim found sleeping by the wayside. "Not Honesty in the abstract, but Honest is my name." There is a difference that grows wider as one ponders it. Truly he had "taken notice of many things," and learned what he knows through many "notable rubs." There is discernment and imagination back of Mr. Standfast, a "right good pilgrim," who "is as his name is," and discernment and human sympathy back of Mr. Feeble-Mind, from the town of Uncertain. By one near miracle after another, he has somehow escaped fatal harm, and has learned "to run when I can, to go when I cannot run, and to creep when I cannot go." Mr. Fearing, a most troublesome pilgrim, carries his Slough of Despond around with him, even in a pleasant meadow, and yet he is "tender of sin," and has "the root of the matter in him."

Bunyan has learned through the years of his pastorate that the church militant has Ready to Halts, Mr. Fearings, and Mr. Feeble-Minds in every membership. It is at best a very uneven body of saints, and all must bear with those whose names appear often among the Discipline Cases. The spirit of Part II is that of a gathered church, in which everyone's conduct is the concern of all, and in theory at least, in a spirit of helpfulness. As the pastor of such a group, Bunyan had gone a long way in his own experience of living in an unfinished world.

Perhaps the portion of this story most readers remember longest is that in which the pilgrims cross the river at the end of the way. Bunyan seldom fitted his ideas into a patterned piece as he does here, but also seldom did he use simple words more nobly than in these few unforgettable moments of farewell. By them he lifts the pilgrimage to the level of dream. When Christiana passes over, the road is full of people to see her take her journey. The children weep, as she beckons farewell and is carried out of sight. Mr. Ready-to-Halt left his crutches behind. He would need them no longer. Mr. Feeble-Mind had nothing to leave, but he crossed safely. Mr. Despondency's daughter, Much-Afraid, went through the river singing, but no one could understand what she said. When Mr. Honest's name was called, the river was overflowing its banks, but he had spoken beforehand to Good-conscience to meet him at the brink and help him over, so that he crossed safely. Mr. Valiant-for-Truth, a younger man, and sometimes a boastful conqueror, was not boastful at the last.

"Then said he, I am going to my Father's; and though with great difficulty I have got hither, yet now I do not repent me of all the troubles I have been at to arrive where I am. My sword I give to him that shall succeed me in my pilgrimage, and my courage and skill to him that can get it. My marks and scars I carry with me, to be a witness for me that I have fought His battles who now will be my rewarder."

So he passed over, and all the trumpets sounded for him on the other side.

Considered by itself and for itself, without reference to its greater predecessor, Christiana's story shows that Bunyan, like Mr. Honest, has learned many things through the "notable rubs" life has brought him. He is not dreaming in this book. His eyes are wide open; he is looking at real people in a real world and in daylight. He has found it a better place than he once thought it could be, and human

John Bunyan

nature, even "lost," as Calvinism had taught him to regard it, was redeemable in more than the conditions for acceptance at Heaven's gate required. The man who wrote this book was himself a good neighbor, warmhearted, tolerant of minor foibles, and often amused by them. His laughter was not loud, but there was a merry ring in it.

A Book for Boys and Girls: or, Country Rhimes for Children

"Man's heart is apt in Music to delight"

Two years before his death, John Bunyan indulged his lifelong delight in music and rhyme by writing a little book of seventy-four brief poems for children. Very probably many, if not most of these, had been written earlier when his own children were young, and they may possibly have been recalled in 1686 when he had grandchildren old enough to enjoy them. The popularity of Abraham Cheare's *Looking-Glass for Children*, since the early 1670's, William Jole's *Father's Blessing*, and James Janeway's *Token* [11] would naturally have suggested to him the importance of preachments adapted to children's understanding, for in this book, as in everything else he wrote, he was the preacher. This time, like Paul, as he said, he was playing the fool that he might "mount" the thoughts of his young readers "from childish Toys

> To Heav'n, for that's prepar'd for Girls and Boys.
> . . . .
>
> I do't to show them how each Fingle-fangle,
> On which they doting are, their Souls entangle,
> As with a Web, a Trap, a Ginn, or Snare,
> And will destroy them, have they not a Care."

He could, if he pleased, he said, "use higher strains, but

> To shoot too high doth but make Children gaze."

He was aiming to catch them, and as his verses show, he knew what he was about.

For a long time ministers have been shooting thunderbolts at children, he said, "counting them not Boys but Men." That will not do. He will try another way, and play with them:

> "My very Beard I cast behind the Bush
> And like a Fool stand fingring of their Toys,
> And all to show them, they are Girls and Boys." [12]

Seventeenth century children, brought up to think that the main business of life was to get ready to die, would have turned these pages with delight. They might have skipped quickly through the rhymed Ten Commandments and the Lord's Prayer to get to the Fish in the Water, the Swallow on Wing,

> "Oh! how she flies and sings,"

the Mole in the Ground "very smooth and slick,

> She digs 'i th' dirt, but 't will not on her stick";

the Cuckoo, "Thou Booby, sayst thou nothing but Cuckoo"; the Boy running after the Butterfly, or another boy with a paper of plums,

> "Which he counts better of than Bread";

the Horse, that snorts and flounces at the sound of the drum, the Hourglass that spins "But just an Hour and then the Glass is run."

One of the very pleasing ones is of the snail:

> "She goes but softly, but she goeth sure,
> She stumbles not, as stronger Creatures do:
> Better than they which do much further go,
> She makes no noise, but stilly seizes on

> The Flow'r or Herb, appointed for her food.
> The which she quietly doth feed upon
> While others range, and gaze, and find no good.
> And though she doth but very softly go,
> However 'tis not fast, nor slow but sure;
> And certainly they that do travel so,
> The prize they aim at, they do procure."

There is no logic back of his choice of subjects, any more than in what by chance arrests the quick interest of a child. The charm is in the unexpectedness of subject and the simple literalness of the jingling couplet.

> "The Watch my Father did on me bestow,
> A golden one it is, but 'twill not go."

Also the frog:

> "The Frog by Nature is both damp and cold,
> Her Mouth is large, her Belly much will hold.
> She sits somewhat ascending, loves to be
> Croaking in Gardens, tho unpleasantly."

Her dampness and coldness all country children know, and once they have been told to look, forever after they will see her sitting aslant. It is a discovery, although not for the strange reason Bunyan assigns. She is like the large-mouthed Hypocrite, he says, who mounts his Head, as if he were above the World, and seeks in Churches for to croak although

> "He neither loveth Jesus, nor his Yoak."

Various other similitudes are likewise devious and strained, as usually they are not in most of Bunyan's other writing. He makes the Bee an emblem of sin, using her sting upon those who seek her honey:

"Now wouldst thou have the Hony and be free
From stinging; in the first place kill the Bee."

It would be a long generation yet before Isaac Watts would give children "the little busy bee" and use her industry instead of her sting in four of the best-loved stanzas of his *Divine and Moral Songs for Children.*[13]

Bunyan's spider is also surprising. She is the same one Christiana saw on the wall at the Interpreter's House, a black, ugly, crawling thing in the sinner's eyes, but she becomes a fount of wisdom, capable of teaching man the way to heaven. Children might miss this rather unexpected turn, for the sinner-spider dialogue is too long, but henceforth they would delight in looking for the spider's den, her bottomless hole, the way she hides herself when she

"for Flies do wait,"

or finds her way through chink or crevice, even to the "Throne where Princes reign," how quickly she makes a new web, when the maid sweeps one down. There is enough detail to challenge sharper peering into the darksome corners, where, Bunyan would have it, she does her evil work. It would not be evil to children.[14]

Not all the subjects are drawn from nature, but enough to justify the title *Country Rhimes.* It is largely an outdoor book:

"All sorts of Birds fly in the Firmament

.   .   .   .

Look how they tumble in the wholesome Air."

There is a cackling hen, a cloudy morning, a fair morning, a sunrise, a sunset, the rose bush, "A world of Blossoms on an Apple-tree." A fair number concern simple household things: the penny loaf, the lanthorn, candles, a pair of spectacles, a weathercock, a looking glass, a spinning top. There is the horse and his rider, "one who rides sagely on the Road,

John Bunyan

> Another rides Tantivy, or full Trot.
> One claws it up the Hill, without stop or check,
> Another down, as if he'd break his Neck.
> Now every Horse has his especial Guider,
> Then by his going you may know the Rider."

There are a few inevitably tempting subjects for the moralist: the disobedient child, the barren fig tree, the boy dull at his books, but for the most part the subjects are unexpected and unstereotyped. Also there is an understanding of the waywardness of children's interest, and a respect for their minds in the working out of a similitude, which is seldom obvious enough for quick perception. Of course, one's eternal fate is not left out.

> "Some go as if they did not greatly care,
> Whether of Heaven or Hell they shall be heir,"

but this is a minor note, surprisingly so, for one to whom the reality was ever present in mind. Children of his day could not remember a time when they did not know about heaven and hell. They knew they had a body and a soul from the time they knew anything at all.

"How do you know it?" Isaac Watts asked in the second question of his second Catechism.

> "Because I find something within me that can think and know, can wish and desire, can rejoice and be merry, which my body cannot do,"

answered every child with complete promptness.[15] Bunyan directed his verses to small readers possessing such knowledge. He also took for granted their ability to understand the allegorical way of thought which was still part of every English child's heritage. Everything still had a dual meaning, the literal and the emblematical:

> "Canst thou sit by the riverside, and not remember that as the river runneth, and doth not return, so is the life of man,"

Elizabeth Grymeston had written in her *Miscellanea* in 1604, and as near the end of the century as 1686, men, women, and children were still seeing double. Very soon they would see only what their eyes told them, but not yet the children for whom Bunyan wrote.

In 1724, thirty-six years after Bunyan's death, the title of this little volume was changed to *Divine Emblems for Children, or Temporal Things Spiritualized.* The new title hardly fits these simple verses. *Emblem,* a word made famous by Francis Quarles, places the book in a literary category to which Bunyan did not aspire. The *emblems* or "silent parables" of Quarles, and those who followed him in this popular fashion, were highly complicated allegorical pictures, accompanied by detailed comparisons in verse. Pictorial detail and verse made one intricate design, wide-ranging in idea. Picture and moral idea were equated, even though the idea be too abstract for concrete symbol to express. Apparently the more abstract the idea, the more intricate the symbol, the greater the reader's pleasure. Bunyan's knowledge of this immensely popular literary confection may have been scanty, but he could not have been unaware of it. For these simple country rhymes, he did not need a literary source. His own compelling habit of mind forced him to give concrete form to abstract preachment, as he had done in the Interpreter's House or at the top of the Delectable Mountains. His unintentional contribution to emblematic verse was to transfer it to the nursery, where it might live a little longer, for the emblem fashion was already fading in 1686.

On Bunyan's shelf of sixty books, this little volume is a pleasant note, not for any striking originality of content or skill in execution, but for something caught between the lines.

"Great things by little ones are made to shine,"

he wrote in one of the stanzas, and something about Bunyan is made to shine from these rhymes. There is a father's tenderness in them, and a gentleness of understanding. It is not a school book. He wrote it to give pleasure to little children. James Janeway's *Token for Children,* which had preceded it by some years, bears a preface signed "By one who dearly loves little children." There is no rea-

John Bunyan

son to doubt that James Janeway, a sad, much-afflicted man, meant what he wrote, and that his care for children's souls deserved to be called a loving care, but he needed to look again, to watch children at their play, and listen to their talk. His own examples of pious boys and girls would be painful indeed to contemplate, were they believable. They wept bitterly at secret prayer, prayed red-eyed, with extraordinary meltings, prayed while other children were playing on Sunday, rebuked their parents for not doing the family duty of prayer, spoke the language of Canaan, not of the playground, and walked as strangers on the earth. In appropriate sequel, invariably they died young.[16]

Bunyan's thought of children was also in the Puritan tradition, and firmly; his concern with their souls was tireless, but his temperament and his honesty of vision that went below the surface called for a different approach. He was not trying to frighten them, but as he said to "Catch" them. He could never have written in the vein of Abraham Cheare's oft-quoted quatrain:

> "Hath God such comeliness display'd
> And on me made to dwell
> 'Tis pitty, such a pretty maid
> As I should go to Hell!"

Pity indeed, even to a Calvinist, and quite unnecessary.[17]

Hints of Bunyan's own childhood are frequent in these verses, although the horrors have now faded. He is the "awakened" child who makes lamentation, but without recall of the devils at his coat:

> "I have in sin abounded,
> My heart therewith is wounded,
> With fear I am surrounded,
> My spirit is confounded.
>
> Had I in God delighted,
> And my wrong doings righted;
> I had not thus been frighted,
> Nor as I am benighted."

He is also the speaker in *Upon a Ring of Bells.* Even in the emblematical part the bells are real bells, and it is his soul that cannot "but bounce and sing":

> "O Lord! if thy poor Child might have his will
> And might his meaning freely to thee tell,
> He never of this Musick has his fill
> There's nothing to him like thy ding, dong Bell."

This is Bunyan, the boy of Elstow speaking, as he stands by the belfry door, longing to pull the rope. It is also Bunyan the grandfather, looking forward, and far sooner than he could know, to the bells of the Celestial City.

It would be a loss not to have this book.

Chapter Twelve

"All the trumpets sounded for him on the other side"

The end came suddenly and without warning. He was apparently in his usual health, and abundant in labors of preaching, writing, and administering the affairs of his ever extending parish, when in August, 1688, he was asked by a young neighbor to intercede with the lad's estranged father at Reading, and prepare the way for a reconciliation. Whatever the cause of the estrangement, it was serious enough to jeopardize the youth's inheritance, even to shut the door to his own direct appeal. Would Mr. Bunyan prepare his father's mind to receive him? Whether the young man was a member of Bunyan's church or not is not known, but even if he were not, Bunyan would not have refused the quest. He mounted his horse and was off on his mission.

Reading was a town in which he was well known from his itinerant days, when preaching at a conventicle had called for extreme secrecy. Tradition tells of one occasion, when disguised as a carter, whip in hand, he had preached here in a house from which escape was possible through a back door, and over a bridge across the Kennet River at this point. In August, 1688, disguise was no longer necessary. His mission with the estranged father successfully accomplished, he preached once more to the Reading congregation, which at that

198

time was meeting in a boathouse by the riverside. The Church Book is not extant for this date, and no record of the sermon survives, but because of the previous peril, this meeting might have been a pleasant landmark in parish history.

Leaving Reading, he continued his journey on to London, where he was expected to preach also. This was a forty-mile journey, only a little less than that from Bedford to London, a distance frequently undertaken by him on horseback. In 1688 he was enjoying the favor of London's Lord Mayor, Sir William Shorter, formerly an alderman of Cripplegate Ward, a member of the Goldsmith's Company, and an active nonconformist. "An Anabaptist," John Evelyn wrote, "a very odd, ignorant person, a mechanick, I think." [1] During his previous term as alderman, he had been removed from office by order of the king for attending a conventicle at Pinner's Hall, and he had been restored only in the preceding year, 1687, by a commission from the king himself. He had recently been knighted. On his election as Lord Mayor, a clause had been inserted in the royal patent, presumably at Shorter's request, stating that he might have whom he pleased to preach for him. Bunyan was one of those he chose, but the tradition that he had been made Shorter's chaplain is an error. This August visit might have given Bunyan one of the opportunities the royal patent provided, but that was not to be. Ten days later Sir John was thrown from his horse, as he rode away after opening the Smithfield Fair. Four days later, he died from his injuries. [2]

Bunyan's forty-mile horseback journey was made in a driving rain, but he kept on, arriving at the home of his friend John Strudwick, a grocer at the sign of the Star, on Snow Hill in St. Sepulchre's parish. He was already a sick man. Nevertheless, he preached as he had expected to do, on August 19th, at the meetinghouse of Mr. Gammon, in Boar's Head Yard, off Petticoat Lane, in Whitechapel. This was to be his last sermon. A brief summary of it is preserved, not from John Bunyan's pen, but from notes set down by a listener. His text was John 1, 13, "Which were born, not of blood, nor of the will of the flesh, nor of the will of man, but of God." [3]

No particular importance need attach to lastness, as such, and there is no reason to think this sermon deserves any special distinction, except as one example of Bunyan's later preaching thought. The summary is of interest for itself, however, as showing what one hearer remembered—enough to make two and a half pages in folio in Bunyan's printed works. It was the text and the similitudes by which his thought survived in the listener's memory that carried the message. "I have used similitudes," Bunyan once wrote on a title page, and he might have written the same statement on every one of his sixty such pages, for this was the method in which he was most fully at home.

"I will give you a clear description," he had said, "under one similitude or two," and the one he had chosen was the relationship between parents and children, first for the mother and then the father:

> "Children, it is natural for them to depend upon their father for what they want. If they want a pair of shoes, they go and tell him; if they want bread, they go and tell him; so should the children of God.
> "When the devil tempts you, run home and tell your heavenly Father. This is natural to children.
> ". . . if you would be the King's children, live like the King's children."

A preacher in any age might be discouraged to read what would probably be an oversimplified, perhaps distorted, report of what he had said, but he could learn from it, and were it still the custom, in fact, the obligation, for the pew to take pencil and paper on Sunday afternoon and invite the memory of the morning, some sermon methods might suffer change. From this summary of the Whitechapel sermon, one gathers that it was gentle in admonition, positive in tone, and with an intimacy of address, even affectionate association. In these directions it would seem to be a fair sample of his later preaching.

After his long exposure in rain and chill, to preach this sermon was a sad mistake. Two days later he became very ill, and twelve days later, on August 31st, he died at the home of his host, John Strudwick. He was within three months of his sixtieth birthday, which would have been on November 30th. He was buried on September 3rd, in the Campo Santo of the nonconformists, then called Bunhill in the Fields, now Bunhill Fields. It is assumed that the funeral sermon was preached by George Cockayne, pastor of John Strudwick. The popularity and fairly wide acquaintance among London nonconformists which Bunyan enjoyed at this date would suggest an impressive number of mourners, but no details are extant.

Bunhill Fields had been consecrated nearly a century and a half earlier as the resting place of many thousands whose bones were brought here from St. Paul's Charnel House. During the Great Plague year 1666, when the city's weekly toll reached five thousand, a countless number of bodies had night by night been thrown in the Great Plague Pit, which lies somewhere under the present forest of tombstones and monuments. The plot was not closed for burial until 1820, when it was estimated that at least a hundred and twenty thousand nameless ones lie here, their bones brought lifetimes after they had lived and died.[4] Since the plot is unconnected with any church, it seemed a fitting place for nonconformists to choose as resting place for their dead. It became an honored place, as one after another of their leaders were buried here: Vavasor Powell, John Owen, Susanna Wesley, Samuel Wesley, Thomas Goodwin, Isaac Watts, Daniel Defoe, William Blake. For their sakes, it became a honored place. Bunyan was one who in his day added to this honor.

According to tradition, he was first buried in the Baptist corner at the back of the plot, and at John Strudwick's death in 1695, according to the order he had left, Bunyan's bones were transferred to the vault upon which his effigy now rests. Eleven bodies lie in this grave. The lowermost coffin is thought to be John Strudwick's, the second, Bunyan's. The vault is one of the most impressive in Bunhill Fields, simple in outline, the stone softly weathered, and the overarching plane trees framing it in sunshine and shadow. The inscription reads,

John Bunyan
Author of
Pilgrim's Progress
Obt. 31 Aug. 1688.
Aet. 60

It was restored by public subscription under the presidency of the Right Honorable the Earl of Shaftesbury, May, 1862, restored again in Bunyan's anniversary year, 1928, and yet again after the serious damage to the face of the effigy in World War II. Within the gates, this is a quiet spot, for the plot is a large enclosure, just on the fringe of bustling London life and heavy traffic along City Road. Once in a while one sees someone, who knows the honor this spot bears, remember by lifting the hat as he passes, just as some do for John Wesley, who lies across the way.

On November 5th, a little more than three weeks before Bunyan would have been sixty years old, the fleet of the Prince of Orange entered Tor Bay, in the English Channel, and a new chapter began for those who had listened to preaching in secret places, and served prison terms when constables had found them. Bunyan had been a victim of persecution for religion's sake, not a crusader to end it. He had let others fight the cause in church and state. His part had been to keep on preaching personal religion, to hearten the Much Afraids, the Little Faiths and Ready-to-Halts, and to increase by many hundreds those who would be ready for the new freedom when it came.

In the beginning many of those most deeply concerned in this new freedom were more bewildered than jubilant. An entry in the much-suffering Thomas Jolly's *Notebook* may serve as not an isolated comment on history in the making. In November, 1688, he wrote:

"The Dutch with the English and Scottish army began to land on the 5th of the 9th m. Concerning the P. of O. and his expedition into England, it was strange to us who were altogether unacquainted with the thing and the grounds of it, yet . . . we must needs wish well to ym as protestants." [5]

The Church Book of Bunyan Meeting records the sorrow of the parish in the death of their pastor, under date of the 4th of September, the day following his funeral:

"Wednesday 4th of September was kept in prayre and humilyation for this Heavy Stroak upon us, ye Death of deare Brother

Bunyan. Appoynted also that Wednesday next be kept in praire and humiliation on the same Account." [6]

At this meeting a week later, still another day was appointed to pray for counsel in finding his successor:

"The whole Congregation fasted and prayed together."

The successor was Ebenezer Chandler, a Londoner, who served them for fifty-seven years. He was not a man of books, writing only a brief preface to the 1692 edition of Bunyan's *Works*. The Meeting Barn continued to be their place of preaching until 1707, when the building later referred to as the Old Meeting House was erected on the same site. The present building dates from 1850.

As one might expect, Bunyan's worldly resources were small. The Bedford Book of Administrations, on October 17, 1688, granted administration of his estate to Elizabeth Bunyan, his wife, and the amount named was £42 19/. According to Charles Doe's statement, which this amount bears out, Bunyan did not preach for money,

"for he hath refused a more plentiful Income to keep his station." [7]

His wife, Elizabeth, lived until early in the year 1691. Of his six children, only blind Mary had died before him. The date is not recorded. His son John, who carried on the brazier's trade, lived until 1728, and was a member of the Bedford church after 1693. His second son, Thomas, is not mentioned in the church record. Joseph belonged to St. Paul's parish, and the church records show the births of his children. There is record of the marriage of his daughter Elizabeth in 1677 and of Sarah in 1686, and for Sarah of children and grandchildren. The name of John Bunyan was still appearing during the nineteenth century, but apparently no man of books was numbered among his descendants.

After his death, as sectarian lines became more rigidly drawn, the Bedford church abandoned the liberal policy he had practiced in the receiving of members without insistence on adult baptism. Similarly the other congregations with which he had been most closely associated. Baptist historians in modern times have expressed the view that his popularity in his own day "did nothing to advance the Baptist cause," [8] a verdict that would not disturb Bunyan's sleep. The spirit of his life and the emphasis of his preaching was non-sectarian in the fairest sense of the word for his own day. A generation later he might have felt differently, but to the end of his life his service to the cause of religion was that of one whose loyalty was first of all to the Bible, not to any human institution or organization. He thought of his congregation in Josias Ruffhead's barn, or in Wainwood Dell, as though they were first-generation Christians to whom the apostles Paul, John, Peter had addressed their letters directly. He brushed away the centuries in between, as though they had not passed. In this immediacy of the Gospel message, as he conceived it, lay some of the power of his preaching. Even more, however, it stemmed from the spirit of his life, divorced as it was from movements, institutional struggles, civil, political, ecclesiastical, and sustained alone by inner certainties which were his own private possession.

Postscript

"It came from mine own heart"

That John Bunyan's originality would be questioned might have been taken for granted. Even in his own lifetime, before anything he had written had won praise as literature, he was accused of being the robber.

"Some say *The Pilgrim's Progress* is not mine,"

he reported, four years after its publication, when its continuing success seemed assured. Tinkers did not commonly write best sellers. Bunyan's name on the title page must be a lie. His answer:

> "I scorn it: John such dirt-heap never was,
> Since God converted him." [1]

"Besides, I am for drinking water out of my own cistern," [2] he had said in an earlier book, and again in the preface to the last publication of his life:

> "True, I have not for these things fished in other men's waters; my Bible and Concordance are my only library in my writings." [3]

In so far as indebtedness is a matter of deliberate use of the printed materials that came to his hand, there is no reason to doubt his truthfulness. Within narrow limits he was more of a reader than has been commonly supposed, and since books beget books, his was the unconscious indebtedness which no reader who is also a writer can quite measure or even know. In addition he was the inheritor of the rich Puritan culture to which he had been exposed, as he sat, a listener in the pew for uncounted hours, more hours perhaps than a university degree would have asked of him. There was also a certain discipline of mind which to some extent he had unconsciously acquired, as a result of the weekly exposition of doctrine in its all-embracing ramifications and yet essential unity of design. Trained men had been his teachers in all this. The limits of his culture were narrow, truly enough, but he was neither an ignorant nor an uncultivated man.

His denial of indebtedness in the line, "It came from mine own heart," however, has deeper implications than those which concern the printed page, or the Sunday sermons of his youth and early manhood. He was original in more than the literal sense of owing little to other men or to books, except the Bible. More than mere denial of our common indebtedness is needed to supply a clue toward understanding a man's life and thought which have become a creative event in history. The uniqueness of his originality lay in something positive, deep in his own individual resources, not in the lack of what a different inheritance and training might have given him.

First in importance, he was original in that he discovered what to him was truth, experimentally. It was his own; he had experienced it. He built his whole life on an intense conviction no one could prove.

"I say again, receive my Doctrine, . . .
I know it to be the way of Salvation. I have ventured my own Soul thereon with gladness, and if all the Souls in the world were mine as my own is, I would through God's Grace venture every one of them there. I have not writ at a venture, nor borrowed my Doctrine from Libraries. I depend on the sayings of no man. I found it in the Scriptures of Truth, among the true sayings of God." [4]

He was original in that a fire burned in him that kindled a fire
in other men. An impulse, compelling in its forcefulness, went forth
from him for which nothing in the facts of his life can account. He
merely told his own story, and said, it may be yours also. By making a man's salvation personal, he became a spokesman for an urge
toward individualism which was just under the surfaces of English
life on his own level, and in so doing he set free an idea and encouraged a confidence which would dignify and enrich the lives of thousands. He contributed no new theological ideas; he led no movement;
he fired men as individuals, not as followers.

He was original in that he translated a complex system of theology
into a way of life simple enough to be understood by the least taught
of those who listened. His hearers and readers were never below
their depth under his guidance. He awakened the imagination of
simple people to something beyond the daily round. Nothing was
trivial in his scale of values. Being a common man himself, he gave
expression to the common man's sense of the mystery of life, so
that those who heard recognized their own inarticulate longings.

One does not live with him very long in his many treatises and
sermons without being struck by the singleness of purpose which
runs through everything he wrote or spoke. More than that, the
subject matter is single. He was not concerned with reform. Unlike
Cromwell, also a deeply religious man, unlike Milton, he felt no
call to public service. He had few marginal interests. Eternal salvation and how to get it was his lifelong theme. Nearly everything
in his life proceeded from this one challenge. Eternal salvation, the
marvel of it, the undeservedness of it, the glory of it; it was enough.
In his unending pursuit of it for himself, and his unceasing proclamation of it, he kept company with high purposes and high thoughts
for the greater part of a lifetime. No one can do that without the
evidence being apparent, even to those who do not share these high
purposes and thoughts. They transform the man who surrenders to
them, and they transformed Bunyan.

Perhaps he did not look the part of what we call a spiritual force.
Neither did Gandhi, his exact physical opposite. Bunyan's big-boned,
sturdy frame, his ruddy complexion suggest, to judge from the
Sadler portrait, something of the artisan-tradesman class to which

he belonged. But his appearance, from what testimony remains, did not conceal the flame that burned within.

As modern religious thought has moved away, for generations now, from the beliefs which shaped his life, it is easy to be caught in things secondary and oblique to his main interest, and to undervalue it, but there is no understanding of this man and his power without treating seriously the faith by which he lived and the convictions which determined his actions. Whether one considers them of continuing validity or not is an entirely different matter.

Nor is this portrait alone enough. To give it depth and meaning, one must show a landscape beyond the window. For his day it was a landscape of confusion, of people with an uneasy conscience, searching for certainty, beset by doubt of former certainties and loss of authority. Politically and religiously, the England of Bunyan's day was tense and bewildered. He himself was strangely immune to the currents of contemporary thought surging around him. Doubt hardly touched him after his pre-conversion days. In his maturity, the age of faith was giving way to the age of reason and common sense. Calvinism had already passed its peak of acceptance. John Locke, only four years younger than Bunyan, was already winning hearers for the new thought and the new ways of thinking it. Anthony Wood commented on the different expression on English faces as early as 1660. A great gulf would presently divide the passionate world of Bunyan from the new age to follow. But he kept to the known and familiar road and did not see the point where the ways diverged.

One must look far enough beyond the window to see Bunyan in his own small country-town setting, speaking the language of his fellow artisan and shopkeeping neighbors, and sharing their lives. We must see him living in the day when there were those among Englishmen who were still looking for the philosopher's stone, when a bishop of the Established Church thought that prayer could overcome the malignity of Mars and Saturn in conjunction, when England had not yet passed a law against the burning of heretics, when touching for the king's evil was still practiced, when no child was spared the sight of death, when Puritan zeal against what was called idolatry could hire a man for a half-crown a day to break painted

windows in churches, when the common people were just learning
how to read, and when only recently "the divine art of Printing
and Gunpowder" had "putt the old Fables out of doors, and frighted
away Robin-Good-fellow and the Fayries." We must see him in an
aristocratic age which had no interest in little men, an age without
newspapers, without a world view in any direction, an age in which
everything in this world was still dwarfed by comparison with the
next.

Bunyan was a prisoner during the early days of the Royal Society,
but even if he had known what the ninety-eight original Fellows
of the Society were thinking and writing about, he lacked the curi-
osity about the world in which he lived to follow their thirst for
knowledge as to the distance of the moon from the earth, the nature
of sea salt, spiders how they spin, the sap, how it rises in the trees,
the nature of light, of the Aurora Borealis, and the first hints that
maybe the earth itself was in motion. He was after "Heavenly"
knowledge, and his eyes and ears were shut to all else. If there had
been light enough in his prison chamber for him to see the eclipse
of 1671, he would merely have taken his Bible and Concordance,
looked up the place, read of the times when the sun was darkened,
and pondered what it did signify. Such singleness of interest has its
pitiful side, perhaps, as well as its comfortable side for those who
can be content with it, but John Bunyan cut a wide swath among
those with whom he labored because of this very singleness. Sometimes one of the things that makes a man important in the history
of ideas is that what he has to say is single, not manifold, and that
this singleness can be reduced to one very simple statement.

To try to see John Bunyan in his own time and place, after many
excursions to and fro in the England of his life span, is not to meet
a giant, or even one who might seem to have significant elements
of greatness in him. He was a quite ordinary man, keen of eye, quick
of wit, obviously a man who worked with his hands, knew his Bible
and in his conversation was seldom out of it. As such a man, he is
not an enigma. There were others like him in his own stratum of
seventeenth century life. To have met and talked with him in a Bedford street or to have heard him preach in Wainwood Dell might
not have been a memorable experience.

John Bunyan

His contemporary, John Aubrey, only three years older, and living nine years longer, collected 426 Englishmen for inclusion in his *Brief Lives*. He passed Bunyan by, with every good reason for so doing. Even though he had included Dissenters, the "preaching tinker" would hardly have been among them. In Aubrey's record Shakespeare was the son of a butcher, but not accounted superior to another butcher's son, his acquaintance. He was given a scant page and a half. Yes, his comedies would live. Spenser had a page. He was a little man, wore short hair, a small band and small cuffs. Sir Walter Raleigh had eighteen pages; Thomas Hobbes had eighty-two.

Some men grow larger as they walk away from their own time; some smaller. Nothing in their time or place quite explains why this is so. To understand such men, perhaps it is just as well after long pondering to put out of mind all that has been unearthed as to the when and what and how and why of their lives, and to contemplate what they have left behind them, as though they were orphans on earth and men without a country.

John Bunyan came into English literature and history by a side door, as it were, and he is there not for any reason that Elstow or the tinker's trade, or Bedford County Gaol or even dissenting Puritanism can quite explain. He is there because he looked deeply enough into himself to learn something about all men. He is there because he discovered one of the great themes which run through human experience in all the ages and then expressed it in simple words. He is there because he organized a segment of human experience in such a way as to give it shapeliness and meaning. (Poets have done that for us and by that token have they qualified as poets.) For many thousands of men and women through three centuries, Bunyan has taken religion out of the realm of confused mystery, made it personal, and given it a relation to life as it is lived in a practical world. He is there also because he obeyed an inner compulsion to tell over and over what to him had been a deeply private experience. In one such telling something in him imparted a radiance to the story, and made it somehow unforgettable. What we call genius in him may be as simple, and also as mysterious, as to have been only his own natural and luminous way of telling it. Listen to his own word:

"It came from mine own heart"

"Thus I put Pen to Paper with delight,
And quickly had my thoughts in black and white.
For having now my Method by the end;
Still as I pull'd it came; and so I pen'd it down.

. . . . Nor did I undertake
Therebye to please my neighbour; no not I
I did it mine own self to gratifie." [5]

Notes

Chapter I The Boy of Bunyan's End

1. From the section headed "De bonis et malis," *Timber or Discoveries,* London, 1641, p. 109.
2. For a summary of known fact concerning the earlier Bunyans, and mention of the documents establishing the family record, see John Brown, *John Bunyan,* revised edition, London, 1928, pp. 18–23.
3. *Grace Abounding to the Chief of Sinners,* London, 1666, Paragraph 2 (hereafter referred to as *G.A.*).
4. This portion of the will is quoted by John Brown, *op. cit.,* p. 31.
5. Celia Fiennes, *Through England on a Side-Saddle in the time of William and Mary,* London, 1888, pp. 291–292. A new edition under the title *The Journeys of Celia Fiennes,* ed. by Christopher Morris, was issued, London, 1949.
6. *G.A.,* Par. 3.
7. Richard Baxter, *Reliquiae Baxterianae,* London, 1696, p. 2.
8. *Victoria History of the County of Bedford,* II, 163–164, 180.
9. Closely paralleling a word of Erasmus, prefaced to his Greek Testament, 1516.
10. Reputedly written by Miles Smith, one of the two final revisers of the text, a noted Orientalist, Prebendary of Hereford and Exeter.
11. Some of these tales are conveniently accessible in John Ashton, *Romances of Chivalry,* London, 1887. For specific details recurring in

212

Notes

Bunyan, the most thorough investigation is that of Harold Golder, "Bunyan's Valley of the Shadow," *Modern Philology*, Vol. 27, 1929; "Bunyan's Giant Despair," *Journal of English and Germanic Philology*, Vol. 30, 1931.

12. *G.A.*, Pars. 5–7.
13. Edward Rogers, *Some Account of the Life and Opinions of a Fifth-Monarchy Man* (John Rogers), London, 1867, p. 7.
14. *Ibid.*, p. 12.
15. *Reliquiae Baxterianae*, p. 2.
16. George Fox, *An Autobiography* (2 vols.), Philadelphia, 1903, 1906, Vol. I, 6.
17. *G.A.*, Par. 4.
18. Rogers, *op. cit.*, pp. 9–11.
19. *Reliquiae Baxterianae*, pp. 11–12; 81, 82. Similar lists of deliverances are common to seventeenth century autobiographies.

For further details of seventeenth century Elstow, Bedford, and environs, see: Vera Brittain, *In the Steps of John Bunyan*, London, 1950; G. Gore Chambers, *Bedfordshire*, Cambridge, 1917; C. F. Farrar, *Old Bedford*, Bedford, 1926; L. M. Hawkins, *Old Bedford and the Silent Tide*, Bedford, 1936; J. H. Mathiason, *Bedford and Its Environs*, Bedford, 1831; *The Moot Hall*, Bedfordshire County Council, 1952; S. R. Wigram, *Chronicles of the Abbey of Elstow*, Oxford, 1885.

Chapter II   Soldier in Cromwell's New Model Army

1. Discovered in the Public Record Office in 1896, by Ernest G. Atkinson, in a volume of Commonwealth Exchequer papers stamped Newport Pagnell Muster Rolls, 1644.
2. *Reliquiae Baxterianae*, p. 44.
3. No date. The king's answer was of Dec. 24, 1642. Apply yourselves to Parliament, he said.
4. Sir Charles Harding Firth, *Cromwell's Army, a history of the English Soldier during the Civil Wars, the Commonwealth and the Protectorate*, London, 1921, pp. 32–33. The plan as officially recorded, *Col. State Papers, Dom.*, 1644–1645, p. 232. *Commons Journals*, Nov. 23, 1644.
5. For historical details concerning the fortress of Newport Pagnell, see Rev. H. Roundell, "The garrison of Newport-Pagnell," *Records*

of Buckinghamshire, 1863, Vol. II, 206–216, 298–312, 354–373. Sir Samuel Luke's Journal to March, 1644, is printed in the *Oxfordshire Record Society*, Vols. 29, 31, 33. His *Letter Book*, Egerton MSS. 785, 786, 787.

6. *G.A.*, Par. 13.
7. Public Record Office.
8. For a general statement of the make-up of the New Model, see Firth, *op. cit.*, Chap. III.
9. *The Writings and Speeches of Oliver Cromwell*, 4 vols., ed. William Cortez Abbott, Harvard Press, 1937–47. June 14, 1645, Vol. I, 360.
10. *The Souldier's Pocket Bible*, London, 1643; Facsimile reprint, London, 1895.
11. *The Souldier's Catechism*, London, 1644; Facsimile reprint, London, 1900.
12. Preface to the Reader, *The Building and Glory of the Truly Christian and Spiritual Church*, London, 1647.
13. *Reliquiae Baxterianae*, pp. 50–53, 58.
14. Printed in full, *Archaelogia*, Vol. XXXV, 1853, pp. 310–334.
15. Firth, *Cromwell's Army*, Appendix, pp. 409 ff.
16. *Letter Book*, June 10, 1645. Quoted by D. R. Guttery, *The Great Civil War in Midland Parishes*, Birmingham, 1950.
17. Egerton, 786. Quoted Roundell, p. 358.
18. Public Record Office.

Chapter III Embattled Tinker

1. In *Grace Abounding to the Chief of Sinners*, 1666.
2. *The Diary of the Rev. Ralph Josselin, 1616–1683*, ed. E. Hockliffe, London, 1908. Camden Society, 3rd Series, Vol. 15, pp. 44–45.
3. Discovered at St. Neots in Huntingdonshire, in 1905, by William Rowlett; after some years offered for sale in London and purchased by Sir Leicester Harmsworth for the Bunyan Meeting in Bedford, where it may be seen among the Bunyan relics in the Museum behind the chapel. The details of this story are summarized by Vera Brittain, *In the Steps of John Bunyan*, pp. 99–100.
4. *G.A.*, Par. 15.
5. *Ibid.*
6. Robert Parsons [the Jesuit], *A Book of Christian Exercise appertaining to Resolution*, London, 1583, Perused by Edmund Bunny, Lon-

don, 1597. The second part, *A Christian Directorie*, was issued separately in 1601. For Baxter's account of his conversion, see *Reliquiae Baxterianae*, p. 3.

7. By Proclamation of James I, 1617. Republished on the accession of Charles I, 1625.

8. Instituted in 1639. He remained until after the Restoration.

9. *G.A.*, Pars. 22, 23, 24.

10. From *Out of My Life and Thought*, New York, 1949, p. 88. Published by Holt, Rinehart and Winston, Inc. Copyright, 1933, by Henry Holt & Co., Inc.

11. *G.A.*, Par. 16.

12. *Ibid.*, 9, 52.

13. *The Plaine Man's Pathway* was first published in 1601; 19th impression, 1625. Arthur Dent was a dissenting preacher of South Shoebury in Essex. He had refused to wear the surplice or to make the sign of the cross. *The Practice of Piety* was first published in 1612. Lewis Bayley was Bishop of Bangor.

14. Pp. 139 ff.

15. P. 374.

16. The 1612 edition was enlarged in 1613, because "many *devoutly* disposed, prevailed" with him "to adde some parts, and to amplifie others." This edition contained 1,031 pages.

17. *G.A.*, Par. 38.

18. *The Journal of*, ed. Norman Penney, Cambridge, 1911, 2 vols., I, 78.

19. *G.A.*, Pars. 129, 130. For Luther's *Commentary on St. Paul's Epistle to the Galatians*, see edition of John Prince Fellowes, London, 1940.

20. *The Confessions of St. Augustine*, trans. by Edward B. Pusey, London, 1909, p. 223.

21. *The Varieties of Religious Experience*, New York, 1902 (Modern Library), p. 186; see Lectures VIII, IX, X. Bunyan's conversion is discussed in some detail.

22. *G.A.*, Pars. 255–260.

See also: Mohandas Gandhi, *An Autobiography, or the Story of My Experiments with Truth*, Kalupur, Ahmedabad, 1945; John J. O'Meara, *The Young Augustine*, London, 1954; Roger Sharrock, "Spiritual Autobiography," *John Bunyan*, London, 1954, Chap. 3; Henri Talon, *John Bunyan*, London, 1951, pp. 49–71.

Chapter IV Field Preacher

1. *G.A.*, Par. 295.
2. Broadside. Included in *Works of John Taylor, the Water Poet*, 4 vols., Spencer Society, 1870, I, No. 6. One cut shows How in his tub encircled by ten others.
3. Its subtitle reads, "A Treatise to prove Humane-Learning to be no Help to the Spirituall understanding of the Word of God."
4. Broadside, *The Cobler's Monument*, 1640; contains also an epitaph. He had been buried in the highway, near Shoreditch.
5. *Autobiography*, London, 1827, p. 17.
6. W. H. Summers, *The Lollards of the Chiltern Hills*, London, 1906, deals with the Bedfordshire region. See also John Brown, *Puritan Preaching in England*, New York, 1900. The first Dominicans came in 1221; the first Franciscans, in 1224.
7. *G.A.*, Pars. 266, 267, 268.
8. *A Brief Account of the Author's Imprisonment*, added to modern editions of *G.A.*, Par. 318.
9. *The Jerusalem Sinner Saved, Works*, ed. Henry Stebbing, 4 vols., London, 1862, II, 466. This edition is used for citations from *Works*.
10. *G.A.*, Par. 282.
11. *Ibid.*, Par. 284.
12. *A Few Sighs from Hell, Works*, I, 131, 133.
13. John Evelyn, *Diary*, p. 90.
14. A summary of known fact concerning this episode and Bunyan's share in it is in the Appendix to William York Tindall, *John Bunyan, Mechanick Preacher*, Columbia University Press, 1934. Difficulty in tracing Bunyan's pamphlet is increased by the fact that its precise title is not given in contemporary references to it.

Chapter V Offender Before the Law

1. *A Discourse of the House of the Forest of Lebanon, Works*, IV, 133.
2. *The Diary of Samuel Pepys*, ed. Henry B. Wheatley, 1893, under date of May 25, 31, and June 1, 1660.
3. *A Relation of the Imprisonment of Mr. John Bunyan*, written by himself, *Works*, IV, 479–489. This account, first published in 1765, contained no description of the manuscript as the source, but the

fact that Charles Doe, in the *Struggler*, lists an unprinted manuscript in his Catalogue-table of Bunyan's works, lends some support to the assumption that this is Bunyan's own account. Bunyan's quoted statements are taken from this account, pp. 483–487.

4. *Commons Journals*, VII, 521. There are many contemporary references to this episode.
5. Quoted, Emelia Fogelklon, *James Nayler, the Rebel Saint*, London, 1931, p. 43.
6. Known as the Conventicle Act, 1593. It had been continued four times, and was made permanent in 1624. It had been invoked frequently.
7. *A Relation of the Imprisonment*, pp. 487, 488, 489.
8. For Sir Matthew Hale, see Bishop Gilbert Burnet, *The Life of Sir Matthew Hale*, London, 1820.

Chapter VI "The Lord's Free Prisoner"

1. Published, 1672. *Works*, I, 415.
2. A Broadsheet. The full title reads *Prison Meditations*, Dedicated to the Heart of Suffering Saints and Reigning Sinners, By John Bunyan, in Prison, 1665. No known copy survives. Its authenticity is attested by Charles Doe's mention in his chronological list of Bunyan's works. Stanzas 3, 4, 6, 7, 20.
3. *The State of Prisons in England and Wales*, Warrington, 1784. John Howard had previously been sheriff of Bedford.
4. *Journal*, I, 124–126, 127; II, 83.
5. *The History of the Life of Thomas Ellwood*, London, 1827, pp. 150–151.
6. Ed. Henry B. Wheatley, 1893, IV, 210.
7. Charles Stanford, *Joseph Alleine: His Companions and Times;* A Memorial of Black Bartholomew, London, 1861, pp. 282–294. Quotations from the letters, pp. 290, 291, 292.
8. *Prison Meditations*, Stanza 18.
9. "To the Godly Reader," *Works*, I, 282.
10. *Ibid.* pp. 337, 293.
11. *Ibid.*, pp., 293–294.
12. The *Church-Book of Bunyan Meeting*, 1650–1821. Reproduction in facsimile of the original folio, London and Toronto, 1928. Intro. by G. B. Harrison. Cf. Brown, *John Bunyan*, pp. 213–214, for entries quoted.

13. *The Christian Progress of George Whitehead*, London, 1725, Part II, 358, 359.
14. For documents connected with the Issue of Licenses under the Declaration of Indulgence, 1672, see *State Papers Domestic*, Charles II, 321 (58), Vol. I, 318–319.

Chapter VII "The Head of Goliath in My Hand"

1. Tibor Mende, *Conversations on India and World Affairs*, New York; Copyright, 1956, by George Braziller, Inc., p. 8.
2. From his Preface.
3. *G.A.*, Par. 92.
4. *Ibid.*, Pars. 93, 137, 144, 173, 174, 201, 215, 235, 250, and many others.
5. *The Life and Death of Vavasor Powell*, London, 1671, the year after his death.
6. *The Work of Jesus Christ as an Advocate*, *Works*, IV, 319.
7. *A True Testimony of Obedience to the Heavenly Call*, London, 1653.
8. There is a detailed account of William Franklin in Humphrey Ellis, *Pseudo-Christus*, London, 1650.
9. Three titles appeared under her name in 1654: *The Cry of a Stone*, *A Legacy for Saints, Strange and Wonderful Newes from Whitehall*, or the mighty visions proceeding from Mistris Anna Trapnel, March 11, 1654.
10. Henry Jessey, *The Exceeding Riches of Grace Advanced by the Spirit of Grace, In an Empty Nothing Creature*, (viz.) Mrs. Sarah Wight, 6th ed., London, 1652.
11. Among many others, Joseph Salmon, *Heights in Depths and Depths in Heights*, London, 1651; Richard Coppin, *Truth's Testimony*, London, 1655; Nicholas Smith, *Wonderfull Prophecyes Revealed to Nicholas Smith Shoemaker*, London, 1652. For a full discussion, with mention of many more such accounts, see William York Tindall, *John Bunyan, Mechanick Preacher*, New York, 1934.
12. Issued previously in three parts, 1660, 1663, 1665, and as a whole in 1664.
13. Pp. 252–273.
14. His *Autobiography* shows many parallels to such language.
15. From "The Dry Salvages" in *Four Quartets*: Copyright, 1943, by T. S. Eliot; *The Complete Poems and Plays*, New York, 1950, p. 136. (By permission of Harcourt, Brace & World, Inc.).

16. For a recent discussion of *Grace Abounding*, see Margaret Bottrall, *Every Man a Phoenix*, London, 1958, Chap. V, pp. 82–110.

Chapter VIII   Pastor of Bunyan Meeting

1. *The Continuation of Mr. Bunyan's Life*, added to the 7th edition of *Grace Abounding*, 1692, *Works*, IV, 490–493. Probably written by George Cockayne, minister at Red Cross Street, Southwark.
2. The gift of the Duke of Bedford in 1876.
3. Several of these entries are included in Brown, *John Bunyan*, pp. 231–232.
4. Portions of his final letter are also in Brown, pp. 89–90. See also *Church Book*, facsimile. For many years this letter was read annually to the congregation on New Year's Day.
5. *Differences in Judgment about Water-Baptism*, *Works*, I, 459. His opponents in print had been William Kiffin, Henry D'Anvers, and Thomas Paul.
6. *Peaceable Principles and True*, *Works*, IV, 465; *The Heavenly Footman*, *Works*, IV, 182.
7. William Urwick, *Bible Truths and Church Errors*, London, 1888, chapter on "Bunyan not a Baptist." See also W. T. Whitley, "The Bunyan Christening," *Trans. Baptist Hist. Soc.*, 1910–1911, II, 255–263.
8. *Works*, II, 220–269.
9. *G.A.*, Pars. 314–317; edition of 1688, 6th.
10. Egerton 2414. First printed in 1760. Another edition, edited by G. B. Harrison, London, 1929.
11. *Works*, I, 475.
12. For a review of known fact as to Bunyan's imprisonments, see W. T. Whitley, "Bunyan's Imprisonments," *Trans. Baptist Hist. Soc.*, London, 1918–1919, Vol. VI, 1–24; Joyce Godber, *Congregational Hist. Soc. Trans.*, 1949, Vol. XVI, No. 1, pp. 23–33, completing the work of Frederick Guiney, who discovered the bond in the possession of Bucks Archeological Society.

Chapter IX   *Pilgrim's Progress*, 1678

1. The edition of James Blanton Wharey, Oxford, 1928, is used for the quoted passages. His edition is based on the text of Bunyan's third

edition. Roger Sharrock has now published a revision of Wharey's work, using the text of Bunyan's first edition; unfortunately received too late for use in this work.

2. *Works*, IV, 183.
3. *Works*, II, 378–379.
4. P. 11.
5. *Works*, IV, 181.
6. The Conclusion, p. 174.
7. P. 172.
8. *The Travalyed Pilgrim*, by Samuel Bateman, 1569.
9. *Epictetus his Manuel and Cebes his Fable*, out of the Greek originall, by J. Healey, London, 1610; *The Tablet of Cebes, or the Embleme of humane life*, Rendered into English by John Davies (from the French of G. Boileau), 1670; Richard Parsons, *Cebes' Tablet*, Boston, 1887.
10. Gerald Robert Owst, *Literature and Pulpit in Medieval England*, Cambridge, 1933, pp. 104–106. See also his *Preaching in Medieval England*, Cambridge, 1926.
11. Harleian MS. 1671. The illustration is on Fol. 5. Mr. Owst's discovery of this analogue was first reported in a letter to *The Times* (London), Nov. 24, 1928. Letter of L. P. Jacks, Nov. 27; Owst's reply, Nov. 29, 1928.
12. P. 103.
13. *The Bookman*, Oct., 1928, Vol. 75, pp. 13–17, "Bunyan—A Revaluation"; Replies, Nov., 1928, pp. 97–106.
14. M. Esther Harding, *Journey into Self*, New York, copyright, 1956 by M. Esther Harding, pp. 13, 100. (By permission of Longmans, Green and Company, Inc.).

Chapter X   "Bishop Bunyan"

1. According to the census of 1676 ordered by Archbishop Sheldon. For the returns as summarized for Bedfordshire, see John Brown, *John Bunyan*, pp. 293–294.
2. *The Struggler, Works*, IV, 499, 500.
3. *Saved by Grace, Works*, II, 159–160.
4. *Ibid.*, p. 144.
5. *The Lord's Free Prisoner*, 4 pp. folio, 1683. Written while he was still in prison. He died in Newgate, 1684. "This letter is a Word-Apology under Patient suffering For a Faithful Testimony, or a necessary Vindication, and a just Defence of F.B."

6. *The Notebook of the Revd. Thomas Jolly*, July 1671–1693, Chetham Society, Manchester, 1895, p. 91.
7. See Brown, *John Bunyan*, pp. 315–325.
8. Reproduced by Brown, *ibid.*, p. 339. Now preserved in the Bunyan Museum.

Chapter XI "Our Author Bunyan"

1. In Doe's Folio, 1692.
2. *The Life and Death of Mr. Badman and The Holy War*, edited by John Brown, Cambridge, 1905, p. 3.
3. Several of these are printed by John Brown, *John Bunyan*, pp. 231, 304, 305, 306.
4. The Author to the Reader, p. 9 (Brown ed.).
5. William York Tindall identifies these, *John Bunyan, Mechanick Preacher*, New York, 1934, p. 278, Note 26. See also: Roger Sharrock, *John Bunyan*, London, 1954, Chap. V, pp. 106–117; Henri Talon, *John Bunyan*, chapter on Badman, pp. 225–239; James Blanton Wharey, "Bunyan's Mr. Badman," *Mod. Lang. Notes,* Vol. XXXVI, No. 2, pp. 65–79.
6. *The Discovery of a New World*, London, 1640, 3rd impression, pp. 237–238.
7. *The Holy War*, p. 293 (Brown ed.).
8. Most easily recognized are the many echoes from Richard Bernard's *The Isle of Man*, a popular allegory before Bunyan was born, more particularly place names and names of actors in the story. Benjamin Keach's *War with the Devil*, 1676, and his *The Glorious Lover*, 1679, were also undoubtedly familiar to him. *The Progress of Sin*, 4th edition, 1684, shows many parallels to Bunyan's *Prilgrim's Progress*.
9. First half of 13th century. The earliest extant religious dialogue. See also Charles H. Firth, "Bunyan's Holy War," *Jour. of Eng. Studies*, I, No. 3, pp. 141–150. Roger Sharrock, *John Bunyan*, Chap. VI, Henri Talon, *John Bunyan*, pp. 240–256.
10. Thomas Sherman (T.S.) wrote a sequel, appearing in 1683, not only extending the story, but aiming to correct what he thought any tendency to "lightness and laughter" such as Bunyan's pilgrim had occasioned in some "vain and frothy minds." A Part III was published in 1693. Tender Conscience, not Christian, was the principal character.

11. Also Benjamin Keach's *The Child's Instructor*, 1664; Henry Jessey, *A Looking-Glass for Children*, 1773 (2nd ed.), included some of Cheare's verses.

12. From "To the Reader," Facsimile, issued by John Brown, 1889.

13. *Divine and Moral Songs for Children*, 1720.

14. The spider-and-the-fly parable tempted Bunyan several times in his sermons. In *Light for them that Sit in Darkness*, *Works*, II, 154, of course, it is an emblem of the soul ensnared by Satan.

15. The first question had been, "DEAR Child, do you know who you are?" and the answer, "I am a creature of God, for he made me, body and soul."

16. In Thomas White's *Little Book for Little Children*, 12th ed., 1703, very popular, there is a *Diary of Sin*, left by a child of eight, who had died. It begins: 1. He had whetted his knife on the Sabbath day. 2. He did not reprove one whom he heard swear. 3. He had omitted prayer and gone out to play. There is more in like vein.

17. Each stanza ends with some variation on these last two lines:
(of her charms)
> "What would become of these delights,
> if I should go to Hell?"

(if she chooses the right way)
> "The promised Spirit would me place,
> safe from the lowest Hell."

(It ends)
> "To what a Glory God hath rais'd
> a Fire-brand pluct from Hell."

See also: F. J. Harvey Darton, *Children's Books in England*, Cambridge, 1932; Rosemary Freeman, *English Emblem Books*, London, 1948; Mario Praz, *Studies in 17th Century Imagery*, London, 1947, 2 vols.; Francis Quarles, *Emblems*, London, 1639; Roger Sharrock, "Bunyan and the English Emblem Writers," R.E.S. Vol. XXI, No. 82, April, 1945.

Chapter XII "All the trumpets sounded for him on the other side"

1. *Diary*, IV, 562–563.
2. John James Baddeley, *The Aldermen of Cripplegate Ward*, gives an account of Shorter.

3. *Works*, IV, 476–478.
4. For various historical details, see Alfred W. Light, *Bunhill Fields*, London, 1915, 2nd edition, 2 vols.
5. *Notebook, op. cit.*, p. 91.
6. Quoted by John Brown, *John Bunyan*, p. 374.
7. *The Struggler, Works*, IV, 497. It appears under Reason X for printing Bunyan's works by subscription.
8. W. T. Whitley, *A History of English Baptists*, London, 1932, p. 141.

Postscript

1. Advertisement to the Reader, end of *The Holy War*, John Brown, ed., p. 432.
2. To the Learned Reader, Prefatory to *The Holy City, Works*, I, 283.
3. To the Christian Reader, Prefatory to *Solomon's Temple Spiritualized, Works*, III, 224.
4. The Author to the Reader, Prefaced to *Light for them that sit in Darkness, Works*, III, 114.
5. *Pilgrim's Progress*, The Author's Apology for his Book, Wharey ed., pp. 1, 2.

Bunyan's Published Works

Acceptable Sacrifice, The 1689
Advocateship of Jesus Christ, The 1688
Antichrist and his Ruine, Of Doe's Folio
Badman, The Life and Death of Mr. 1680
Barren Fig Tree, The 1688
Book for Boys and Girls, A 1686
Case of Conscience Resolved, A 1683
Caution to Stir Up, A (broadside) c. 1684
Charles Doe's Folio 1692 (12 pieces left in MS.)
Christ a Compleat Saviour Doe's Folio
Christian Behaviour c. 1663
Christian Dialogue, A [?] No copy known.
Collected Works Doe's Folio, 1692. 12 pieces prepared for the press
before his death and 10 formerly printed.
Come and Welcome 1678
Concordance, A New and Useful [?] c. 1672 or earlier. No copy
known.
Confession of My Faith, A 1672
Defence of the Doctrine of Justification by Faith, A 1672
The Desires of the Righteous Granted, The Doe's Folio
Differences in Judgment about Water-Baptism . . . 1673
Discourse . . . of the House of God, A 1688
Discourse upon the Pharisee and the Publicane 1685

Doctrine of the Law and Grace Unfolded, The   1659
Exposition of the first 10 Chapters of Genesis, An   1692
Fear of God, A Treatise of   1679
Few Sighs from Hell, A   1658
Fig Tree, The Barren   1688
Good News for the Vilest of Men   1688
Gospel Truths Opened, Some   1656
Grace Abounding to the Chief of Sinners   1666
Greatness of the Soul, The   1683
Heavenly Footman, The   1698
Holy City, The   1665
Holy Life, A   1684
Holy War, The   1682
House of the Forest of Lebanon, Of the   Doe's Folio
Instruction for the Ignorant   1675
Israel's Hope Encouraged   Doe's Folio
I Will Pray with the Spirit   n.d. (3rd ed., 1663)
Jerusalen Sinner Saved, The (See *Good News*)
Justification by Faith, A Defence of the Doctrine of   1672
Justification by Imputed Righteousness, Of   Doe's Folio
Law and a Christian, Of the   Doe's Folio
Life and Death of Mr. Badman, The   1680
Light for Them that Sit in Darkness   1675
Mapp of Salvation and Damnation, A   c. 1664
Mr. John Bunyan's Last Sermon   1692
One Thing is Needful   1683
Paul's Departure and Crown   Doe's Folio
Peaceable Principles and True   1674
Pharisee and the Publicane, The   1685
Pilgrim's Progress, The, Part I   1678
Pilgrim's Progress, The, Part II   1684
Prison Meditations   1665
Profitable Meditations   c. 1661
Questions about the . . . Seventh Day Sabbath   1685
Relation of the Imprisonment of Mr. John Bunyan, A   1765
Reprobation Asserted   n.d. c. 1674
Resurrection of the Dead, The   c. 1665
Saint's Knowledge of Christ's Love, The   1692
Saint's Privilege and Profit, The   Doe's Folio
Saved by Grace   c. 1676

John Bunyan

Sermon, Mr. John Bunyan's Last 1692
Sighs from Hell, A Few 1658
Solomon's Temple Spiritualiz'd 1688
Some Gospel Truths Opened 1656
Strait Gate, The 1676
Treatise of the Fear of God, A 1679
Trinity and a Christian, Of the Doe's Folio
Vindication . . . of Some Gospel Truths, Opened, A 1657
Work of Jesus Christ as an Advocate, The (see *The Advocateship of*) 1688
Works of Mr. John Bunyan, The 1692

For complete bibliographical information see F. M. Harrison, *A Bibliography of the Works of John Bunyan*, Supplement to the Bibliographical Society Transactions, No. 6, 1932.

Collected Works.

Complete Works of John Bunyan, edited by George Offor, 3 vols., London and Edinburgh, 1860–1862.

The Entire Works of John Bunyan, edited by Henry Stebbing, 4 vols., London, 1862.

The Holy War and The Life and Death of Mr. Badman, edited by John Brown, Cambridge, 1905.

The Pilgrim's Progress and Grace Abounding, edited by John Brown, Cambridge, 1905.

The Pilgrim's Progress, edited by James Blanton Wharey, Oxford, 1928.

Selected Bibliography

Adams, Thomas, *The Sermons of Thomas Adams,* ed. by John Brown, London, 1909.

Alleine, Richard, *Vindiciae Pietatis,* London, 1664.

Ashton, John (ed.), *Romances of Chivalry,* London, 1887.

Aubrey, John, *Aubrey's Brief Lives,* ed. by Oliver Lawson Dick, London, 1949.

Augustine, St., *Confessions,* trans. by Edward C. Pusey, London, 1909.

Bacon, Nathaniel, *A Relation of the Fearful Estate of Francis Spira in the year 1548,* London, 1653.

Barclay, Robert, *The Inner Life of the Religious Societies of the Commonwealth,* London, 1876.

Baxter, Richard, *Reliquiae Baxterianae* or, Mr. Baxter's Narrative of the most memorable Passages of his Life and Times, London, 1696.

———, *A Treatise of Conversion,* London, 1657.

Bayley, Lewis, *The Practice of Piety,* Directing a Christian How to Walk that he May Please God, London, 1685. First published, 1612.

Beaumont, Agnes, *The Narrative of the Persecution of Agnes Beaumont in 1674,* Egerton MS. 2414; ed. by G. B. Harrison, London, 1929.

Bernard, Richard, *The Faithfull Shepheard; or The Shepheard's Faithfulnesse,* London, 1607.

———, *The Isle of Man, or Legall Proceedings in Manshire, against Sin,* London, 1627.

Bloom, J. H., *Pulpit Oratory in the Time of James the First,* London, 1831.

John Bunyan

Bottrall, Margaret, *Every Man a Phoenix*, London, 1958. Chapter V, "Bunyan's Grace Abounding."

Brailsford, Mabel Richmond, *A Quaker from Cromwell's Army: James Nayler*, London, 1927.

Braithwaite, William C., *The Beginnings of Quakerism*, London, 1912.

Brittain, Vera, *In the Steps of John Bunyan*, London, 1950.

Brown, John, *John Bunyan, His Life, Times and Works*, London, 1885; reissued with addenda, ed. by Frank Mott Harrison, London, 1928.

———, *Puritan Preaching in England*, London, 1900.

Burnet, Gilbert, *Bishop Burnet's History of His Own Time*, 2 vols., London, 1724.

———, *The Life of Sir Matthew Hale*, London, 1820.

Burrage, Champlin, *The Early Dissenters in the Light of Recent Research*, (1550–1641) 2 vols., Cambridge, 1912.

Burrough, Edward, *The True Faith of the Gospel of Peace*, London, 1656.

———, *Truth the Strongest of all, Witnessed Forth in the Spirit of Truth, against all Deceit*, London, 1657.

Calamy, Edmund, *The Nonconformist's Memorial*, abridged and corrected by Samuel Palmer, 2 vols., London, 1775.

Campbell, Mildred, *The English Yeoman*, New Haven, 1943.

Canne, John, *A Voice from the Temple*, London, 1653.

Cebes, *The Embleme of Humane Life*, Rendered into English by John Davies of Kidwelly, London, 1670, from the French of Boileau; reprinted, Glasgow, 1901.

Chambers, G. Gore, *Bedfordshire*, Cambridge, 1917.

Chillenden, Edmond, *Preaching without Ordination*, London, 1647.

Church-Book of Bunyan Meeting, Facsimile edition, ed. by G. B. Harrison, London, 1928.

Clarke, Samuel, *A Generall Martyrologie containing a Collection of the greatest Persecutions which have befallen the Church of Christ*, London, 1651.

———, *Mirrour or Looking-Glasse Both for Saints and Sinners*, London, 1671.

Cockett, C. B., *Bunyan's England*, London, 1928.

Cocks, H. F. Lovell, *The Nonconformist Conscience*, London, 1943.

Cragg, Gerald R., *Puritanism in the Period of the Great Persecution*, Cambridge, 1957.

Cromwell, Oliver, *The Writings and Speeches of Oliver Cromwell*, 4 vols., ed. by Wilbur Cortez Abbott, Harvard Press, 1937–1947.

Darton, F. G. Harvey, *Children's Books in England*, Cambridge, 1932.

Davies, Godfrey, "The Parliamentary Army under the Earl of Essex, 1642–45," *English Historical Review*, XLIX, 1934, pp. 32–54.

——, *The Restoration of Charles II, 1658–1660*, Huntington Library, 1955. (See also Firth).

Dekker, Thomas, *The Bel-Man of London*, London, 1608.

——, *Lanthorne and Candlelight*, London, 1609.

Dell, William, *The Building and Glory of the truely Christian and Spiritual Church*, London, 1646.

——, *The Tryal of Spirits*, London, 1653.

Dent, Arthur, *The Plaine Man's Pathway to Heaven*, London, 1625. (19th Impression)

Doe, Charles, *The Struggler*, London, 1692.

Edwards, Thomas, *Gangraena, or a Catalogue and Discovery of Many of the Errours, Heresies, Blasphemies and Pernicious Practices of the Sectaries of this Time*, London, 1646.

Ellwood, Thomas, *History of the Life of*, London, 1827.

Evans, Arise, *An Eccho of the Voice from Heaven or a Narrative of the Life and Special Calling and Visions of Arise Evans*, London, 1652.

Evelyn, John, *Diary*, ed. by Austin Dobson, 3 vols., London, 1906.

Farrar, C. F., *Old Bedford*, Bedford, 1926.

Fiennes, Celia, *Through England on a Side-Saddle in the time of William and Mary*, London, 1888.

Firth, Charles Harding, "John Bunyan," in *Essays Historical and Literary*, Oxford, 1938.

——, "Bunyan's Holy War," *Journal of English Studies*, I, 1913.

——, *Cromwell's Army; or a history of the English soldier during the Civil Wars, the Commonwealth, and the Protectorate*, London, 1921, 3rd edition.

——, (with Godfrey Davies), *The Regimental History of Cromwell's Army*, 2 vols., Oxford, 1940.

Foster, Albert J., *Bunyan's Country*, London, 1901.

Fowler, Edward, *The Design of Christianity*, London, 1671.

——, *Dirt Wip't Off or a Manifest Discovery of the Gross Ignorance, Erroneousness and Most Unchristain and Wicked Spirit of one John Bunyan, Lay-preacher in Bedford*, London, 1672.

Fox, George, *An Autobiography*, ed. by Rufus M. Jones, 2 vols., Philadelphia, 1906.

—— , *The Journal of George Fox*, ed. by Norman Penney, 2 vols., Cambridge University, 1911.

Foxe, John, *Actes and Monuments of matters most speciall* [Book of Martyrs], 3 vols., London, 1641 (the edition Bunyan read in prison).

√Freeman, Rosemary, *English Emblem Books*, London, 1948.

Froude, J. A., *John Bunyan*, London, 1880 (English Men of Letters Series.)

Gardiner, Samuel Rawson, *History of England, 1603–1642*, 10 vols., London, 1883–1884.

Godber, Joyce, "The Imprisonments of John Bunyan," *Congregational Historical Society Transactions*, XVI, April, 1949, pp. 23–33.

Golder, Harold, "John Bunyan's Hypocrisy," *North American Review*, Vol. 223, 1926.

———, "Bunyan's Valley of the Shadow," *Modern Philology*, Vol. 27, 1929.

———, "Bunyan's Giant Despair," *Journal of English and Germanic Philology*, Vol. 30, 1931.

Griffith, Gwilym, *John Bunyan*, London, 1937.

Guttery, D. R., *The Great Civil War in Midland Parishes*, Birmingham, 1950.

Haller, William, *The Rise of Puritanism*, New York, 1938.

Harding, M. Esther, *Journey into Self*, New York, 1956.

Harper, Charles G., *The Bunyan Country*, London, 1928.

Harris, Benjamin, *The Protestant Tutor*, London, 1679.

Harrison, F. M., *John Bunyan, A Record of Recent Research* (typescript), 1940.

√Harrison, G. B., *John Bunyan, A Study in Personality*, London, 1928.

Hawkins, L. M., *Old Bedford and the Silent Tide*, Bedford, 1936.

√Hobbes, Thomas, *Leviathan*, London, 1651.

Hobson, Paul, *Practicall Divinity*, London, 1646.

———, *A Garden Inclosed, and Wisdom Justified of her Children*, London, 1647.

√Hooker, Richard, *The Laws of Ecclesiastical Polity*, 1593. Everyman Edition.

How, Samuel, *The Sufficiencie of the Spirits Teaching without Humane-Learning*, London, 1640.

Howard, John, *The State of Prisons in England and Wales*, Warrington, 1784.

Hubberthorne, Richard, *A True Testimony of Obedience to the Heavenly Call*, London, c. 1653.

√James, William, *The Varieties of Religious Experience*, 1901–1902. Lectures VIII, IX, X.

Selected Bibliography

Jessey, Henry, *The Lord's Loud Call to England*, London, 1660.

Johnson, Richard, *The Famous Historie of the Seaven Champions of Christendome*, London, 1616.

Jole, William, *A Father's Blessing and a Guide to Heaven*, London, n.d.

Jolly, Thomas, *The Notebook of the Revd. Thomas Jolly*, July 1671–1693, Chetham Society, Manchester, 1895.

Josselin, Rev. Ralph, *The Diary of, 1616–1683*, ed. by E. Hockliffe, London, 1908.

Keach, Benjamin, *War with the Devil*, London, 1676.

———, *The Glorious Lover*, 1679.

———, *The Progress of Sin, or Travels of Ungodliness*, London, 1736.

Kelman, John, *The Road, A Study of John Bunyan's Pilgrim's Progress*, London, 1917.

Kiffin, William, *A Glimpse of Sion's Glory or the Churches Beauty Specified*, London, 1641.

Knollys, Hanserd, *The Life and Death of Hanserd Knollys*, London, 1692.

Knox, John, *John Bunyan in Relation to His Times*, London, 1928.

Leavis, F. R., *The Common Pursuit*, London, 1952. Contains an essay, "Bunyan through Modern Eyes," pp. 204–210.

Lilburne, John, *The Christian Mans Trial*, London, 1641, 2nd edition.

Luke, Sir Samuel, *Journal of Oxfordshire Record Society*, Vols. 29, 31, 33.

———, *Letter Book*, Egerton MSS. 785, 786, 787.

Luther, Martin, *Commentary on St. Paul's Epistle to the Galatians*, ed. by John Prince Fellowes, London, 1940.

Macaulay, T. B., Essays on Bunyan, *Works*, London, 1806, Vols. V, VII.

Masson, David, *Life of Milton*, London, 6 vols., 1877.

Matthiason, J. H., *Bedford and Its Environs*, Bedford, 1831.

Mende, Tibor, *Conversations on India and World Affairs* (with Nehru), New York, 1956.

Merril, Elizabeth, *The Dialogue in English Literature*, New York, 1911.

Miller, Perry, "John Bunyan's Pilgrim's Progress," in *Classics of Religious Devotion*, Boston, 1950.

Moot Hall, The, Bedfordshire County Council, 1952.

Muggleton, Lodowick, and John Reeve, *A Divine Looking-Glass*, London, 1661.

Neal, Daniel, *A History of the Puritans*, London, 1732.

Noyes, Alfred, "Bunyan—A Revaluation," *Bookman*, Vol. 75, Oct., 1928, pp. 13–17; replies, Nov., 1928, pp. 97–106.

Nuttall, G. F., *The Holy Spirit in Puritan Faith and Experience*, Oxford, 1946.

Ogg, David, *England in the Reign of Charles II*, 2 vols., Oxford, 1934.

John Bunyan

O'Meara, John J., *The Young Augustine*, London, 1954.

Owst, Gerald Robert, *Literature and Pulpit in Medieval England*, Cambridge, 1933.

———, *Preaching in Medieval England*, Cambridge, 1926.

Parkes, Joan, *Travel in England in the Seventeenth Century*, Oxford, 1925.

Patrick, Simon, *Parable of the Pilgrim*, London, 1663.

Paul, Robert S., *The Lord Protector, Religion and Politics in the Life of Oliver Cromwell*, London, 1955.

√Pepys, Samuel, *The Diary of Samuel Pepys*, ed. by Henry B. Wheatley, 8 vols., London, 1893.

Perkins, William, *The Art of Prophesying*, London, 1603.

Powell, Vavasor, *The Life and Death of Vavasor Powell*, London, 1671.

Rogers, Edward, *Some Account of the Life and Opinions of a Fifth-Monarchy Man*, London, 1867.

Roundell, Rev. H., "The Garrison of Newport-Pagnell," in *Records of Buckinghamshire*, Aylesbury, 1863, Vol. II, pp. 206–216, 227–241, 299–312, 354–373.

Schlatter, Richard B., *The Social Ideas of Religious Leaders, 1660–1688*, London, 1940.

Schweitzer, Albert, *Out of My Life and Thought*, trans. by C. T. Campion, New York, 1949.

√ Sharrock, Roger, *John Bunyan* (Hutchinson's University Library), London, 1954.

———, "Bunyan and the English Emblem Writers," *Review of English Studies*, April, 1945, pp. 105–116.

Shaw, George Bernard, *Dramatic Opinions and Essays*, Dedicatory Epistle to *Man and Superman*, London, 1907.

Sibbes, Richard, *The Bruised Reede and Smoaking Flax*, London, 1632.

Simpson, Joseph, *History of the Town of Newport Pagnell*, Newport Pagnell, 1868.

Smith, Nicholas, *Wonderfull Prophecyes Revealed to Nicholas Smith Shoemaker*, London, 1652.

Souldier's Catechism, The, London, 1644, Facsimile reprint, 1900.

Souldier's Pocket Bible, The, London, 1643, Facsimile reprint, 1861, 1895.

Stanford, Charles, *Joseph Alleine, His Companions and Times*, London, 1861.

Summers, W. H., *The Lollards of the Chiltern Hills*, London, 1906.

√Talon, Henri, *John Bunyan, the Man and his Works*, London, 1951.

√Tawney, R. H., *Religion and the Rise of Capitalism*, London, 1926.

Taylor, John, *Works of John Taylor, the Water Poet*, 4 vols., Spencer Society, London, 1870.

Tindall, W. York, *John Bunyan, Mechanick Preacher*, New York, 1934.

Tomason, George, *Pamphlets, Books, Newspapers, and Manuscripts*, collected, 1640–1661, British Museum; *Catalogue*, 2 vols., London, 1908.

Trapnel, Anna, *The Cry of a Stone*, spoken in Whitehall by Anna Trapnel, being in the Visions of God, Jan. 1653.

———, *A Legacy for Saints*, being several experiences of the dealings of God with Anna Trapnel, London, 1654.

Trevelyan, G. M., *A History of England*, Vol. II, *The Tudors and the Stuart Era*, New York, 1953 (Anchor Books).

Trotter, Eleanor, *Seventeenth Century Life in the Country Parish*, London, 1919.

Tulloch, John, *English Puritanism and Its Leaders*, Edinburgh and London, 1861.

Underhill, Evelyn, *Mysticism*, London, 1930.

Urwick, William, *Bible Truths and Church Errors*, London, 1881; contains a lecture on "Bunyan not a Baptist."

Watson, Philip S., *Let God Be God, An Interpretation of the Theology of Martin Luther*, London, 1947.

Wharey, James Blanton, *A Study of the Sources of Bunyan's Allegories, with Special Reference to Deguileville's Pilgrimage of Man*, Baltimore, 1904.

Wharton, Nehemiah, "Letters from a Subaltern Officer of the Earl of Essex's Army written in the Summer and Autumn of 1642," *Archeologia*, Vol. 35, 1853, pp. 310–334.

White, Thomas, *A Little Book for Little Children*, London, 1703.

Whitehead, George, *The Christian Progress of George Whitehead*, London, 1725.

———, *Jacob Found in a Desert Land*, London, 1656.

Whiting, C. E., *Studies in English Puritanism from the Restoration to the Revolution*, 2 vols., New York, 1931.

Whitley, W. T., "The Bunyan Christening," *Trans. Baptist Hist. Soc.*, 1910–1911, Vol. II, pp. 253–263.

———, "Bunyan's Imprisonments," *Trans. Baptist Hist. Soc.*, London, 1918–1919, Vol. VI, 1–24.

———, *A History of British Baptists*, London, 1923, 1932.

Wigram, S. R., *Chronicles of the Abbey of Elstow*, Oxford, 1885.

Wilkins, John, *The Discovery of a New World*, London, 1640.

Willey, Basil, *The Seventeenth Century Background*, London, 1934.

Wood, Anthony, *The Life and Times of Anthony Wood, Antiquary*, 1632–1695, 5 vols., Oxford, 1891.

Index

Act of Conformity, 96
Act of Indulgence, 137
Act of Uniformity, 114
Actes and Monuments (John Foxe),
104, 164
Adams, Thomas, 72
Allegory, as mode of thought, 150;
the vogue passing, 177, 194–195
Alleine, Joseph, arrested and impris-
oned, 108–109, 110
Alleine, Richard, quoted, 125–126
Alypius (Augustine's friend), 61
Anabaptist, confused with Baptist, 86;
applied to Bunyan, 133; to Sir
William Shorter, 199
Anatomy of Melancholy, The, 16
Andrewes, Lancelot, 72
Apologia pro vita sua, 120
Arabian Nights, The, 16
Arcadia, 16
Archer, Thomas, 14
Attar, Farid Uddin, 147
Aubrey, John, quoted, 76, 210
Audley, Robert, 167
Augustine, his conversion, 50, 60;
quoted, 61–62; mentioned, 127,
128
Aylesbury, Lord, 167
Aylesbury Gaol, 107

Bacon, Francis, 16; quoted, 105
Bampfield, Francis, 166–167
Baptist, 63, 86, 95, 108, 131–132, 133,
203–204
Baxter, Richard, early education, 13;
reading of Bible, 13–14; of medi-
eval romances, 16; boyhood sins,
21; deliverances, 22; of civil war
violence, 26; religion in the army,
34; his conversion, 47–48; men-
tioned, 50, 67, 71, 134, 161
Bayley, Lewis, 53
Beard, Thomas, 173, 175–176
Beaumont, Agnes, 134–135, 136
Beaumont, Captain, 37–38
Bedford, 9. *See also* Bedfordshire en-
virons, *under* John Bunyan
Bedford Church Book, 73, 74, 160
Bedford County Gaol, 5, 94, 104, 139,
140, 210. *See also* Imprisonment,
under John Bunyan
Beecher, Sir William, 96
Bell-ringing, 57, 126
Bel-Man of London, The, 171–172
Bellman's Second Night's Walke, The,
172
Bentley, Anne (aunt of John Bunyan),
7
Bentley, Elizabeth (aunt), 6

Bentley, Margaret (mother), 6, 7

Bentley, Mary, née Goodwin (grandmother), 6–7

Bentley, Mary (great-grandmother), 6

Bentley, William (grandfather), 6

Bernard, Richard, 148

Bevis of Hampton, Sir, 16, 17

Blake, William, 59, 127, 201

Blaney, Robert, 139

Blundell, Sir George, 96

Boehme, Jacob, 127

Book for Boys and Girls, A, Or Country Rhimes for Children, 190–197; quoted, 12, 190–194, 195, 196–197

Book of Common Prayer, The, 90, 97

Book of Sports, The, 48

Boulton, Major, 29

Bratts, Ned, 72

Breda, Declaration of, 88

Bridewell, 108

Brief Lives, 210

Browning, Robert, quoted, 72

Bruised Reede, The, 122

Buckingham, Duke of, 7

Bunhill Fields, 10, 200–201

Bunny, Edmund, 47–48

Bunyan, Anne (3rd wife of Thomas Bunyan), 6

Bunyan, Elizabeth (half-sister of John Bunyan), 6

Bunyan, Elizabeth (2nd wife of John Bunyan), marriage, 84; plea for her husband, 99–101; Deed of Gift, 168; death, 203

Bunyan, Elizabeth (daughter), 64, 203

Bunyan, John (son), 64, 160, 203

Bunyan, John
contemporaries, 1
portents of ill, 1, 8
estimate, relation to Puritanism, 1, 2, 136, 207; relation to his own time, 1–2, 177, 178, 209; relation to Dissent, 2; relation to English culture, 2, 210; religious leadership, 2, 136–137, 204, 210; his originality, 205–207
known ancestry, 4–7

birthplace, Bunyan's End, 4, 5, 8

parentage, Thomas Bunyan, "Braseyer," 5; Margaret Bunyan (née Goodwin), 6–7; their marriage record, 7

birth date, 1628, and christening record, 7; the year 1628, 7–8; national background, 8, 208–209

Elstow, the Green, 9–10; at fair time, 10; on the High Road, 11–12

Bedfordshire environs, Bedford town, 9; surrounding country, 11; prototypes of House Beautiful, 12–13

boyhood, early education, 13–14; the Bible, 15–16; reading of romances, 16–19; habit of swearing, 21; night terrors, 19; deliverances, 22–23; death of his mother, 23; forecast for life, 23; religious influences, 52

army experience, enlistment, 24, 25, 26; garrison of Newport Pagnell, 28–29; fighting experience, 29; soldier companions, 29–30; religious influences, 31–34, 37–39, 52–53; army discipline, 34–36; understanding of issues, 39–40; significance for life of army experience, 40–42; associations for life, 42; end of military life, 42

return to Elstow, 44–45; tinker's trade, 45–46; marriage, 46–47

conversion, a five-year struggle, 47–48; the tipcat game, 48–50, 126; reading of pious books, 53–56; bell-ringing, dancing, given up, 57; meeting four poor women, 57; acquaintance with Ranters, 57–58; mental struggles, 58; counsels of Pastor Gifford, 59; reading of Luther's *Commentary*, 60–61; joining Bedford Church, 62–63; forecast for life, 64

move to Bedford, 64

as itinerant preacher, current attitudes toward unlearned preacher, 67–72; power in the pulpit, 67, 76–77; modest beginning, 73–74; secret meeting places, 74–75; early sermons, 75–76

as controversialist, with Edward Burrough, 78–80; first printed treatise, 78–80; concerning witchcraft, 82–83

death of first wife, 84

marriage to Elizabeth, 84

arrest at Lower Samsell, 89–91

hearing before Justice Wingate, 92–94

trial at the Chapel of Herne, 96–98

wife's plea at August Assizes, 99–101

imprisonment in Bedford County Gaol, sense of innocence, 102–103; daily life, 104–105; jail conditions, 104, 105, 106; prison sermon, "The Holy City," 111–114; release, 114; help of Quakers, 115–116; fruitfulness of prison experience, 115–116; writing of *Grace Abounding*, 118–119

pastor of Bedford Church, election, 114–115; license to preach, 116; evidence of Church Book concerning discipline, 130–131; concerning baptism as membership qualification, 131–133; Agnes Beaumont affair, 134–135

second imprisonment in Bedford County Gaol, an ecclesiastical offense, 137–138; completion of *Pilgrim's Progress*, 141 ff.; release, 158

eleven years of freedom, pastoral activity, 159–160; preaching success, 160–161, 162–166, 168; writings (See *The Life and Death of Mr. Badman, The Holy War, Pilgrim's Progress*, Part II, *Country Rhimes for Children*); journey to Reading, 198–199; last sermon, 199–200

death, 200; mourning of Bedford Church, 202–203; children, 203; death of wife, Elizabeth, 203; his estate, 203

writings:
    Confession of My Faith, A, 102–103, 132–133
    Country Rhimes for Children, 190–197
    Defence of the Doctrine of Justification by Faith, A, 133–134
    Few Sighs from Hell, A, 81
    Forest of Lebanon, The, 87
    Grace Abounding to the Chief of Sinners, a personal record, 19, 21, 22, 44, 46, 48–50, 58–59, 60, 61, 62; mentioned, 63, 134, 136, 145–146; a conversion example, 64, 118, 128, 166; a prison book, 117; motive in writing, 118–120; seventeenth century parallels, 121–126; modern interest, 128
    Heavenly Footman, The, 133, 143–144
    Holy City, The, 111–114
    Holy War, The, 177–183; local history, 167; quoted, 177, 179, 181; war reminiscences, 180, 181, 182
    Instruction for the Ignorant, 138
    Life and Death of Mr. Badman, The, 169–176; Bedford reality, 170–171, 176; compared with Dekker, 171–172; revelation of Bunyan, 176; compared with *Pilgrim's Progress*, Part II, 184
    Peaceable Principles, quoted, 133
    Pilgrim's Progress, The, Bedfordshire background, 11; debt: to medieval romance, 17, to contemporaries, 150, to medieval heritage, 151–152; quoted: 144, 146–147, 154, 155, "Author's Apology," 211, "Conclusion," 146–147; questions of date, 145–146; the pilgrimage idea, 147–148; estimate, 155–158, 166; help to his fame, 161;

Bunyan, John (*continued*)
    contrast with *Badman*, 169,
    176
  Pilgrim's Progress, The, Part II,
    motive in writing, 183-184; a
    gentle journey, 184; quoted,
    184, 185, 186, 187, 189; realistic
    cast, 184-185, 188-189; man
    with muckrake, 185-186;
    lightness of touch, 186-187;
    music, 187-188; revelation of
    Bunyan, 188-189; the crossing
    over, 189
  Prison Meditations, quoted, 103-
    104, 110
  Saved by Grace, 162-164
  Some Gospel Truths Opened, 78-
    79
  *Vindication of the Book Called
    Some Gospel Truths Opened*,
    78
Bunyan, Margaret (mother of John
  Bunyan), 4, 6, 7, 13, 23. *See also*
  Margaret Bentley
Bunyan, Margaret (sister of John
  Bunyan), 8, 23
Bunyan, Mary (half-sister), 6
Bunyan, Mary (daughter), 47, 64, 203
Bunyan, Thomas (ancestor), 4-5
Bunyan, Thomas (father), 4, 5, 6, 7,
  8, 13, 14, 23
Bunyan, Thomas (half-brother), 6
Bunyan, William (ancestor), 4
Bunyan, William (ancestor), 5
Bunyan, William (brother), 8
Bunyan Meeting Museum, 106
Bunyan's End, 4, 8, 45
Burrough, Edward, 72, 77, 78
Burton, Robert, 16

Calvin, John, 128
Calvinism, 157, 180, 189-190, 208
Calvinist, 196
Camden, Viscount, 24
Carlyle, Thomas, 30, 48
Castle, The (Kafka's), 147
Castle of Perseverance, The, 183
Cebes, The Tablet of, 149-150
Cervantes, Miguel de, 16
Chandler, Ebenezer, 203

Chapel of Herne, 96, 154
Charles II, 88, 99, 167
Chaucer, 151
Cheare, Abraham, 190, 196
Chester, Sir Henry, 96, 100
Christian Progress, The (of George
  Whitehead), 115
*Church-Book of Bunyan Meeting,
  The*, quoted, 115, 160, 202-203;
  mentioned, 119, 130, 131
Cicero, 60
Clarendon, Earl of (Edward Hyde),
  68
Clarke, Samuel, 173, 174, 175-176
Claxton, William, 124
Cobb, Paul, 98
Cockayne, George, 201
Cockayne, Lieut. Col. Richard, 24, 25,
  28, 39
Colloquy of the Birds, 147
Colman Green, 75
Commentary on the Galatians (Lu-
  ther's), 60-61
Common Prayer, The Book of, 90, 97
Commonwealth Mercury, The, 81
Confession of My Faith, A, quoted,
  102-103, 132
Confessions (Rousseau), 126
Conformity, Act of, 96
Conrad, Joseph, 152
Conventicle Act, The, 119
Conventicles, 73; laws against, 68, 86,
  91-92, 96-97
Cooper, Thomas, 129
Country Rhimes for Children, quoted,
  12, 190, 194, 195, 196-197; men-
  tioned, 185. *See also A Book for
  Boys and Girls*
Cowley, Mathias, 41, 78
Crocker, Thomas, 129
Crompton, Justice, 129
Cromwell, Elizabeth Hampden, 30
Cromwell, Oliver, quoted, 27, 30-31;
  mentioned, 7, 15, 24, 28, 39, 44, 63,
  80, 121, 207
Cry of a Stone, The, 124

Dante, mentioned, 147; quoted, 153
D'Anvers, Henry, 133

Debate of the Body and the Soul, The,
 182–183
Deed of Gift, 168
Defence of the Doctrine of Justifica-
 tion by Faith, A, 134
Defoe, Daniel, 11, 176, 201
Dekker, Thomas, 171–172
Dell, William, 34, 75, 83–84
Denne, Henry, 83
Dent, Arthur, mentioned, 53, 173, 186;
 quoted, 55
Derby Prison, 107
Design of Christianity, The, 134
Diary (of Samuel Pepys), quoted, 108
Dickens, Charles, 187
Differences in Judgment about Water
 Baptism, 63
Dirt Wip't Off, 134
Divine Emblems for Children, 195
Divine and Moral Songs for Children,
 193
Doctrine of the Law and Grace Un-
 folded, The, 41
Doe, Charles, quoted, 160–161, 166,
 203; mentioned, 162
Domesdale Prison, 106
Dominican friars, 72
Don Quixote, 16
Donne, John, 75
Dreadful Warning to Lewd Livers,
 A, 174
Duck Mill Lane, 63

E, of Toft, Mr. 83
Earl of Shaftesbury, 202
Ecclesiastical Polity, The Laws of, 16
Edwards, Jonathan, 66
Eglamoure of Artoys, Sir, 16
Eliot, T. S., quoted, 127
Elizabeth, Queen, the 35th of, 111
Ellwood, Thomas, 72, 107
Elstow, 9, 25, 45; the green, 9–10, 48;
 the annual fair, 10, 154; the High
 Road, 11–12; mentioned, 37;
 changes of war, 45; wife not of
 Elstow, 46; Bunyan's cottage, 47
Essex, Earl of, 26, 35
Epictetus, 2
Evelyn, John, quoted, 80–81, 199
Everyman, quoted, 153

Faerie Queene, The, 16, 148
Fairfax, Sir Thomas, 28, 38, 44
Father's Blessing, A, 190
Fenne, John, 129, 130
Fenner, William, 19
Few Sighs from Hell, A, 41, 81
Fiennes, Celia, quoted, 8–9, 10
Fifth Monarchists, 30; his view of
 Fifth Monarchy claims, 86–87,
 113; Bunyan under suspense, 89;
 Venner affair, 95; Nayler punish-
 ment, 95–96
Fleetwood, Capt., 38
Foster, Sir William, 93, 139
Fowler, Edward, 133–134
Fox, George, mentioned, 7, 50, 67, 72,
 73, 77, 83, 123; boyhood inno-
 cence, 21; conversion, 59–60; his
 prison experiences, 106–107; his
 religious ecstasies, 127
Foxe, John, *Actes and Monuments,*
 90, 104, 164
Franciscan friars, 72
Franklin, William, 124
Fuller, Thomas, 127

Gadbury, Mary, 124
Galatians, Commentary on the (Lu-
 ther's), 60–61
Gandhi, 104, 207
Garden Inclosed, A, 39
Garrison, William Lloyd, 76
General Martyrologie, A, 174
Gibbs, John, 41, 75; quoted, 80, 82
Gifford, John, 14, 59, 129; Bunyan's
 pastor, 63; his liberality of view,
 131–132
Glorious Lover, The, 148
Goodwin, Thomas, 73, 201
Gough, James, 96
Grace Abounding to the Chief of
 Sinners. See under Bunyan, writ-
 ings
Great Plague year, 106
Grymeston, Elizabeth, quoted, 194–
 195
Guilleville, Guillaume de, 148, 153
Guy of Warwick, 16, 17

Hale, Sir Matthew, 99, 100–101
Hall, Christopher, 48–49

Hamlet, 123
Harding, M. Esther, quoted, 156
Harlington House, 92
Harpur School, 13, 14
Harrowden, 4, 25
Harvey, Thomas, 1, 7
Heavenly Footman, The, quoted, 133, 143, 146
Hensman, Samuel, 130
Heresies (listed), 70–71
Hillersdon, Sir Thomas, 12–13
Hobbes, Thomas, 16, 210
Hobson, Paul, 37–38; quoted, 39
Holinshed, Raphael, 16
Holles, Denzil, 35, 37
Holy City, The, 111–114
Holy War, The, 121, 167, 178–183; quoted, 41–42, 176–177
Hooker, Richard, 16
Hortensius, 60
Houghton Conquest, 14, 25
Houghton House, 13
House Beautiful, 12–13
How, Samuel, 68–70, 85
Howard, John, 105
Howgill, Francis, 77
Hubberthorne, Richard, 77, 113
Hyde, Edward, Earl of Clarendon, 68

Ilchester Prison, 109
Index Purgatorius, 56
Instruction for the Ignorant, quoted, 138
Instrument (of release), 115
Ireton, 44
Isle of Man, The, 148

Jacob Found in a Desert Land, 122
James, William, 62
Janeway, James, 190, 195–196
Jerusalem Sinner Saved, The, 121
Johnson, Dr. Samuel, 158
Jole, William, 190
Jolly, Thomas, 202
Jonson, Ben, 4
Josselin, Ralph, *The Diary* of, quoted, 44–45, 80
Jung, Carl Gustav, 156

Kafka, Franz, 147–148
Keach, Benjamin, 148
Kellie, John, 20
Kelsey, Thomas, 139
Kelynge, John, 96, 97, 98
Kempis, Thomas à, 55, 56, 156
King James Version, 14–16

Landy, Sister, 171
Langland, William, 153
Laud, William, 7, 22
Lawrence, Brother, 50
Lawrence, Robert, 90
Laws and Ordinances of War, The, 35–36
Lay preaching, in the army, 33–34; of Paul Hobson, 37–39; popularity of, 67–68, 72–73; ridicule of, 68–69; confutation of, 69–71. *See also* Bunyan as itinerant
Leicester, Siege of, 29
Lenthal, Speaker, 30–31
Lessing, Karl Friedrich, 156
Leviathan, 16
Life and Death of Mr. Badman, The, 169–176. *See also* Bunyan, writings
Lindale, Dr., 93
Lives of Ten Eminent Divines, The, 174
Lollards, 73
Looking-Glass for Children, A, 190
Lower Samsell, 89, 91, 97
Luke, Sir Samuel, governor of Newport Pagnell, 24, 29, 30, 88; on the New Model soldier, 36; on Hobson and Beaumont, 38
Luther, Martin, 50, 60–61
Lying Wonder Discovered, A, 82

Machiavelli, 132
Manchester, Second Earl of (Edward Montagu), 25, 26, 27
Marco Polo, 177
Marshall, Stephen, 20
Marston Moor, 27, 29
Mayflower, 15
Medieval romance, 16–19
Meeting Barn, 129–130, 203
Mercurius Britannicus, 28
Milton, John, 151, 207

Mirrour or Looking-Glasse, for Saints and Sinners, 173
Miscellanea, 194–195
Mobb's Hole, 75
Monk, General, 88
Monmouth's Rebellion, 168
Montaigne, Michel de, 16, 126
Moot Hall, The, 9, 10, 12, 48
More, Henry, 71
More, Sir Thomas, 16
Moses and the Promised Land, 147
Mozart, 145
Münster, riots of, 86

Naseby, battle of, 30, 38
Nayler, James, 72, 95–96
Nehru, Jawaharlal, 118
Newbury, battle of, 27
Newgate Prison, 107
Newman, James Henry, 16; quoted, 48, 50, 66, 120
New Model army, authorized, 26, 28; make-up of, 29–30; discipline in, 35–36; equipment of soldier, 36–37; Denzil Holles on, 37; social status, 37
New Model soldier, Sir Samuel Luke on, 36; mentioned, 182
Newport Pagnell, fortified, 28–29; unrest at, 39; mentioned, 41, 141, 180, 183; ordered demolished, 42
Norton, Roger, 125
Notebook of the Rev. Thomas Jolly, quoted, 167, 202
Noyes, Alfred, 155–156

O'Doyly, Lieut. Col. Charles, 39
O'Hara, Capt. Charles, 42
Old Meeting House, 130, 203
Owen, John, 201
Owst, Gerald R., 151

Parable of the Pilgrim, The, 153
Parsons, Robert, *Resolution*, 48. *See also* Edmund Bunny
Pascal, Blaise, 50
Patrick, Simon, 153
Paul, Thomas, 132–133
Peaceable Principles, quoted, 133
Pèlerinage de la vie humaine, Le, 148–153

Pennington, Isaac, 72
Peoples Army, The, 29, 33
Pepys, Samuel, quoted, 88, 108
Perkins, William, 72, 122
Petition of Right, 1, 7
Philips, Mary, 82
Pilgrim's Progress, The. See John Bunyan, writings
Pinney, Anne (Thomas Bunyan's first wife), 7
Plaine Man's Pathway, The, 57; quoted, 53–55; dialogue method, 173; man with the muckrake, 186
Plato, 61
Ponder, Nathaniel, 141
Powell, Vavasor, 122, 201
Practicall Divinity, quoted, 39
Practice of Piety, The, 53, 56, 57
Preston, Thomas, 72
Prince of Orange, 202
Prison Meditations, quoted, 103, 104, 110
Puritanism, 136, 157, 210

Quaker No Papist, The, 83
Quakers, Bunyan's controversy with, 77–79, 82–83; mentioned, 95, 108, 125, 136; help in his release, 115–116
Quarles, Francis, 195

Raleigh, Sir Walter, 210
Ranters, 57–58, 71
Resolution (Robert Parsons, the Jesuit), 47–48
Robert the Devil, 18–19
Rogers, John, 19–22
Rolle, Richard (of Hampole), 127
Rousseau, Jean Jacques, 126
Royal Society, The, 209
Rubáiyát, The, 147
Ruffhead, Josias, 116, 129, 130, 204
Russell, Sir William, Governor of Worcester, 35
Russell, Lord William (the Patriot), 167

Sadler, Thomas, 207–208
St. Cuthbert Street cottage, 64, 159, 160, 168

St. Cuthbert's Church, 137, 139, 171
St. Francis, 50
St. John of the Cross, 127
St. John's Church (Bedford), 59, 62–63, 129
St. Teresa, 127
Saint's Everlasting Rest, The, 56
Saved by Grace, 162, 163–164
Savonarola, 165
Schoolhouse Chapel, 96
Schweitzer, Albert, 51–52
Sedgwick, Obadiah, 35
Seekers, 71
Seven Deadly Sinnes of London, The, 172
Shakespeare, 7, 16, 151, 210
Shorter, Sir William, 199
Sibbes, Richard, 122
Sidney, Sir Philip, 16
Smith, Nicholas, 124
Smith, Thomas, 83
Smithfield Fair, 199
Snagg, Thomas, 96
Socrates, 149
Some Gospel Truths Opened, 41, 78
Souldier's Catechism, The, quoted, 32–33
Souldier's Pocket Bible, The, quoted, 31–32
Spenser, Edmund, 16, 148, 151, 210
Stanton, John, 171
Strait Gate, The, 143, 144
Strange and Terrible Newes, 82
Strudwick, John, 200, 201
Struggler, The, 161
Sufficiencie of the Spirit's Teaching, The, 69
Swan Inn, 12, 24, 99
Swinton, William, 171

Tablet of Cebes, 149–150
Test Act, 137
Theatre of God's Judgments, The, 173
Theologia Germanica, 60
Thomas à Kempis, 55, 56, 156
Timely Warning to Drunkards, A, 173–174
Tinker's Hill, 75

Tipcat game, 10, 49–50, 126
Token for Children, A, 190, 195
Torner, John, 109–110
Trapnel, Anna, 124
Travalyed Pilgrim, The, 148
True Faith of the Gospel of Peace, The, 78
Truth the Strongest of All, 78
Twisden, Judge, 99
Tyndale, William, 15

Ulysses, Journey of, 147
"Upon a Ring of Bells," 197
Utopia, 16

Vane, Sir Harry, 96
Varney, William, 13
Venner, Thomas, 86, 95, 96, 138
Vergil, 147, 155
Vindication of the Book Called Some Gospel Truths Opened, A, 41, 78

Wainwood Dell, 75, 204, 209
Waller, Sir Hardress, 26
War with the Devil, 148
Watts, Isaac, 193, 194, 201
Wesley, Charles, 50
Wesley, John, 62
Wesley, Samuel, 20
Wesley, Susanna, 201
West Chester Prison, 123
Weye to Paradys, The, 151
Wharton, Nehemiah, quoted, 35
Wheeler, William, 75
Whitefield, George, 66
Whitehead, George, 77, 83; quoted, 115–116; similarity of his experience to Bunyan's, 122
Whittier, John Greenleaf, 76
Wight, Sarah, 124
Wildman, John, 171
Wilkins, Bishop John, 177
Wingate, Judge Francis, 89, 90; Bunyan's hearing before him, 92–94
Witt, Brother, 171
Wood, Anthony, 208
Wycliffe, John, 73

Zoar Chapel, 168